THE $100,000 TEACHER

THE $100,000 TEACHER

A Teacher's Solution
to America's Declining
Public School System

Brian Crosby

CAPITAL
BOOKS, INC.
Sterling, Virginia

Copyright © 2002 by Brian Crosby

All rights reserved. No part of this book may be reproduced or utilized in any form or by any means, electronic or mechanical, including photocopying, recording, or by any information storage and retrieval system, without permission in writing from the publisher. Inquiries should be addressed to:

Capital Books, Inc.
P.O. Box 605
Herndon, Virginia 20172-0605
ISBN 1-892123-55-X (alk.paper)

Library of Congress Cataloging-in-Publication Data

Crosby, Brian (Brian Franklyn)
    The $100,000 teacher : a teacher's solution to America's declining public school system / Brian Crosby.—1st ed.
        p. cm.
    Includes bibliographical references and index.
    ISBN 1-892123-55-X
    1. Teachers—Salaries, etc.—United States.   2. Public schools—United States.   3. School improvement programs—United States.   I. Title: One-hundred-thousand-dollar teacher.
    II. Title.
LB2842.22 .C76 2001
371.01'0973—dc21   2001043755

Printed in the United States of America on acid-free paper that meets the American National Standards Institute Z39-48 Standard.

First Edition

10   9   8   7   6   5   4   3   2   1

Dedicated to all hard-working teachers
who deserve better,
most especially my mentors,
John Sage and Sidney Kolpas.

CONTENTS

FIGURES

ix

ACKNOWLEDGMENTS

Not all the examples used in this book come from my own personal experience and so I thank those teachers across the country who shared their opinions and "war" stories and for obvious reasons had to remain anonymous. Thank yous to Ron Goldfarb for believing in my ideas; Kristen Auclair who helped polish them; Kathleen Hughes for taking a chance; and Noemi Taylor, who guided me with patience through this whole process. I am indebted to Casey Maddren and Jim York for making me believe I could do this, to Sherry Joe for being the best editor a husband could have, and to Benjamin Harvey for letting Daddy work on his book.

Grateful acknowledgment is made for permission to reproduce the following figures and excerpts that appear in this book:

Figures 5 and 12 from *Quality Counts 2000: Who Should Teach?* Reprinted with permission from *Education Week.*

Figures 3a, 3b, 4, 6, and 14 from "Survey & Analysis of Teacher Salary Trends 2000." Reprinted with permission from the Research & Information Services, American Federation of Teachers, AFL-CIO.

Excerpts from "Target Time Towards Teachers" by Darling-Hammond. Reprinted with permission of the National Staff Development Council, 2001.

One stylistic note: for simplicity's sake I chose the "he" pronoun when referring to a teacher, even though I recognize that the vast majority of kindergarten through 12th grade educators are women.

PREFACE

"Public schoolteachers should earn six-figure salaries."
Thus began my nationally syndicated op-ed piece in
the *Los Angeles Times* back in November 1998 that trig-
gered a firestorm of controversy across the country, from
C-SPAN's *Washington Journal* to KABC/WKABC Talk-
Radio's Larry Elder. Letters and faxes poured in, mostly
in support of my position and many from veteran teachers
who have been waiting for one of their own to speak up
about the hard work of teaching and the few rewards for
staying in it. The concept of the $100,000 teacher had
struck a raw nerve in the public's psyche, compelling me
to write this book.

The basic premise for *The $100,000 Teacher: A
Teacher's Solution to America's Declining Public School
System* is that good teachers deserve $100,000—and
more—if society demands higher student achievement.
The book spotlights a truth policy makers would rather
not confront: that increasing teachers' salaries significantly is the best way to markedly improve the state of
public education. It doesn't take a space shuttle engineer
to realize that the more money offered to people in a given
profession, the more that will attract people, both in quantity and, most important, quality since the prestige of that
profession will likewise increase. Many of the best and
brightest college graduates continue to choose careers
such as engineering and computer animation, where
22-year-olds can earn starting salaries of $40,000—a salary
teachers in large metropolitan areas earn only after ten

years of work. Until the applicant pool is enlarged to attract more talented individuals from more lucrative fields, the most critical job in America will remain in critical condition.

Things must change if public education is to survive.

I know because I am chairman of the English department at a suburban high school in the Los Angeles area and have been a teacher for 13 years. I have spent half of my career mentoring dozens of teachers and facilitating numerous workshops.

Hundreds of books have been published on the public school system and how to fix its problems, but these are written by so-called experts, such as university professors or education think tank personnel who think they have the right solution, despite their distance (geographical and philosophical) from the problem. Without ever having taught one day in a public school, these reformers nevertheless have strong opinions on the problems with teachers and the education structure. It's as if classroom teachers lack the credentials to write about their own profession.

Well, it's time for one of the nearly three million public school teachers in this country to tell his story—not a union leader, not a university professor, not a paid educational consultant, not anyone else who has spent little time teaching America's youth, but one who spends every day on the front lines, to speak up for all good teachers out there, and respond to all the criticism and negative press about how incompetent teachers are and how they are responsible for the poor academic performance of this country's children.

I interviewed dozens of teachers from around the country, elementary and secondary, public and private, and spoke with many school administrators, district officials, and union leaders. I asked the teachers to respond to 100 questions covering the scope of the material in this book. For obvious reasons, the people I questioned wished to remain anonymous, so they are referenced either by the area of the country they are from or the grade level or subject matter they teach.

While my experience is at the secondary level, my proposals would work for the whole of public education, kindergarten through 12th grade.

Ever since the federal government's 1983 report, *A Nation at Risk,* decried the shortcomings of public education, education pundits have clamored for myriad reforms—yet, none of them have worked in the long term. The key is something so basic most people can't see it. The teacher is the foundation of a productive learning environment and, if that teacher is no good, the students suffer. All the reading programs and computer hook-ups will be wasted if that classroom teacher is not capable of performing at an optimum level. For too long, education reformers have overlooked (or refused to believe) that the quality of the instructors matters most. I know of teachers who are given wonderful curriculum guidelines yet cannot (or will not) use them either because of a lack of proper training or a lack of commitment.

Creating a more private sector–like pay schedule with a true career ladder is the most immediate change that needs to be implemented. Unions must give up the notion of protecting the rights of all teachers no matter how bad they are and allow teachers to be paid according to their performance. Politicians have to relinquish taxpayers' money earmarked for special programs, be it Title I or Internet connections, and pool the money to create a legitimate professional pay scale. And teachers themselves need to be willing to be evaluated by peers and sweep out the incompetent instructors who make all teachers look bad. After all, a U.S. Department of Education study released in January 1999 revealed that only one in every five full-time public school teachers feels well qualified to teach in today's classroom of technology, multicultural diversity, and disabled students.

How can teachers be looked up to unless they have the respect of students, parents, and school support staff?

In addition to pay, the daily working conditions of the teacher need upgrading. Teachers should not have to do secretarial work such as answering phones and photocopying. Teachers need to be an integral part of the decision-making process at their work sites. Until these important changes are implemented, respect for teachers as professionals will remain weak.

The idea of "professionalizing" teaching is gaining popularity as the key to a better public school system. The public is becoming increasingly aware that the professional teacher is the key to a better public school system. Polls all across America show that people believe the best way to improve student learning is through improved teacher quality. A recent California public opinion poll shows that residents favor higher pay for qualified teachers, ranking teaching as the most beneficial profession to society by a three to one ratio, yet a *New York Times* article (Bronner, 1998) reports that "the U.S. ranks among the lowest [industrialized nations] in teacher pay per capita." Teachers in Germany, Ireland, and South Korea earn twice or more of their nations' gross domestic product per capita, while U.S. teachers earn 1.2 times the GDP. In Australia, France, and Britain, the average teacher earns more than other university graduates; in the United States, that same teacher earns less. A teacher in Japan earns the same salary as an engineer, but a U.S. teacher earns only 60 percent of an engineer's wage.

Surveys also show that Americans are willing to pay more in taxes to get better teachers.

This book is for:

- Parents who see children (theirs and others) getting by but not receiving the education they need to succeed.
- Policy makers who continue voting on pet education projects to enhance their resumes.
- Union leaders who need a wake-up call that their backs are against the wall. Closer scrutiny of

teachers is imminent, and unions either will jump on the bandwagon or be disbanded.

- University credential directors who should realize the drastic need to revamp their curriculum to make it more relevant.
- Unknown number of college students right now who have thought about teaching but know that parental and societal pressure forces them to choose a more lucrative though less enriching career.
- Good teachers who need, more than anyone else, a morale boost.

It is time to stop throwing more tax dollars at programs to teach phonics or grants to wire schools for the Internet. The most important component in the classroom to make a true impact on the student is not the 2.0 gigahertz Pentium IV computer; it is the well-paid and much more thoroughly trained teacher.

Good teachers deserve $100,000—and more—if public education is to serve its customers, the students, well into the twenty-first century.

America, We Have a Problem

> **WANTED**
> **2,000,000 TEACHERS BY 2012**
>
> Need minimum five years of college, including bachelor's degree and teaching credential. Meet the individual needs of 175 young people every day. Create engaging lesson plans that follow state and local standards. Teach only to the curriculum. Prepare students to excel on all standardized tests. Take work home daily. Be willing to forgo promotion. May need to provide own supplies and photocopy services. Starting pay: $25,000

FACT: Half of all teachers will retire in nine years.

FACT: One-fifth of new teachers quit within three years.

FACT: Half of all new teachers quit within five years.

All across the country "help wanted" signs have gone up for teachers. Maryland needs 11,000 teachers, and North Carolina is short 10,000. In trying to fill 3,500 vacancies, Chicago is recruiting from 35 countries. Last year, New York City hired 8,000 new teachers—10 percent of its workforce (Coeyman, 2001).

Three significant factors have contributed to the greatest teacher shortage in this country's history:

1) The average age of today's teacher is 44.

2) When new teachers entering the field do not receive support during their first few years, they are twice as likely to quit.

3) According to Tom Leveless of the Brookings Institution, 20 million kids will enter high school within the next four years, a one-third increase over current enrollment (Coeyman).

With so many veteran teachers retiring, so many new teachers quitting, and so many more students entering the public schools, this country is facing an unprecedented demand for new teachers. By 2012, conservative estimates put the number of available teaching positions at two million, while others claim the need may reach two and a half million. All of these facts have created a formula for disaster unless action is taken immediately.

Why is America facing such a crisis?

When the federal report on the public school system's shortcomings, *A Nation at Risk,* came out in 1983, it ignited a debate on how to improve student learning. Never mentioned in its discussion of how many days students were in school and which programs should be created to combat the decline in tests scores was the important role of the teacher—the most central, crucial, influential individual at a school, the one with the most impact on student achievement. Such an oversight has been duplicated by other proposals on how to fix public education.

For too long the dialogue swirling around public education has skirted the teacher's critical place. Too much money has been wasted on experts, consultants, programs, and computers.

It is time to focus on the teacher for there is a teacher crisis in America. It is a crisis of quality and quantity. And if enough people do not wake up to this realization, especially those with the power to influence real change, then this country's children will suffer substantially.

What's wrong with teaching? Why is it considered the poor stepchild among professions? Why don't smarter people enter its workforce? Does America really want the adults who come in contact with 53 million school children six hours a day to continue to be low-paid, middling-competent, powerless workers?

The $100,000 Teacher addresses these issues and puts forth a dramatic proposal to transform the teaching profession and raise it up to the level of law and medicine.

In a country where an 18-foot-long SUV isn't big enough, a 25-inch TV isn't too large for a bedroom, and each member of the family carries a pager and cell phone, it is time for education to be a top priority. Why should it take the annual release of standardized scores for the public to pay attention to what's going on in America's classrooms?

In a recent California poll, 59 percent of respondents said they would consider going into teaching if average salaries were $60,000. This is an important finding because that state, which employs one-tenth of the country's public school teachers, anticipates over a quarter of a million teacher openings in the next ten years. In a 2000 nationwide poll conducted by Recruiting New Teachers, Inc., for the report, *The Essential Profession: American Education at the Crossroads* by David Haselkorn and Louis Harris (2001), 82 percent of Americans would recommend that a member of their family go into teaching if the job paid $60,000.

However, with the average teacher salary at two-thirds of that figure—$41,000—who will fill these two million jobs? Fully credentialed, highly qualified, intelligent people? Looking at the teaching profession's record, that is highly unlikely to happen.

All the books on education reform (and there are nearly as many as there are diet books) overlook and understate the lack of respect and pay the teaching profession experiences. Good teachers are grossly underpaid, while bad ones are living on easy street. Many people believe there are too many terrible ones, but the fact is, there are too many average ones. For a job as important as teaching, average doesn't cut it; yet that number of average instructors will continue to rise as long as the pay, working conditions, and respect aren't there. Paying a college graduate with an additional year of credential coursework a starting salary of $25,000 will not have Ivy League alumni rushing to fill out teaching applications. As stated in the book, *Who Will Teach?*: "Bright, well-educated graduates will seek and obtain opportunities in other fields, leaving the weakest graduates to teach our children." Who wants their son or daughter taught by someone who just barely passed an easy state teacher test?

Teachers shouldn't barely be able to do their job— they should be the experts in their field. Unfortunately, other fields pay much more, so that's where many smart people go.

Give bright college students a real choice among law, medicine, and education. "My son, the teacher" should carry just as much weight as "my son, the doctor." Do college students attend Princeton for their credential program? What is wrong if a Yale graduate teaches eighth-grade science?

As a high school English teacher at a suburban high school in the Los Angeles metropolitan area for the past 13 years, and a mentor teacher for nearly half that time, I have seen plenty of good, average, and bad teachers. With smaller class sizes becoming the nationwide trend, the search for qualified instructors is difficult, forcing many districts to place increasingly less qualified people in front of school children.

Many students are being fed a fast-food education by noncredentialed teachers who provide only drive-through service. Sixty percent of New York City schools' new teachers in 2000–01 were not certified. Keep in mind that this is the largest school system in the country and employs 80,000 teachers. One-fourth of all 36,000 teachers working for Los Angeles Unified, the second-largest district, have no credential.

In January 1999, the U.S. Department of Education released a survey of more than 4,000 full-time public school teachers that revealed that only one out of every five felt well qualified to teach. If a similar study came out regarding unqualified physicians, the president would declare a national state of emergency.

To improve student learning you have to improve teacher quality, period. In terms of positively affecting student achievement, technology, reading programs, and even smaller classes rank a distant second to a gifted teacher. Look at figure 1 at what Americans said when asked in the Recruiting New Teachers (RNT) poll about this issue.

Quality teachers ranked second at 89 percent, one percentage point behind school safety. Instead of more computers, smaller classes, and school choice, people want more talented teachers and principals (ranked fourth).

Common sense dictates that a highly competent teacher is able to help students to achieve more than an instructor who isn't. And many studies have proven just that, linking good teaching to improved student learning. Well then, public education should ensure that all students receive good teaching.

What needs to be done is what has not been done before:

- Teachers should be paid based on competency, not on years of service or units of college credit. This means that some teachers deserve to earn more money than others regardless of experience.
- Principals should be able to fire incompetent teachers, another long-standing taboo in public education. Why allow bad teachers to infect students year after year?
- Exceptional teachers should be able to earn more money than principals. Everyone agrees that the

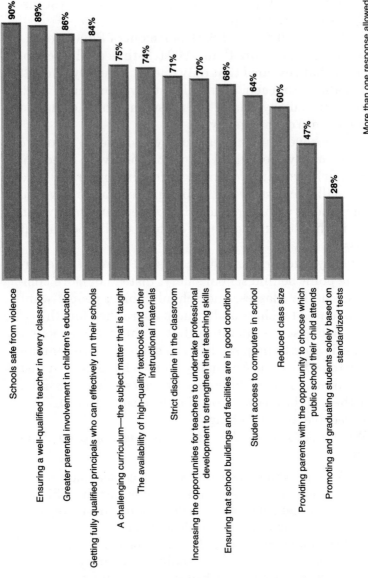

Figure 1. Measures to Lift Student Achievement Deemed Very Important
Source: Recruiting New Teachers, Inc.

- Schools safe from violence — 90%
- Ensuring a well-qualified teacher in every classroom — 89%
- Greater parental involvement in children's education — 86%
- Getting fully qualified principals who can effectively run their schools — 84%
- A challenging curriculum—the subject matter that is taught — 75%
- The availability of high-quality textbooks and other instructional materials — 74%
- Strict discipline in the classroom — 71%
- Increasing the opportunities for teachers to undertake professional development to strengthen their teaching skills — 70%
- Ensuring that school buildings and facilities are in good condition — 68%
- Student access to computers in school — 64%
- Reduced class size — 60%
- Providing parents with the opportunity to choose which public school their child attends — 47%
- Promoting and graduating students solely based on standardized tests — 28%

More than one response allowed

teacher is the primary caretaker of schoolchildren's learning, so it's time the teacher's salary reflected that.

- Teachers in high-demand fields, such as math and science, should be paid more. Public education must remain competitive with more lucrative fields. If such a policy is good enough for city governments to use, why not school boards?
- Teachers should know (and be held accountable for knowing) the subject area they teach. Teachers need to be willing to trade job security for job quality, and the only way for that to happen is to be evaluated according to a set of teaching standards, not standardized test results.

But the centuries-old, politically charged public education establishment has to be uprooted. No longer should a lawmaker or school board member tell a teacher what to do in the classroom, any more than a city council member should tell a surgeon what to do in the operating room.

The $100,000 Teacher explores in part 1 an average work day that I and millions of other teachers go through. Few people outside of education can comprehend what it is like to work in a classroom. Teachers are high-octane performers; they have to disguise teaching in the form of entertainment to maintain student interest, slicing and dicing hours of instructional time into bite-size bits. Teachers are major decision makers, answering dozens of questions a day and confronting numerous more situations requiring jurisprudence. Teachers are counselors helping students with personal problems. And some teachers are parents for those children for whom school is a haven, the only place they feel secure. Teaching is merely one of many tasks teachers perform daily.

On top of the hectic work schedule, teachers work in substandard conditions, from not having access to a telephone to not being able to use the bathroom when needed. The poor working conditions account for much of the lack of respect the profession receives from society at large and the support staff where the teacher works.

By improving salaries and working conditions, teaching will attract top talent. Part 2 focuses on steps that need to be implemented to transform teaching into a full-fledged profession.

Only by paying outstanding teachers a six-figure professional wage can the teaching profession truly become professional. Society pins too much hope on the kindness of benevolent strangers to enter the teaching field.

Teachers need a bold career ladder so that becoming administrators is not their only promotion option. The $100,000 plan presents a professional pay scale based on competence, not seniority, with incentives to promote ambition and innovation in teachers.

Higher salaries will maintain the good teachers and keep them there, and higher accountability will get rid of the bad apples.

With financial incentives in place, evaluating teachers becomes most important. Despite the teachers unions' long-standing opposition to a true teacher evaluation process, that is the only way for teachers to earn more money and respect. The belief that one cannot judge objectively what constitutes good teaching must vanish.

Following the model of medical internships, university credential programs must rethink how they train teachers by having college students work side-by-side with real classroom teachers in real settings with real students. Mickey Mouse coursework does little to prepare one to connect with 175 individual minds daily. Teacher interns should produce an impressive portfolio of videotaped lessons and written analysis of student work. Then they need to pass a rigorous subject-matter test to ensure their competence. It should be a challenge to get a teacher's license, just as it is to pass the bar exam, and having a teaching certificate should carry weight.

Most important, teachers need to gain control over their own profession, just as doctors did nearly a century ago. As long as others dictate to them what they should be doing, teachers will remain oppressed professionals.

Teachers themselves should be developing curricula, determining the best ways to assess student achievement, even have a hand in designing their own workspace in schools. Their opinions should count and be listened to.

Part 3 deals with the obstacles in the way of professionalizing teachers. As far as paying higher salaries, tax increases can be avoided through redistributing and properly managing current funding and including more private-sector participation.

Teachers unions need to step out of the way and let true reforms take place before the dam bursts. Their protection of the weakest instructors to the detriment of the strongest ones has run its course. Unions should also focus more energy on gaining true power for their clientele.

School administrators must relinquish their hold on the decision-making process and involve the brightest people on campus. Treating teachers as grown-up students does not encourage them to do their best work.

And parents, and even teachers themselves, must allow these reforms to flourish. Parents need to tell their children to view teachers respectfully, encouraging them to consider teaching as a career choice, not as a last resort. It's time for teachers not only to demand to be called professionals, but also to act the part. If they want more money and better working conditions, they need to demand that their unions act more like professional associations along the lines of the American Medical Association instead of the AFL-CIO. Otherwise, they need to separate themselves from the unions and create an elite branch of teachers who truly are empowered.

As the Carnegie Forum on Education and the Economy stated in its 1986 report, *A Nation Prepared: Teachers for the 21st Century*, "The teaching profession is the best hope for establishing new standards of excellence as the hallmark of American education."

The reforms delineated in *The $100,000 Teacher: A Teacher's Solution to America's Declining Public School System* may seem daunting. It's not so much a change in money as a change in attitude before a true revolution in the teaching profession can take place. The powers that be, from politicians to school boards to principals, need to rethink how they perceive teachers. And teachers are going to have to rethink how they view themselves and develop a vision of what direction their profession should take.

One of the more valuable lessons I have learned after 13 years as a teacher is that you can't truly judge something in life unless you have firsthand knowledge of it. None of us can possibly have a full understanding of the inner workings of police departments, government agencies, military operations, or social services. Yet, within five minutes, taxpayers can come up with a long list of ways to correct their deficiencies.

Well, anyone who has ever worked for one of these publicly paid organizations will tell you it ain't that easy. No important problem in life can be fixed easily; otherwise, it would have been done so already.

Unless you are a teacher, or have one in the family, you cannot know how it feels to walk into a classroom with 30 small faces looking at you waiting for the show to begin. What other professional sees up to 200 clients in a day?

How ironic that at a time when the teaching shortage is approaching epidemic levels, the job appears even less attractive because of all the pressures on the teacher, from implementing content area standards to standardized testing. While the bait has improved—starting salaries in a few major cities now hover around $40,000—the pressure cooker on the teacher has been turned higher than it has ever been before. It's showtime, and it's time to show results. According to Arthur E. Levine, president of Teachers College, Columbia University,

America is looking for a quick fix for its schools. But if we really believe that higher standards, which definitely are needed; better testing, which ideally should assess the full range of student skills and talents; and technology literacy, a vital requirement for the Information Age, will add up to a remedy for what ails far too many of the nation's schools, then we're thinking wrong. Something significant is being left out. To get it right, we have to get serious and put the teacher at the center of any equation to reform education.

This book is not just designed for retired teachers to nod in approval or current ones to shake their heads in disagreement; rather it is more for the students who are in America's classrooms right now, some of whom have brilliant minds and should consider teaching as a viable option.

I recall as a new teacher sitting among the seasoned pros who often talked about waiting for the revolution to change education like the coming of the messiah. And as history has shown, the education establishment (which does not include teachers, by the way) moves more slowly than the line at the post office on April 15.

Is it realistic then to think that the 160-year-old public school system will be magically reformed with some of the suggestions contained in this book?

The revolution is not going to happen today or tomorrow or even in the next few years. But it could happen within the next decade. And that is when the young people of today will be deciding what they want to be when they grow up.

Ever since I became a teacher, I have wanted to be a role model, not only for students, but for the profession, from the way I dress to how I organize lessons. I want my job to look attractive, and students to look up to teaching. I want many of them to consider becoming teachers.

There is no more opportune moment than a millennium in its infancy to reevaluate the role of the most important school employee. Poll after poll shows that Americans rate education as the number one priority among all issues, including the economy, crime, health care, and family values.* The RNT survey revealed that 62 percent of the American public ranks teaching the number one profession that provides the most benefit to our society, compared to doctors (22 percent), nurses (3 percent), business people (3 percent), public officials (2 percent), lawyers (2 percent), journalists (1 percent), and accountants (1 percent). If this is how Americans truly feel, then the time has come to give teaching its professional due.

---

*This was before the tragic terrorist attacks occurred on September 11, 2001.

PART 1

An Industry,
Not a Profession

Bell schedules, assemblies, public address announcements, staff development—all part of the education vernacular more in line with an industry rather than a profession.

Spending time with children all day long, leaving work at 3:00 P.M., and having the summer off gives the misleading impression that teaching is an easy, part-time profession.

The public views the nonpaid 11-week summer break, all of the holidays (Veterans Day, Thanksgiving, two-week winter break, Martin Luther King Jr., Lincoln, Washington, one-week spring break, Memorial Day), and the nontraditional hours, and thinks teachers are lucky. Despite all of this time off, though, teaching, when done well, is a very demanding profession, requiring a sharp mind to answer impromptu questions, high energy to create an electric ambiance in the room, and sensitivity in making untold number of decisions when working with up to 175 unique and sometimes fragile young minds.

What follows is not an extraordinary day in my career, but rather a typical one. I have had many much busier and some less so. This window into my classroom reflects what goes on in thousands of other classrooms in this country, and people need to know what it takes to teach young people.

As if the job of teaching weren't tough enough, the working conditions of the educator are shameful.

- Physical plant—It all begins with the environment, the physical plant that houses both teachers and students. Often the school campus does not make the statement that education matters. If the maintenance of the outside of the buildings can't be kept up with peeling, institutional color paint a common sight, at least the classrooms should be swept and vacuumed regularly.

14

- Classroom climate—Teachers lack space to do their work. With more students and computers, space to simply walk around desks has diminished, forcing many educators to just stand motionless at the front of the room. Some schools have created makeshift classrooms in cafeterias, libraries, and storage areas due to cramped quarters. In addition to the physical space limitations, the classroom environment is interrupted frequently by intercom announcements and phone calls, destroying the carefully constructed learning ambiance.
- Lack of support—Essentials of any working professional—an office, a secretary, a telephone, supplies, and photocopiers—are luxury items for the teacher. The teacher's classroom doubles as an office. The majority of teachers still do not have real telephones that can dial out. Supplies are of poor quality and in limited quantities. Most schools have several photocopy machines for administrators and support staff, but usually only one for the largest group of employees at the work site.
- Lack of respect—Teachers are not naturally granted the same respect as other professionals. Many tasks are asked of teachers beyond teaching to children, such as supervising hallways and student bathrooms. Adults who work at schools forget that teachers are professionals, not simply grown-up kids. Their practices are regularly challenged by some administrators and parents. After awhile, such lack of respect takes its toll.
- Meetings—The reason why so many teachers abhor meetings is that they come right after a full day's work. The last thing a person wants to hear when he is exhausted is how poor of a job he is doing. Besides, teachers are very protective of their time and how it is used, especially those few moments when they are not teaching.
- Staff development—The idea that teachers constantly need staff development is a slap in the

face to all those educators who worked hard for their credentials and master's degrees. After awhile, the sense that one does not have the skills to teach children and therefore needs ongoing training transforms into a self-fulfilling prophecy, making teachers feel they are not smart or competent.

Society needs to wake up to what is happening to teachers across the country. If it is affecting the teachers and their work environment, then it definitely affects the students and their learning environment.

CHAPTER 1

The Daily Struggle:
Life in the Trenches

7:00 a.m.   Arrive at work: the blizzard begins
Sign in and pick up mail. It's not uncommon to receive
12–15 pieces of correspondence a day, several of which
need some kind of response:

- teacher's request for books
- two-page printout of yesterday's students who were absent
- request for the name of a senior for an academic award
- two-page assembly schedule and seating chart
- memo from principal excusing students to attend assembly
- teacher's clearance list for those students attending the assembly
- second memo from principal regarding a graduation planning meeting
- memo from a teacher excusing students to attend a field trip
- note regarding music concert by students during lunch
- a district newsletter

7:10   Teachers' workroom
Go to workroom to photocopy a study sheet on *The Great
Gatsby*. Some days I'm lucky to find the copy machine

free. No such luck today, even at this early hour, because four other teachers are waiting in line for the school's only copying machine accessible to teachers. I decide to return later.

7:15   Classroom

Rush into classroom to check voice mail, write down important phone messages, return calls, respond in writing to any notes, verify today's class agendas written on the white board at the end of yesterday, check e-mail, respond, grade papers, review lesson plans, be prepared to bump into a colleague for a quick conversation or receive a call from an administrator or English teacher asking for something, interact with students trickling in who have questions or need one-on-one help.

8:00   Passing bell for period 1

Welcome students to classroom, collect homework, answer questions from students, arrange items needed on podium, have the vocabulary "word of the day" ready to go at bell.

8:05   Period 1 begins (sophomore English)

Start class with vocabulary word.

8:06   Remind students to take careful notes when they work in their collaborative groups. Each day students choose a different task, such as character motivation or famous quotes, so that all will have experience doing vocabulary or plot summaries or quotations.

8:10   In four-member groups, students discuss Act III of Shakespeare's *Julius Caesar*. Roam up and down each row listening in on their answers to yesterday's study questions, complimenting them on good responses, correcting them when necessary.

8:25   Students present information from their Shakespeare groups. As each group speaks, the rest of the class takes notes.

8:40   Ask students if they have any questions on the act. Highlight key lines they need to know. Instruct how to identify and explain figurative language. Assign them ten figures of speech for homework.

8:45 Show Antony's famous "Friends, Romans, countrymen . . . " speech as dramatized by Marlon Brando from the 1953 film *Julius Caesar*. Students take notes on Antony's persuasiveness. Right in the middle of a key line the phone rings: BRRRING!BRRRING! "This is Tracy. Did you turn in that scholarship paper? It was due yesterday." (Why was such a call made in the middle of a class period? Not only was it unimportant, but it just as easily could have been done between periods, or better yet, with a written note.) The mood I carefully created for this critical moment in the play has been shattered.

8:55 Have students write down in their journals a definition of persuasiveness and traits of a persuasive speaker. Then they are to evaluate Antony's speech according to those traits.

9:00 Period 1 ends; period 2 passing bell
Class ends while students are still writing. They will finish their responses for homework and share them tomorrow.

As students exit, several come up to talk to me about that night's homework assignment or that day's graded work. Simultaneously, the next class is filing in. A few students greet me with a "Good morning, Mr. Crosby" that I try to acknowledge as I continue answering students' questions: one student wants homework for the next three days due to an absence, another student wants me to read her introduction, another wants me to review a bibliography, another needs my signature on a weekly progress form. Multitasking for teachers is not just a buzzword—it's a survival skill.

9:05 Period 2 begins (sophomore English)
Again, start the class with vocabulary word. Must be finished before the bulletin is read. The school bulletin is read over the P.A. three times a week, even though it's printed daily. Announcements usually last between five

and 15 minutes, even during shortened 35-minute periods (one reason why period 2 is slightly longer).

9:16   Period 2 really begins

On this day students are presenting poems they've been studying in groups during the week. I sit at my desk listening for correct grammar and content and observing proper public speaking skills. I comment on each student's presentation. Take roll during breaks between speeches.

9:23   In the middle of one of the presentations, the phone rings. The attendance office wants me to remind one of my students to go there after class.

9:31   In poetry groups, students explicate three poems each. I sit in with each group, guiding them when necessary.

9:51   Each group makes a three-minute presentation on one of the poems. I evaluate each group on three bases: 1) how well they organize their material, 2) how well they present it in terms of correct poetry terminology, and 3) how interesting they make their presentation.

9:55   P.A. announcement: Representatives of a certain college will be available to talk with students during snack.

9:59   New poetry terms—synecdoche, assonance, poetic inversion—are discussed. Examples for each are given from students' poems.

10:02   P.A. announcement: Bathrooms on the first floor will be unlocked during snack.

10:04   Tonight students will locate five figures of speech, identify and explain them, and paraphrase three new poems from their anthology.

10:05   Period 2 ends; snack begins

This 15-minute break allows a teacher time to go to the bathroom, walk to the faculty cafeteria (which takes at least four minutes to get to through a throng of teens), stand in line usually ten people deep to get a cup of coffee, sit down, gulp down the coffee, and make it back to the classroom. Even if a teacher is sure-footed and is able to be at the door at 10:05 ahead of the students exiting, not much time is available to grab a chair and communicate with one's peers, only one of two such daily opportunities for teachers to talk to colleagues (the other is lunch).

I'm the adviser to the school newspaper, so during nearly every snack and lunch, journalism students come in to work on the computers, which means I have to be in the classroom. After speaking to students from period 2 and to the journalism kids, it usually is 10:20, and I have lost the one legal time I am allowed to leave the classroom until lunch begins at 12:20. And to think that in some school districts teachers are required to do yard duty. Imagine an attorney being called on during his lunch hour to sit at the security guard station in the lobby of an office building.

10:20   Snack ends; passing bell for period 3
I swing by the workroom to make my copies, but a technician is fixing the machine.

10:25   Period 3 begins (journalism)
Staff meeting with student reporters begins. Discuss the progress of articles for the next issue, offer suggestions for getting additional information.

10:41   Phone rings: A business wants to advertise in the school newspaper.

10:42   Phone rings: A teacher wants some books.

10:43   Phone rings: The principal wants suggestions for scholarship candidates.

10:45   Work with a student on a news article.

10:50   Work with an editor on a layout.

10:54   The fire alarm system mistakenly goes off. Two things occur: A blinding strobe light blinks incessantly, and a throbbing siren sounds near dangerous decibel levels for humans. Because of the number of false alarms at my school, teachers are instructed to wait for an announcement before escorting students to emergency locations on campus. So while we wait, no teaching or learning can take place until both the lights and sirens are turned off.

10:56 P.A. announcement: False alarm; remain in room.

11:00 Walk around to the reporters on the computers and offer assistance; answer questions.

11:02 A teacher calls asking for books.

11:10 Evaluate articles and speak to the writers.

11:20 **Period 3 ends; passing bell for period 4**

11:25 **Period 4 begins (journalism)**
This class includes most of the editors, so there is an editors' meeting. Discuss the progress of the current issue, where the ads fit into the layouts, and any problems encountered with reporters meeting deadlines.

11:40 A student teaching assistant (T.A.) from the counseling office delivers a summons for a student.

11:45 The same student T.A. from the counseling office returns with another summons for a different student.

11:54 Fill out a deposit slip for advertising money for the newspaper account and a check reimbursement form for the supplies I purchased last night.

12:03 P.A. announcement: Tickets to the winter formal go on sale at lunch.

12:15 Phone rings: A teacher wants me to put an article in the paper about one of her students.

12:20 Period 4 ends; lunch begins

We have a 30-minute lunch that begins immediately at the end of period 4 and finishes at the beginning of the passing bell of period 5. After assisting students, I can usually leave my room around 12:35, meaning I arrive at the cafeteria at 12:40, if I don't have to stop at the restroom. By this time there is no waiting, so I get my food quickly and rush back to my classroom to avoid the crush of students and staff when lunch ends. I finally sit down at 12:45 to swallow my food hurriedly so that in five minutes I can rush to the faculty bathroom and be back by the 12:50 passing bell, energetic and ready to go.

However, today I skip lunch because I have two students coming in to take make-up tests. Afterward, I rush downstairs to get the books that teacher requested—and can't find them. I get back upstairs and type out a memo to all English teachers trying to locate the books. I also type up the list of scholarship candidates requested earlier by the principal. Back downstairs, I stuff the memo into the teachers' mailboxes and give the list to the principal's secretary.

On my way to the restroom, I check in again on the copier. This time two people are in line.

12:50 Lunch ends; passing bell for period 5

A reporter working on an article during lunch has her computer freeze. Another can't get her computer to print. I work on the computers until the next class starts.

12:55 Period 5 begins (American literature)

Before the bell rings, students already have their vocabulary sheets out; they know they can earn points for saying the word, reading the word in context from the book, and defining it.

1:00 Go around the room and have each student mention an important fact about John Steinbeck from the research assigned for last night.

1:14 Discuss *The Grapes of Wrath* as an example of proletarian literature. Answer students' questions.

1:22   The school's telephone operator inadvertently puts through a parent's call. The parent is not willing to allow me to get off the phone as quickly as possible, so I must wait while the parent goes on about the recent progress report of her daughter. I quickly take down her number so I can resume teaching. Meanwhile, during the two-minute call, the students are talking to one another.

1:24   Finish historical background on Steinbeck's book. Then students get into study groups to work on themes, characters, and symbols. Walk around and sit in on groups, assisting them when needed.

**1:50   Period 5 ends; period 6 passing bell
          (conference period—end of teaching time
          but not end of work day)**

If I've done my job right, I'm physically exhausted. It may only be two in the afternoon, but already my voice is hoarse, my legs tired, my neck tight. I have just taught five straight classes to 175 students. It is exactly like giving five one-hour performances. Any teacher who doesn't feel fatigued each day is not giving 100 percent, period. Of course, just like any seasoned pro, through the years I've learned to pace myself. Once I even took a vocal class to learn how to use more of my diaphragm as a way to diminish stress on my vocal chords.

All day long you try not to stand stationary in front of the room by walking up and down the rows, yet with 40 desks shoved in a 30 × 24 room, every row is littered with backpacks, making a teacher's movement tricky at best. Stepping over the 20- to 30-pound bags is like walking through a minefield. With the trend toward eliminating lockers, some students carry two backpacks plus an athletic bag or instrument case.

Teaching drains your brain as well. Few jobs demand so much in the way of instantaneous decision making. Your eyes and ears always must be focused on each of the 175 customers you work with every day. Unlike politicians who get debriefings before press conferences, teachers must be ready to answer extemporaneously dozens of questions each day covering a range of topics.

It is presumed that during the 55-minute conference or preparation period I will be able to create lesson plans for three different courses, work on the student newspaper, photocopy any handouts, answer mail, return phone calls, meet with parents, call students' parents if their children need help, conduct office business with principals, deans, and counselors, grade tests and essays, pick up stray books left in book bins under desks and paper on the floor, straighten desks, and clean the whiteboards. In actuality, I do much of this work after regular working hours late into the afternoon.

No matter how well planned my prep may be, there is no predicting which teacher may walk in for some help, or which administrator may phone with some problem, thereby depleting precious minutes.

2:45   Period 6 ends; students go home

I do know teachers who leave at approximately the same time as their pupils, pejoratively referred to by administrators as "five and drive"—teach five periods, then leave immediately. The number of hours spent on campus is not necessarily an indication of one's level of dedication because some people need to pick up their own children from schools or child-care centers, so they take work home.

3:10   Department chair meeting

Now that the teacher's official workday has ended, the meeting day begins. Picture this: You've gone through a full day of work and now you'll sit in a room for at least an hour and a half listening to people talk at you. Usually there are ten or 15 agenda items. We're lucky to get through half of them, partially because of one or two chatty teachers who lengthen the proceedings. Not only is it difficult to concentrate during these long meetings, but many agenda items pertain to what teachers *are not* doing correctly and what they'd better start doing correctly or else. In other words, the message, geared for that minority of teachers who don't belong in the classroom, is preached to the choir, the department heads, the instructional leaders on campus, who for the most part are some of the school's best employees. Every time I have to sit there hearing the condescending and derogatory tones of an administrator after having taught my heart out, I feel a giant hammer pounding my entire body into the ground. If only these former teachers could hear themselves.

4:50   Return to classroom

Write down tomorrow's agenda on the board and pack up briefcase. Tonight, I'm taking home three sets of papers (35 per class, 105 papers, 315 pages total) and my lesson planning book.

5:00   Teacher's workroom

After three earlier attempts, I pop my head in, discover no one around, and quickly run to the machine to make my 35 copies, only to discover a hand-scrawled note, "Service call has been placed."

5:05 p.m.   Leave work

Total pay: $194.44 before taxes, based on a $35,000 annual salary.

So, what do you want to be when you grow up?

CHAPTER 2

The School as a Workplace: Today's Sweatshops

One of the most popular episodes of *I Love Lucy* shows the title character and her best friend, Ethel, working in a candy factory, frantically trying to wrap chocolates moving increasingly faster on an assembly belt. Instead of wrapping the mouthwatering chocolates, Lucy and Ethel stuff them into every place they can find—their mouths, clothes, hats—and prevent them from reaching their ultimate goal: sale to the general public.

The same fate has befallen American schoolchildren: Like widgets on an assembly line, they are rushed from classroom to classroom for periods lasting less than an hour. By the time teachers take attendance and bulletins are read over the public address system, most students have barely 30 minutes in which to learn. There may be a hubbub of activity at a school, but not much learning is taking place.

This anachronistic assembly line structure of educating young people has remained virtually unchanged during its 160-year history. The status quo prevents any real revamping of public education, from the size of the buildings to the duration of the class periods. The institution conditions students for the relatively brief time they attend school, yet wreaks a heavy toll on both pupils and teachers.

What an eye-opener it was when I realized that it wasn't only the students who were on the assembly line— the teachers were as well. They are pushed involuntarily from one meeting, to the next announcement, to the next class, and so on, filled, wrapped, and packaged with eduspeak, and put into boxes—their classrooms.

As Philip Bigler and Karen Lockard describe the situation in *Failing Grades: A Teacher's Report Card on Education in America* (p. 73), the teacher "is always behind, always has papers to grade and return, always has work to prepare. Not only do teachers become demoralized . . . students also feel discouraged by a situation when their voices are not heard, their papers not read, and their needs not met."

It's not that much of an exaggeration to claim that public schools today are America's sweatshops. If schools were office buildings and housed only adult workers, Congress would pass a law denouncing the conditions, and the Occupational Safety and Health Administration would draw up guidelines to clean them up, closing some schools down.

If schools want to attract more talent, then they need to appeal to those who have the greatest influence on student learning: teachers.

Having worked in the private sector for ten years before entering teaching, I know how much better other professionals are treated than teachers, who must deal with everything from inadequate materials and unreliable copying service to condescending administrators. So much of this mistreatment of teachers is inculcated that those in charge often fail to see the situation clearly.

It is an injustice that those entrusted to teach the youth of America have been treated as second-class workers for nearly two centuries. For too long, society has taken them for granted, assuming future students will get a good education despite the challenge of passing ballot measures that provide for school improvements via an increase in property taxes.

In some respect, it's even more important for teachers to demand better treatment and improved working conditions than to demand higher pay, because school environment directly affects job performance.

Following are prime examples of the inadequacies, disgraces, and inhumanities that befall what many refer to as the most important job outside of the military in terms of the security of this country's future.

The Physical Plant—America's Trailer Parks

Imagine a classroom with no air conditioning, 40-year-old textbooks, insufficient supplies, peeling paint, and aisles so narrow it's impossible to walk between the desks. Where are you? Uruguay? Tibet? The Congo?

Try any school district here in America.

The country that houses the world's best universities also boasts a third-world kind of kindergarten through 12th grade (K–12) public education system. These are the conditions in which children learn and teachers work. One look at the dilapidated condition of public school buildings speaks volumes about the low priority our society places on education.

In many communities, school buildings are neighborhood eyesores. Drive around town and examine the elementary, middle, and high schools. Many are surrounded by rust-stained concrete walls, the result of moisture from decades-old chain-link fences. If the schools were houses, homeowners associations would call their city representatives in horror.

How can the public expect top-notch education when the buildings that serve students are the oldest, most outmoded public structures in town? Chipped paint, leased bungalows, crumbling asphalt, overflowing toilets, inoperable drinking fountains, dirty walls and floors, dimly lit hallways, banged-up lockers, and lopsided lunch tables abound. Even when a school gets the rare paint job, the drab shade reminds one of a prison more than an exciting place to learn. Schools need to look inviting, not depressing. Just as workers should feel pride in their workplace, so should children feel pride in their schools.

Bathrooms have graffiti with no soap, no paper towels, and no stall doors. And that goes for the student bathrooms as well. In fact, some schools have converted faculty bathrooms into storage areas.

Here is one description from a New York teacher with 31 years' experience on the condition of her workplace:

> Our buildings are old and in poor condition. Windows don't open, lighting is poor, ventilation is terrible. Usually you are freezing or roasting. The building I'm in—almost a hundred years old—was finally remodeled three years ago. It is much brighter and you can recognize someone at the other end of the hall. But there are too many buildings at the school that still need updating. Some have not had any interior paint for 30 years. The halls reek of urine from the boys' bathroom. At our school they were continually giving the boys lectures on proper bathroom use until they finally realized that the pipes were corroded (100 years old, what a surprise!) and the liquid was running down the walls. We have too many crumbling facilities.

Faculty lounges resemble thrift stores. In them you will find old, beat-up avocado green couches with stained, mismatched pillows, manual dial microwaves that are filthy and never cleaned, refrigerators with broken climate controls, chairs fit for children (usually the old ones too broken for even the students to use). Try sitting in a wooden chair made for a first grader.

Society shovels students and teachers into cramped quarters that any mid-sized business would be ashamed to invite clients to. Schools in major cities such as New York, Chicago, and San Francisco must ignore legal limits on the number of students in a class because of lack of space. If classrooms posted the legal limit of persons allowed for occupancy as restaurants and elevators do, they would be cited. What good is reducing class size if there's no place to house the students?

Visitors are amazed at how close to each other students have to walk—no wonder physical altercations happen so frequently at overcrowded schools. The scarcity of open space on campuses is at epidemic proportions, with former playground areas taken up by portable classrooms. Many schools resemble housing projects rather than places for students to learn.

Look at how beautiful college campuses tend to be. Notice how construction is an ongoing event, even for such nonessentials as coffee houses and recreational facilities. The University of Virginia has a $18.5 million aquatic and fitness center with three pools, Occidental College used $14 million to create a food court offering a bakery and sushi bar, and Temple University spent $10.5 million on a sports complex with a motorized climbing wall. Meanwhile, in the K–12 world, students in year-round schools swelter in rooms with no air conditioning, and schools located near airports take "jet noise breaks" in nonsoundproof buildings.

At schools where custodial help is wanting, teachers have to clean their own floors, wash their black or white boards, line up the desks each day, even paint their own rooms. Some teachers are expected to hang maps and bulletin boards themselves.

Would you allow your child to sit at a table that's never wiped off? Or sit in a never cleaned chair? Or sit on a rarely vacuumed floor? You do if your child goes to public schools.

Education's dirty little secret is that the rooms aren't that clean. Classrooms don't have dust bunnies—they have dust elephants. Clumps of hair can be seen all over the floor, along with bits of paper, crushed candy residue, dried gum bits, and caked-in dirt. It's not the custodians' fault; districts fail to allocate enough funds for house-cleaning.

The one time a year teachers can count on their rooms being cleaned is right before an open house. One teacher said that bungalows at her school are hosed down once every three years.

A longtime fifth grade teacher from the East Coast discussed cleanliness at her facility:

> If you have a principal willing to fight, the building is clean, but the cleaning staff is in short supply. The building I'm in has three cleaning ladies for three floors. In 1970 this building had seven cleaning ladies. Our rooms are swept every other day, and we empty our own trash. We even supply our own liner bags. Nothing is ever moved and the floors are *never* mopped until the next summer recess—even in classrooms where students eat lunch in them. If a cleaning lady is out, no substitute is assigned until she is out for three consecutive days. My room has gone 11 days without being cleaned.

How can you boost state standardized scores when rooms are filthy? How can you implement state standards when fights break out regularly during lunch? Schools are stuck in a perpetual survivor mode, just trying to get through the day without a major incident that might make the next day's newspaper or, worse, newscast.

Because many schools no longer employ full-time gardeners, coaches do manual labor such as dragging the field, setting up batting cages, erecting bleachers in the gym, chalking the field, repairing broken-down equipment, even weeding. It is degrading to ask teachers to do yard duty, let alone the yard. What's next—having teachers be crossing guards? Is this the best use of college-educated employees? Too often the bottom line is forgotten.

Before any discussion about improving test scores takes place, schools' physical buildings need to be maintained properly so they aren't a distraction. Not too long ago one of those education waves that floods everyone's classrooms hit: the concept that schools should help build a child's self-esteem. Well, how good can that child feel about himself when he is dropped off each day at a building that looks like a prison, and then he sits in a filthy classroom? According to a 2001 public opinion poll by Peter D. Hart and Robert M. Teeter for Educational Testing Service, 78 percent of people favor spending tax dollars on fixing up schools and building new ones. Schools should show children how much society cares about where they are every day of 13 years and the value of education in our country.

Classroom Climate

Inadequate space in the classroom also makes teaching difficult. The vast majority of school buildings have been made obsolete by today's higher student-teacher ratios and computer equipment. Rooms designed for 25 students now hold as many as 40, along with tables laden with computers, printers, and other hardware. When districts build new schools, they need to take into consideration how much larger the classrooms need to be. And with more and more schools eliminating lockers because of their high maintenance cost, there is the problem of overstuffed backpacks mentioned earlier. How can teachers do their jobs when there isn't enough room for them to serve their clients—the students?

Many schools are so overcrowded that classes are held in auditoriums, cafeterias, libraries, and storage rooms. Some schools have a makeshift library in the hallway, which makes learning difficult for students.

Overcrowding affects teachers as well. Some don't have their own classroom, requiring them to travel from room to room each period. Without fail, the brand-new teachers are not given rooms and are forced to move around. The group that needs the most support must struggle not only with disciplining students and grading an avalanche of papers, but also with packing and unpacking their work tools. Some secondary school teachers travel as much as five times a day. Due to some teachers' unwillingness to share their rooms, the traveling teacher must be sure to have at all times basic supplies, including chalk, staplers, paper clips, tape, and paper. There are even science teachers who have to lug shopping carts of lab materials down crowded corridors.

The inability to stake a claim to a room rocks a teacher's foundation. No matter how many hours teachers put into hanging up motivational posters and student work, they are left with the thought that at any given time another teacher can use that room. This situation is already the norm at year-round campuses, where every couple of months a teacher strips his room down only to rehang everything a few weeks later.

Some schools rent out classrooms in the evenings and on weekends. This makes it quite stressful when the regular teacher comes back to find desks in the wrong place, materials missing, and writing on the board. The one area in which a teacher can feel secure is no longer a refuge.

Even when one feels somewhat secure within the confines of one's classroom, a teacher is not safe from distractions. Teachers experience "an endless stream of interruptions, assemblies, P.A. announcements, and other disruptions of instruction, making it difficult for even the most talented teachers to effectively plan or complete required curriculum objectives" (Bigler and Lockard, p. 25).

The message is subtle but clear: What teachers do in their classrooms isn't all that important and can be interrupted at any time.

Student messengers walking into a classroom to pick up attendance folders may not seem like a big deal. However, children are easily distracted. Every time the door opens, watch how all the students' heads instinctively turn away from the teacher or the board or wherever their attention had been focused on. The teacher has to pause the lesson and wait for the door to close and the students to regain concentration.

One day during a 20-minute period when my students were delivering oral presentations, a student messenger arrived with boxes of books returned from another teacher. Minutes later, a second student walked in with a calendar of counseling sessions, followed by a third delivering a schedule for another student.

All of these messengers interrupted students delivering timed speeches that required two weeks of research. Each student speaker lost his concentration, as did the rest of the class.

Not a single one of these interruptions merited disrupting the classroom. Each easily could have been taken care of at another time. It's not uncommon to have two to four student teaching assistants walk into a room during one class hour, and frequently the same student comes in twice.

P.A. announcements in particular are distracting. They can occur at any time during the school day (even testing periods aren't immune) and for inane reasons such as announcing where and when sporting events will take place, or repeating information already distributed in memos or printed in the daily bulletin. It's a feature more akin to working in a factory than a learning environment. And some principals don't seem to know when to stop talking. The P.A. acts as a controlling device for them.

What administrators, who formerly taught, fail to recall is how disruptive such announcements are to the classroom environment that has been established by the teacher. Intercom announcements are annoying, rude, and not conducive to a focus on learning. They damage the delicate instructional atmosphere, extinguishing any flame of knowledge, which is then difficult to rekindle. Since there's no way to turn off the speaker, they stop dead the lesson that's going on, the lesson the teacher meticulously planned to bring out "educating moments," those times when students have stopped paying attention to the wall clock and are highly engaged. Likewise, students don't care for such interruptions, leading many to ignore them and, in turn, lose respect for the administration.

"Interruptions on the P.A. are constant and annoying," said one New York teacher. "It often sounds like a hospital. This interferes with the flow of your teaching day."

Having the ability to make important announcements to an entire school, especially when there is a real emergency, definitely has its place. Mostly, however, what is broadcast is mundane and repetitive. For example, many schools use their P.A. system to read aloud from announcement bulletins already printed and posted. Such announcements commonly run ten to 15 minutes long, eating away precious instructional minutes. This is especially harmful during minimum days. Once during a shortened 36-minute period, it took 12 minutes to read the bulletin aloud, leaving 24 minutes for learning to take place.

Teachers are taught from day one to plan out lessons carefully. What's the use if on any given day at any given time an interruption can ruin the momentum of the lesson.

As a 33-year veteran teacher describes intercom interruptions, "It makes you angry, and you can't help but roll your eyes. The students don't like them, either." Some teachers cover up their speaker boxes or disconnect the P.A. system altogether. To ward off student messengers, this teacher and many of her colleagues have resorted to hanging "Do Not Disturb" signs on their doors.

Often personal information meant only for faculty ears is revealed on the P.A., admonishing teachers in condescending tones: "Do not excuse students from class before the passing bell." "Be sure to turn in paperwork no later than 3:00 P.M." "Make sure all books have been returned." Instead of seeking out the specific teachers who are letting their students out early, which would take more time to do and necessitate discreet human resource skills in personal meetings with individual teachers, these principals choose to broadcast their criticisms, stabbing the heart of the teaching rank's morale. It is a cheap and easy way to administer. Publicly humiliating teachers sends a terrible message to the students about how to treat other people. Insulting the one group of adults on campus whom young people spend the most time with infects a school's spirit and creates an overall unpleasant atmosphere.

Administrators making announcements willy-nilly has gotten so out of hand that some collective bargaining agreements allow for only a single interruption per day at specific times of the day—such as first thing in the morning or just before the end of the school.

With added pressures on schools to administer mandatory standardized testing, it is imperative that classroom time remain as free from interruptions as possible. The ambiance in a classroom should be like that of a library or church in terms of respect for one's surroundings. Administrators should treat the P.A. system as the public is asked to use 911—only for emergencies.

Lack of Support

Offices

Lack of privacy and workspace presents another challenge for teachers. Very few have private space or even a common room where they can photocopy lesson plans and get supplies. Even conference rooms are rare on school grounds because of overcrowding.

With teachers expected to do more, including contacting parents before and after student progress reports, private offices are crucial to their job. Teachers need offices —at least one for each department—where they can visit quietly and tutor students, have parent consultations, or even make an occasional doctor's appointment. One teacher tells of calling her gynecologist in the school's only teacher room, where several of her colleagues listened in as she tried to explain in a hushed tone why she needed to see the doctor.

Teachers are expected to contact parents for a variety of reasons, with some schools insisting that a parent receive not just a follow-up call to a teacher action, but a call beforehand as well to let a parent know some action *may* be taken. Failing the course? Phone home. Didn't do homework? Phone home. Going to change the policy on work handed in late? Phone home. What's next? Informing parents of a change in color of dry erase markers?

If teachers are going to be asked to do more, then they need to be given adequate tools to do their job. They need privacy to make these calls. Imagine receiving a parent's call during class when all student ears are listening in on your private conversation. A classroom is a poor substitute for a professional work area.

Supplies

Lack of supplies and access to equipment as basic as photocopiers also dampens teachers' enthusiasm. In fact, schools should be renamed Office Min for their dearth of basic necessities. Many do not have enough dictionaries, maps, or even current American flags reflecting the existence of 50 states.

One school made front-page news when a group of indignant veterans learned that the campus had classroom flags bearing 48 stars and promptly replaced them with today's stars and stripes.

The creative teacher can forget about elaborate art projects or science experiments. Most schools do not stock unusual items such as colored markers, glitter glue, or even beakers.

Sometimes teachers have to bring items from home to do their job. During California's energy crisis, a memo circulated asking teachers to bring in flashlights in case of a blackout. Shouldn't that item be provided for the teacher?

Petty cash or reimbursement is out of the question for most instructors. Unless they have prior approval, teachers must purchase supplies at their own expense. A biology teacher routinely purchases $32 dissecting packets on her own giving up on any chance of being reimbursed. As she puts its, "It's a battle not worth fighting." In fact, it is estimated that the average teacher spends $400 annually from his own wallet, while many others spend upwards of $1,000. While these are legitimate business-related, tax-deductible items, some teachers do not have enough deductions to itemize so that every dollar they spend on their job is out of their own pocket.

Even if a teacher is reimbursed, it can take quite a long time—two to three months in some cases.

Many schools run out of supplies before the end of the school year, claiming there is no more money to buy pens or paper. One wonders if the central office has a similar problem in serving upper management.

During a severe paper shortage at one school, the vice principal mentioned that he found reams of paper stored in a teacher's closet, so every teacher's room was going to be searched. He assumed that because one teacher did it, all did. Such jumping to conclusions is a common symptom among administrators: A few do it; therefore, all do it. Meanwhile, the real problem not being addressed is that the district does not give its teachers enough paper, and is more interested in a witch-hunt than a solution. How about stopping to think why a teacher would store a few reams of paper in a cabinet in the first place?

Perhaps if teachers were trusted with a well-stocked supply closet, they wouldn't feel they have to hoard paper. Perhaps if teachers weren't watched so carefully whenever they needed supplies, they wouldn't take more than they need for fear the supplies will dry up (as they do at many schools, sometimes as early as three months into the school year).

Veteran teachers end up resorting to guerrilla tactics, including leaving faculty meetings early to stock up on supplies and making friends with the book clerk. A Los Angeles–based teacher said, "Supplies depend on your relationship with the supply clerk, who is the assistant office secretary. If she likes you, you'll probably get the things you ask for."

At one school in the Midwest, teachers had to purchase all of their duplicating paper for the entire school year themselves because the school didn't send the order to the district office on time. "Teachers were told to write everything on the board if they didn't want to spend their own money," said one of the teachers.

Even when an item is in stock in a district warehouse, a teacher first needs to write up a requisition, have it approved, have a check cut, and wait for its shipment—all for a box of markers. Because there is such a long lead time between placing an order and receiving an item, any inspiration a teacher has goes unrealized. It is not uncommon for teachers to wait as long as six months to receive an ordered item.

Teachers should have the authority to get what they need for their classrooms without wasting time filling out forms. This bureaucratic way of doing business adds to the overriding powerlessness felt by educators who feel they can't get easily what they need to teach. Sometimes when they take a pencil, teachers are reminded by the supply clerk that it cost the district 12 cents. This is why so many teachers throw their hands up in the air and just buy the box of pencils with their own money. Besides, if teachers buy their own supplies, they can count on having a pen that writes when they need one. School supplies often are of the poorest quality. "The markers are so cheap they are dried up before you ever open them," said a New York elementary school teacher. "I have gotten colored construction paper that rips if you try to fold it, and a stapler that fell apart the first time I tried to use it."

Because of so many textbook shortages, not to mention the horrendous bureaucracy involved in ordering new books, teachers end up illegally photocopying copyrighted material so that their students have access to it. Book shortages became so bad in the Los Angeles Unified School District that superintendent Roy Romer installed a special hotline for schools to call when they need books.

Public schools finally have followed the lead of public libraries in bar-coding books due to the loss of so many expensive textbooks, often costing nearly $75 each. It only makes sense that if you are losing books, you need to figure out a better way of tracking them. However, even with a computer system, some schools have no way of knowing how many books have been checked out or how many are in the bookroom, frustrating teachers who need to make sure each student has a book. One has to hand count those on the shelves, then go into the rooms of the teachers and do likewise.

Some schools refuse to dedicate an employee to dole out supplies and books, so teachers are left to fend for themselves. In some cases, a stipend is paid to a teacher who, without the help of students, hand delivers supplies during his conference time.

To put it bluntly, society expects teachers to perform minor miracles at an embarrassingly low professional salary and in even more shameful working conditions. How can parents expect their children to maximize their learning when there aren't enough books? How can teachers do an effective job if they are wasting their valuable professional time tracking down scan-trons or filling out requisitions for books or rationing reams of paper to last an entire year?

Equipment

Ask any teacher what he would wish for if he had a magic wand, and photocopiers would be the unanimous choice.

Having only one or two copiers for an entire teaching staff means long lines, and long lines mean precious time wasted when educators could be doing something more productive. How many businesses with 50 or 100 employees could survive with one photocopier?

Because schools don't trust teachers to work with such heavy-duty equipment, they sometimes provide a clerk, who usually needs anywhere from four days to two weeks to turn copying jobs around. Then a form must be filled out, sometimes requiring a host of signatures, from department chair to principal. In some cases, teachers need written approval from their principals before they make a single photocopy. If a teacher gets a brainstorm of an idea the night before class and wants to do something innovative for students, such a Byzantine system kills the spontaneity of that idea.

Waiting in line has become a ritual in a teacher's workday. Upon seeing a colleague at the photocopy machine, animal instincts take over. Teachers in line eye the person at the machine warily, trying to determine how long the user will be. A dance occurs between the waiting teacher and the user. Will the person at the copier make eye contact with those waiting and be courteous enough to announce how much longer he will be, or will he not even recognize the existence of colleagues in the room? A quick glance at the copy counter may give those standing in line the information they seek: the number of copies being made by the user. Or, one can count silently to oneself as the machine spits out the copies. Of course, who knows how many originals there are? Quickly look at what's in the teacher's hand. Should you stick it out and waste away your 30-minute lunch or conference hour? What happens if, when it's your turn, there's no more paper, or the toner runs out, or a terrible misfeed occurs that you won't be able to fix, thus eliciting the burning ire of those behind you in line? Or should you leave now and come back after 5:00 P.M. or before 6:00 A.M., when surely no one will be waiting? It's like the exercise bikes at the health club: there almost needs to be a courtesy sign that reads, "When others are waiting, please limit your copies to 20."

Administrators lecture teachers about overdoing photocopies and, at some schools, teachers are given strict quotas on how many copies they can make for the entire year. That's akin to telling an attending physician in the emergency room to watch the number of syringes used on patients. Photocopied material is used so commonly it's like a second textbook for students.

One copier also means that whenever the toner runs out or the machine malfunctions, teachers have no place to go to make copies. And schools traditionally purchase less-than-stellar equipment to begin with. As a cost-saving measure, schools frequently accept second-hand copiers from private businesses looking for a tax deduction; then the copiers often break down.

A high school teacher said, "They usually break down once every two weeks. And teachers who don't know how to use them usually break them and leave a mess for the next person." An elementary teacher discussed several problems she has had to face in trying to use the school's sole copier:

> There is one machine that overheats continuously, and it is out of order so much that there is a laminated sign next to the machine ready to put right into place (almost daily). I teach in a portable, which means I have to put on my winter clothes, pack up my supplies, and walk upstairs—only to find out that the machine is not working. I have stayed at school until 6:00 P.M. just to try and get at the copy machine. There is a line at 7:00 A.M. in the morning, the earliest we can get into the building.

Without fail, a school's copier malfunctions toward the end of the school year, which is particularly troublesome for secondary teachers readying for final exams. No wonder so many teachers just head over to Kinko's, where there's no wait, no quota, no problem.

As a result of such inconveniences, teachers simply adapt their teaching to the supplies and equipment at hand. No overhead projector? Write on the board. No more photocopying privileges because you're over your copy quota? Dictate to the students. Teachers are very cunning adapters to their situation, making do with what they have. It's like creating Michelangelo's *David* out of Play-Doh.

Unlike photocopiers, providing teachers with computers for classroom use is not a problem. Thanks to computer companies' donations and schools receiving technology grants, a majority of schools have plenty of computer equipment. The problem lies in how the technology is applied, and how the blazing spotlight on computers have been misdirected, neglecting the importance of the teacher.

While schools do a good job of providing computers, they do a poor job of figuring out what to do with them. A distinction needs to be made between teaching with computers and using computers as a work tool. Should school libraries have computers? Yes. Should business classes instructing use of software programs have computers? Yes. Should schools offer courses in desktop publishing and web page design? Yes. Should every student in every classroom have a computer? No.

Look in classrooms across the country and there will be computers—sitting there unused. A 1995 study found that only one-fourth of teachers were using technology (Darling-Hammond, 1997a, p. 37). Many teachers are simply not interested in using computers as part of their daily lesson plan. With the exception of math and science teachers, most faculty members have a more liberal arts background, which explains why they are not that computer savvy. Even when districts train their employees on computers and software programs, unless the teacher goes back into the classroom and immediately practices these skills, whatever information was learned quickly evaporates. Additionally, with the available class time already shrinking due to increased testing, teachers are scrambling to cover the whole curriculum as it is without having to incorporate computers.

As wonderful as computers are, they're like showing a video in class. They are a nice break from the routine and they can "wow" students for a short time, but then you have to return to developing strategies on getting students to grasp the material. A teacher creating an exciting computer demonstration or presentation is fine. But you can't shove students in front of PCs; it's just as wasteful as shoving them in front of TVs.

The most powerful use of computers in the classroom is when students incorporate them in their work, such as science simulations, revising their writing, using Power-Point for oral presentations, or conducting research as long as they've been taught how best to navigate through the overwhelming amount of information. Using computers for drill practices, however, is as wasteful a learning tool as workbooks. Having computer classes is also useful in teaching students skills as long as the software is current; otherwise, it's as if students were learning from a history book that has Jimmy Carter as the most recent U.S. president.

For the most part, schools have been sold the proverbial bill of goods when it comes to computers. They are not the panacea to improving student learning, as some have claimed. This comes from one who used computers for ten years before becoming a teacher, whose master's degree focused on technology, and who has taught college-level computer courses.

Computers alone do not make students smarter. Having access to the Internet does not automatically translate into knowledge learned. It's similar to TV newscasts showing reporters live on location. They have reporters on remotes because they have the technology to do it, not because any breaking information has just been revealed.

Someone somewhere started a trend to ensure that all school children had access to computers. The idea was

that if America's schoolchildren all got hooked up to the
Information Superhighway, all poor student achievement
would be wiped out.

   Over the past decade, school districts quickly tried to
catch up with the rest of the business world. Suddenly,
IBM and Apple were gladly giving millions of computers
away to gain a market advantage over each other. In an industry already riddled with computer-phobes, any teacher
who could hook up a CPU to a printer was anointed the
school's computer guru. Remember, really smart computer people do not go into public education; districts
can't afford to pay them. "The people in charge of technology at the school are somewhere between competent and
inept," said a Spanish teacher. Soon teachers were trained
in how to turn on a computer and use a mouse.

   All through this transition to technology schools
looked good. At open houses, parents could see the shiny
computers and feel that their child was receiving a
state-of-the-art education. As more and more households
were able to afford their own computers, the luster of the
school's technology began to dull. No longer were computers a novelty. Unlike individuals who can upgrade
their PCs inexpensively, school districts, which serve
large populations, are unable to keep up with the computer industry's frequent breakthroughs in speed and
memory. It's not uncommon for students to have more
current equipment than their schools. Because they are
unable to keep up with the rapid changes in technology,
schools would be better off maintaining a smaller number
of computers that continue to be upgraded rather than
put a PC on each student's desk that starts to age immediately. Once the equipment becomes antiquated, using it
to teach is no longer conducive to fostering a working
knowledge of any current technology once students enter
the workforce. Having up-to-date equipment is a peren-
nial problem for schools, many of which still house film-
strips and 16mm film projectors. That's like shooting family memories on 8mm film instead of video. Besides, when

given a choice, teachers would rather have more paper, pens, and books than computers, printers, and scanners.

Districts should provide their teachers with the technology for their staff, not waste money on trying to get a computer in the hands of every student who walks through their doors. Providing teachers with laptops as part of their routine equipment paraphernalia is the best use of technology, allowing those most comfortable with the medium to create lessons and presentations. It would also encourage teachers to work on lessons at home, eliminating any compatibility problems between a teacher's home PC and the one in the classroom. Unfortunately, too many districts don't trust teachers to take any equipment home.

Getting equipment fixed or replaced takes a long time as well. Recently, a Los Angeles Unified School District high school hadn't replaced its damaged computers when school started in September, so students taking a computer class had nothing to work on. After a while, the district was able to get computers from the defunct $175 million Belmont High School and some from a prison, but guess what? No proper wiring came with them so the new computers sat on the students' desks unused for weeks— until the district acted after the story appeared in the newspaper.

The most insulting thing about the lack of supplies and equipment is that there isn't a sense of outrage on the part of states and districts that their teachers lack the most essential basics. What are they thinking? If students can go without enough books and sit at desks that are falling apart, then teachers surely can be more creative without access to a photocopy machine?

Teaching is tough enough without having to search for a pencil or a copy machine. A district would not go bankrupt by providing its teachers with sufficient supplies and equipment. So what's the problem?

Before they hire one more teacher specialist or one more consultant or go after one more grant, districts need to take care of teachers' most basic needs.

Teachers need the basics if they are going to teach the basics.

Telephones

Having a phone is not often a concern for the lowest-level office worker. One may not have a company car, an expense account, a secretary, perhaps not even a computer, but everyone has a phone. It is as much a part of standard office equipment as air conditioning is standard automobile equipment. Unless you're a teacher.

It is very inconvenient to have to go to the faculty lounge or the main office to use a phone, especially when you can only leave a classroom during certain times of the day. And there is no privacy in those places.

"Having to wait until after school to go to the main office and contact parents or anyone else is a real pain," said a ten-year veteran teacher.

While some schools provide no phones whatsoever to their teachers, other campuses give their staff phones that can be used only to call internally. Phones that offer internal connections are more of a nuisance than an aid, adding to the endless daily interruptions of the educational environment. What are districts afraid of? That teachers will make personal calls during all the free time they have?

It is vitally important that the teacher who is legally responsible for the students' welfare have easy and immediate access to 911. Why ask the teacher to call the school operator first, who then notifies an administrator? During a crisis, time is of the essence, and sometimes 30 seconds can be the difference between a tense situation and a deadly one.

Earlier the issue of interruptions of the classroom environment was discussed as detrimental to the learning atmosphere. So, wouldn't installing phones in classrooms add to that problem? A basic policy of phone etiquette would eliminate their concern (similar to P.A. usage). At some schools outside calls are automatically blocked out during teaching hours. It's important to remember the difference between teaching and other businesses; a teacher at work is with his clients nearly all the time. Would an accountant accept calls during a meeting with a client?

Another aggravation is when the school operator asks whether the call is personal or business-related. The teacher feels he is being treated as a child. At some schools, teachers receive a list of all their phone calls, requiring them to initial each personal call made, amounts usually in the 25- to 50-cent range. Such pettiness is an unnecessary aggravation.

In addition to adequate equipment, teachers need access to classroom phones with an outside line. School shootings underscore the urgency of ensuring that teachers have access to the world outside their classroom.

It's the twenty-first century: Give teachers phones.

Secretaries

Abundant paperwork also burdens already overworked teachers. That's why teachers need secretaries.

While administrators enjoy bragging about how much support they offer teachers, it is really the secretaries who keep a school functioning. A competent secretary should be given a raise, but a competent secretary who types forms and even mails letters for teachers—not part of her job—deserves to have a school building named after her.

Unfortunately, there aren't enough of these kind-hearted souls to go around. Some principals' secretaries bark at teachers, act domineering, and belittle teachers, making them feel unworthy. One secretary always greets teachers with a belligerent "What!" whenever approached. Those who are not helpful make the teacher's already difficult job unbearable. If you can't even get respect from those with whom you work, no wonder the outside world looks down at what you do for a living.

Public education is a bureaucracy, so everything requires multiple paperwork. The most minute action needs to be documented these days. Which part of the teacher's work time should be shortened to increase the amount of time to document everything: lesson planning, evaluating student work, researching subject matter?

Here's what one teacher from Pennsylvania does: "I keep a phone log of each parent phone call I make. I record time of day, whom I spoke to or if an answering machine picked up, and the reason for my call. This way, parents cannot come back to the district and say that they were never notified about a particular grade or situation. It's to protect myself in addition to keeping track of whom I have already called and how many times."

In Ohio, as a way to prove whether teachers are doing anything about students who score poorly on state tests, teachers need to document the intervention techniques they use from the beginning of the school year. Each and every student conference needs to be written down on official state forms. Explaining how this makes her feel, a middle school English teacher said, "If I'm a professional and they give me the students and respect me, then they should assume that modifications are being done without having to leave a lengthy paper trail. My time would be better spent grading papers or organizing my classroom. It looks like a tornado went through it because I don't have time to organize my room."

If a teacher doesn't document, he could find himself in a situation similar to this Florida educator: "I called a parent from my home because the student didn't do his homework. The parent used abusive swearing over the phone loud enough for my husband to hear. The next day the parent told my principal that it was me who used abusive language—and the principal believed the parent, referring me to anger management classes."

Filling out forms is pure drudgery for anybody, but especially so for the overworked teacher who is gasping for some extra time. A longtime elementary school teacher summed it up this way: "Every time a new position is created, that person creates some form they want for each student. These forms seem to sit in folders all year and never are looked at again."

One teacher from New York was astonished to discover the required paperwork she had to fill out was to benefit the district monetarily. "I resent filling out long forms on students for SSI or special evaluations and discovering that the district (not the teacher) is paid $15 for every form that is completed."

For those teachers who wish to expand their students' knowledge through field trips and guest speakers, or their own through conferences, the resulting red tape discourages many from doing any of these actions, because each one requires multiple forms. There is the form for a field trip that needs school board approval. The form for the parent that the student will be going on a field trip. The form for using private transportation. And God forbid you invite a guest speaker. Plus, the teacher must call the bus company, arrange for payment, and correspond with guest speakers ensuring that the main office knows you will be having a visitor.

Searching for all the required forms eats up time as well. A teacher shouldn't have to see three secretaries to locate the proper paperwork. If schools will not perform these tasks for the teachers, then at the very least, give teachers all the forms they may need.

Even the physical task of filling out the forms takes more time than necessary. At some districts, the forms are so antiquated one needs a typewriter to fill them out. And if you have to charge a few dollars per student for the bus, each child needs to receive a receipt filled out by, you guessed it, the teacher.

Having a secretary do this work for the teacher would relieve stress and free up time for the teacher to work on more critical matters. "What a treat having a secretary would be," said a New York middle school teacher. "I spend half my day on clerical duties. Having someone to alleviate those tasks would free me up to develop better lessons, and work with students." Plus, providing this kind of support would prompt other educators to expand learning opportunities for their students. Instead, many don't even try to be creative because they know the amount of effort it would take.

It wouldn't be necessary or financially feasible for each teacher to have a secretary. One secretary could support a dozen teachers. Certainly, large departments such as math and English at the secondary level deserve at least one secretary.

Teachers who head departments could also use secretaries. Filling out forms, arranging for conferences and substitutes, putting memos in teachers' mailboxes, and retrieving supplies and books all take away countless hours from the teacher who should be working on teaching-related material.

When it was suggested to a principal that one of the six secretaries in the main office be dedicated to helping teachers with paperwork, he reacted as if the teacher had asked for a year's supply of staples. "We can't do that" was the response.

Why should it be so shocking to provide teachers with the barest minimum of support? It's as if teachers are another breed of worker. The thinking goes something like this: "Since you work with kids all day, your job isn't that stressful. You don't need accoutrements like other professionals. You use puppets, sing songs, have recess, read stories, have nap time. Come on, you don't have a real job."

Superintendents are quick to point out that job number one is taking care of the students, a nice politically correct sentiment but somewhat vacuous. If teachers are not being taken care of, how can they work effectively with students?

States and districts need to provide teachers with ample supplies in the most stress-free way possible; offices with reliable, up-to-date equipment; a team of support personnel whose main job is to be there for the teachers; whatever they need to perform their jobs at a high standard of quality in the classroom. Only then will superintendents be taking care of the students.

Lack of Respect

If teachers had these things, it would go a long way toward improving their work environment. And it's all really a matter of budgetary priorities. But when it comes to such issues as respect, it takes more than money to fix; it would take a change of attitude.

An English teacher from Ohio was at a podium hosting a student writers tournament for the school district when she noticed her principal mouthing everything she was saying as he sat in the audience. "He was totally bored, so he decided to act like Chevy Chase, mimicking me. Keep in mind I'm doing this on a Saturday without compensation and that there are important district officials in attendance. When I approached him about this, he said, 'Oh, I was just joking around.'"

A teacher from Florida described how an entire district treated a teacher at her school when pornography was discovered on her computer. "They sent the middle school science teacher home immediately without telling her why. Later they called her to explain and had her stay home all week until the district could figure out who was responsible for it. It turned out to be a janitor."

When teachers from Los Angeles Unified who headed what turned out to be that year's winning academic decathlon team flew with their students to the national championship, their airfare and hotel were not paid for by the school. And the days off work to attend the event were charged against their own personal time, despite the yearlong commitment it took to coach the team, from after-school sessions lasting into the late evening to all-day Saturday sessions.

Teachers are asked for more than is reasonable: supervising lunch, doing bus duty, patrolling student bathrooms, even remaining on the lookout for PDAs (public displays of affection) during their conference periods. Why are teachers asked to do these things anyway? Would the head of a hospital ask doctors to patrol the patient parking lot during their breaks?

Listen to the voice of a 30-year fifth-grade teacher:

> The elementary teacher is the most downtrodden, beaten-up member of the teaching profession. The day starts early, and there is no end, no free periods, no duty-free lunch. We get 30 minutes for lunch, out of which we walk the students to the lunchroom, often waiting in line for five minutes. Then we have to pick them up and listen to the list of "wrongs" they have committed during lunch. I have been called, paged, asked to unlock my room for a child who has forgotten his ice cream money, and called down because a parent has stopped by to see about a child. In 30 years I don't think I have ever gotten to finish a lunch. I can't pack an orange because it takes too long to eat. Elementary teachers make sure their students are clothed, fed, and pay for student field trips. We are surrogate moms, and we never leave our job, often doing things on weekends or evenings with students.

All too often, teachers are viewed as older students. It's easy to lump teachers and students together because they are physically together all day long, whereas everyone else, from custodians to secretaries to principals, is not.

How else can one explain administrators chastising teachers in front of their students? One dean admonished me in front of my entire class for not having them underneath their desks during a lockdown drill, only the second such drill we had ever had. I looked over the memo carefully and nowhere did I see anything about having students crouch under desks. Any lack of common sense on my part did not give her carte blanche to lash out verbally while the young people I teach looked on. Even if I was dead wrong, did she think about her role as an administrator and how the children perceive her in that role?

The next day I received a call from one of my students' mothers who was outraged that this incident occurred in front of her son.

When I told the mother that the administrator did apologize later on, the mother replied, "But she didn't apologize to your students."

One of the more glaring examples of how teachers are treated like children comes at the end of the school year when myriad items need to be checked off before the teacher can leave for the summer.

At a school district in Florida, teachers have to get 12 signatures before they are given their last paycheck. "The librarian checks to see if all books have been returned, someone else checks that the computer has been turned in, and the department chair checks that the room is left tidy and clean."

Teachers are also expected to follow school policies developed for the students. No pagers and no cell phones makes sense for students, but for adults? "The teacher needs to be a role model for the student" is the thinking. But that teacher is no longer ten years old and may have a child in a day-care setting who demands immediate contact.

Once when the administration was considering uniforms for students, the idea came up, "Hey, what about uniforms for teachers!"

Schools bend over backward to give the appearance of fairness with no special treatment of teachers and, in so doing, end up tarnishing teachers' stature. During a meeting about parking assignments, an administrator said that no one class of workers should have priority in those assignments—that is, a secretary with more seniority should have a better parking space than a new teacher— except when it came to administrators. Whatever their seniority, they always get the most convenient parking spaces.

This lack of respect begets a lack of trust. Teachers are not trusted to be constructive on their own time, to know what's best for their students, to be out of the classroom, to arrive and leave their work site at the proper time, to know how to teach. Any teacher who does not follow the rules is to be mistrusted.

Most teachers have no access to their own workplace after hours or on weekends. A 33-year veteran teacher still has to "call ahead to get in. Only coaches have master keys." If that's the case, then maybe what needs to be restarted is the old timecard accounting system. Those teachers who stay on the job longer to grade papers or work on lessons would clock out later and get paid more. Isn't that the next logical step?

Some schools demand that teachers turn in their keys at the end of the school year. Obviously, the district does not trust its highly educated professionals. School secretaries have to collect all the keys in June and pass them out again in September, and teachers have to stand in lines both times.

Not allowing teachers keys to their own classrooms during the summer discourages them from working in their rooms, which also serve as their offices. It also reinforces the notion that teachers are expected to be on the job at an exact starting time until an exact ending time, and anything beyond that is not encouraged.

Even how teachers are paid disheartens many educators. While some districts pay their teachers every other week, even spreading the ten-month salary over a 12-month period, other schools pay teachers once a month. That translates to only ten financial pats on the back for the entire year. Who else besides armed service personnel deal with that? When you aren't compensated that much money to begin with, at least being paid more frequently would help.

While direct deposit is widely used nowadays, for some teachers picking up one's check requires a trip to the principal's office and receiving it without its even being placed in an envelope. Not providing for the most basic privacy adds to the feeling that one is more a hired hand than a professional.

Teachers receive few kudos. If one doesn't receive financial rewards, perks, or appreciation, pretty soon that person isn't interested in doing a good job. Why work hard when it doesn't get recognized? Are teachers supposed to be martyrs? There are so many things districts can do for teachers to make them feel appreciated. How many of them reward special gifts to their ten-, 20-, and 30-year teachers for staying with the profession for so long? How much money would it cost to provide small signs of appreciation? With the current trend among rookie teachers not to spend their entire career in education, wouldn't it make sense for districts to do everything they could to entice people to remain with the "company" and to make a big deal whenever a teacher reaches a milestone?

A teacher with ten years of experience said that appreciation is rarely shown "apart from the occasional apple from our leadership students or a lunch by the PTA." While many parents across the country try very hard to show appreciation toward teachers, whether it's on Teacher Appreciation Day or at the end of a school year, by giving teachers a cup, office supplies, or a free lunch, teachers would give all of that up in a second for more respect from their superiors.

Unfortunately, administrators aren't the only ones who demonstrate a lack of respect for teachers. Some parents look at teachers as second-class workers, the "B" actors of the professional world, disregarding their pedagogical knowledge. These parents feel they have leverage to challenge the methodology behind a teacher's assignments, tests, or grading system since the common perception is that teachers don't know what they're doing and, therefore, their practices need to be monitored closely. Also, the fact that teachers are paid with tax money seems to give parents the right to raise that "I pay for your salary so you serve me and do as I say" sentiment.

Some parents have sent teachers detailed, multiple-page letters explaining how their lessons are flawed and what they should be teaching instead.

Often the parents' complaints are quite amusing. One called a teacher to complain that her daughter had an assignment due the day after the Memorial Day holiday. When the parent was informed that the girl was assigned the work a week before the holiday, she still wasn't appeased. The family had planned a three-day vacation, and their child was not to be bothered with schoolwork.

Other teachers report having seen parent anger with their own eyes. "At one point, while discussing his son's lack of progress in my class, the father stood up, picked up a desk, and threw it across the room," said an English teacher.

Today's age of rage, whether it be on the highway or in the courthouse, has spilled into the classroom. In Great Britain Prime Minister Tony Blair has proposed harsher sentencing for abusive parents who threaten school staff. This has been called "school rage," and more than 140 cases of parents being banned from school grounds because of violent episodes were reported in England during 2000. Blair said, "There should be zero tolerance of abuse and harassment of nurses, paramedics, teachers, doctors, and other public servants" (BBC website). According to the U.S. National Institute of Justice in 1996, almost one out of five public school teachers reported being verbally abused in a 30-day period. One Georgia teacher said, "I was threatened to be assaulted and put in the hospital."

Students disrespecting teachers is so common nowadays that it's difficult for most teachers to think of just one example. A young teacher with only a few years teaching experience relates this story:

> Once I had a challenging, tough, disrespectful student
> who said the "f-word" in class out loud. He was

swearing because he was upset that I marked him late
for the third day in a row (three tardies equals one
detention). This particular student did not take
responsibility for his own lateness; as his teacher, it
was my fault in his opinion. Not to mention, he was
exceptionally late, and he totally disrupted the class
upon his extremely late arrival by yelling and throwing
books, etc. After his swearing episode, I asked him to
stay after class, so I could speak with him. I wrote
him up on a yellow disciplinary referral card, and
submitted it to the principal's office. The principal
called this unruly child down to his office, and asked
the student for his rendition of what happened in class.
Of course the child denied using any profanity and told
the principal he wanted other students in the class
interviewed to verify who was telling the truth. So the
principal asked me to get four or five student witnesses
from the class to tell him if the unruly student had in
fact used the "f-word" in class and was late three times.
I did get the witnesses, but this put several students
in an uncomfortable situation. Kids do not want to
"rat" on each other, let alone go to the principal's
office as a witness. I felt the principal should have
respected my classroom authority as one of his
teachers. He should have supported me from the
beginning and taken disciplinary action ASAP. The
student was given too much power . . . in this
particular situation. Eventually the child was
disciplined, but it was four days after the fact.

What's disheartening isn't the student's behavior but the
principal's.

The point is that from the most critical areas to the
most trivial, teachers are the Rodney Dangerfields of the
professional world: They get no respect.

Respect will only come once the profession reinvents
itself as one that doesn't just accept anyone, so that outsiders view teachers as specialists. In the meantime, as

long as anybody can become a teacher, everybody will continue taking turns putting teachers down.

Meetings

Teachers view meetings as the enemy. Besides keeping them from working with students, they require working with one another; something they are not used to doing regularly. Most good teachers take away little from these meetings except headaches and aggravation—understandable when one hears what goes on at them. At best, they are mildly tolerable; at worst, they are teacher-bashing sessions that feature verbal abuse about the terrible job teachers do.

Teachers also dislike meetings because they're scheduled after everyone has put in a full day's work. People are tired, cranky, and unreceptive to new ideas and approaches to teaching.

What administrators urge teachers to do while teaching students they commonly don't model during meetings. The techniques teachers have learned about how to vary lessons—that is, not to lecture the whole period, but to actively engage the students instead, is mysteriously missing from these meetings as teachers sit uncomfortably in a library, cafeteria, or auditorium setting because schools provide no professional space for their staff to meet. Such settings originally designed with students in mind provide uncomfortably small chairs and poor acoustics. As an elementary school teacher from New York describes her meetings in the student cafeteria, "The small, round lunchroom stool is extremely uncomfortable, and often it is difficult to see or hear." Of course, if teachers were able to meet regularly to discuss their practices, perhaps such a space would be provided. And an inordinate amount of the agenda revolves around "administrivia": attendance procedures, book collecting, how to fill out forms, etc.

"Most meetings just take up valuable time," said a high school teacher from California. "For most teachers in my school, meeting time is time to correct papers or fix roll books."

One of the more annoying things an outsider would see at a faculty meeting is when the administrator raises his hand and expects teachers to do likewise. This technique for quieting a group, taught as part of classroom management training, might be fine with seventh graders. But to use it with grown adults, college-educated instructors, is condescending.

Meetings are organized and facilitated for the lowest common denominator—how a gifted child feels sitting in a boring class that doesn't challenge him. So often, the same information is presented in a variety of ways: giving handouts to teachers, using overhead transparencies with the same material on them, and the administrator reading aloud word for word what's on the transparencies. Even for PowerPoint presentations, every slide is printed and distributed. It's as if the administration is tempting the teachers to not pay attention. Teachers want to rebel against such childish behavior, which is insulting to their intelligence.

Frequently a handful of chatty teachers monopolize the conversation. One 31-year veteran complimented her new principal's way of conducting meetings because "no one person or group is allowed to run away with the discussion, or to hijack the agenda with personal viewpoints." For her, "nonproductive meetings do not start on time and wander all over the place. You realize you've been sitting in an uncomfortable chair for two hours and nothing has been accomplished. The same people who disrupt every meeting have taken over the discussion, and everyone is ready to leave feeling angry and discouraged."

And if teachers decide to miss a meeting to work with students or on other work-related business, they are chastised with threatening memos and their pay is docked.

Too many worthless meetings scheduled at the worst times also hurt America's teachers. While these meetings may look good on paper, they rarely help teachers improve student learning.

Some schools bank time, that is, add minutes to the school day; then every other week or once a month have a minimum day for students so that staff meetings can take place, often in the afternoon. The problem with this format is that by the time the meetings begin, teachers are burned out. During minimum days for students, teachers actually work harder. Good teachers will try to shoehorn a 55-minute lesson into a 35- to 40-minute time period so as not to lose precious educational minutes. It is exhausting to have students fly in and out of your room every half hour; you're breathless by noon.

If districts want teachers to be receptive to meetings, why schedule them after the workday? Why schedule them on Mondays or Saturdays? Why schedule them at the worst possible times when most people are tired and not open to hearing presentations?

One meeting was scheduled to begin at the precise moment the last class ended, which meant that just by walking from your classroom to the meeting you were guaranteed to arrive late without even a five-minute bathroom break.

Meetings are arranged and scheduled haphazardly without considering people's time or energy: the first day of the month (payday, when teachers are anxious to deposit their checks), the first day of the semester (exhausting for teachers), and Mondays (exhausting for everybody).

One year, every faculty meeting occurred on payday. As the meeting drew closer and closer to 4:00 P.M. the pit in my stomach grew because I knew I wasn't going to be able to get to the bank before it closed to deposit my check (this was before automatic deposit became commonplace). I had to wait until the following afternoon to make the deposit.

At department chair meetings, teachers are told to "share with your department" so many items that if a truly conscientious teacher were to relay the information, no time would remain to discuss pertinent curriculum issues. One sits there and wonders, "Don't they know this?"

The only monthly meeting where real discussion of day-to-day practices take place is the department meeting, yet time is wasted even there on the minutiae and trivial organizational fuzzballs that educators can't seem to eliminate. So much time is consumed on noneducational classroom material that it prevents real dialogue about important teacher-student issues. Instead of allowing teachers to spend an hour once a month (only an hour!) discussing how to improve lesson plans or assess student achievement better, meetings get bogged down in the sludge of venting. This is not to belittle those who get caught up in this, for how can a teacher keep focused on the curriculum when there aren't enough books or supplies? What should be the small stuff is magnified to elephantine proportions, preventing the advancement of good teaching.

What's more, food and drinks are not commonly provided at meetings. Teachers are lucky if they get bags of chips and cans of soda. While not nutritionally sound or what high-priced attorneys have catered at their conference table, at least it is a gesture on the administration's part, a recognition that people need nourishment, especially when they're tired after working all day and don't really want to be there.

Usually the only way teachers get fed at meetings is when they bring in the food themselves. That's why one of the first tasks at hand whenever teachers meet is to circulate a snack sign-up sheet.

When teachers are treated to a rare free lunch, it usually consists of those sliced-up three-foot Subway sandwiches and plastic tubs of cookies from Cotsco. Otherwise, doughnuts are the most common cuisine offered free to teachers. That's because they're one of the least expensive food items that can be provided. Usually, they are the cheapest, worst-tasting variety. Where are the Krispy Kremes? It may seem trivial, but the quality of doughnuts is a microcosm of how the whole teacher profession is viewed: low quality. Public education is like a big box store: trying to offer everything to everybody with only sporadic service. Quality is not the focus, only quantity.

One particular eight-day period for me illustrated the distinction between the way a school treats teachers and the way the private sector operates.

One Saturday morning I had an in-service training at work, and the following weekend I had one hosted at the Getty Museum, the subject of a field trip.

At my school, market-brand doughnuts, graham crackers, and juice boxes were provided, all laid out in their original containers, not even put out on a paper plate.

At the Getty were fresh bagels, fresh fruit invitingly laid out, along with freshly squeezed orange juice and free posters of Van Gogh's *Irises,* a video, and an attractively designed teaching packet.

Even though the Getty workshop lasted only three hours, half of that time was allocated to the teacher to "continue to explore on your own, visit the teacher resource center, and plan for your visit," completely entrusting the teacher to judge best how to spend the rest of the day.

At my worksite, only the last two hours of the seven-hour day were left open for the teacher to decide for himself what he needed to do best for his development. The organized part of the Getty day revolved around creating lesson plans tailored to each teacher's subject area to maximize student learning during the visit.

The organized section at my school dealt with test-taking strategies, how to use e-mail, and discussion of an educational article, all with little relevance to a teacher's specific area, which is part of the problem with mass hit-and-run staff development: It must hit all subject areas and, in doing so, it barely hits the mark, skimming the surface of the actual goings-on in the classroom.

In a business where time matters so much, if you're going to take precious hours away from a working teacher's schedule, make sure it's for a good reason and that it is done in an attention-getting way; otherwise, it encourages teachers to bring papers to grade or to discuss the sports page in the back row. No wonder a colleague of mine refers to staff planning days as staff punishing days.

Productive meetings "would concentrate on specific departmental issues or training," said a ten-year veteran teacher. "Nonproductive meetings are administration-centered." Maybe there doesn't need to be a meeting one month, or maybe discussing two or three issues thoroughly in an hour is more productive. How about allowing teachers to come up with agenda items? Without the inclusion of instructors, meetings end up becoming a meaningless exercise to show the public that teachers have meetings, just like the rest of the working world.

Staff Development (Two Words That Make a Teacher's Skin Crawl)

The concept that teachers need regular training several times a year on how to teach flies in the face of the college degree and teaching certificate that teachers earned to get the job. If there is so much useful information that all teachers need, then lengthen the licensing process and have them all learn it before entering the classroom. I'm not implying teachers shouldn't stay abreast of new developments in learning. As doctors renew their licenses every ten years, so should teachers—and they do every five years. However, when training occurs on a monthly basis, it not only saps the energy and morale of teachers, but makes them question what it is they do know and why it isn't good enough.

In Susan Moore Johnson's *Teachers at Work: Achieving Success in Our Schools,* teachers often describe their staff development or in-service experience as "a haphazard sequence of speeches and workshops addressing unrelated topics" (1991, p. 254). Teachers are herded like cattle from emergency practices training to e-mail seminars to multicultural sensitivity workshops.

Too often the information dispensed is "a response to one of the latest educational trends or politically popular concepts" (Bigler and Lockhard, 1992, p. 95). There is hardly any follow-up to staff development. It's simply dumped on the teachers with no time to develop actual material for the classroom. It should be called staff-arrested development.

Other times the most obvious information is dispensed over a protracted length of time, giving the teachers the sense that they are seen as stupid. According to a science teacher, "One day all the teachers were taught how to turn on a computer. It was a complete waste of time." When something is not challenging, a person tends to tune out. As a high school teacher pointed out, "30 percent of it is productive; 70 percent wasteful."

A 30-year teacher from the East Coast has seen just about all varieties of staff development:

> Because there is tremendous pressure from Central Office to submit development plans, often hastily thrown together packages have been put together. One year we spent a whole day bouncing balls in the parking lot and playing games in the name of team building. Three days before you are to greet 28 new faces in your classroom, you are hardly in the mood for this type of team building. Working on grade-level curriculum would have been more my idea of team building.

Many districts choose to bring in "nationally renowned" (in other words, expensive) speakers to kick off the school year, sometimes referred to as "spray and pay," with no lasting impact once the meeting (misting) ends.

How strange that schools often don't use the best experts to conduct workshops: their own teaching staff.

Other schools try to compact everything for the entire year into opening meetings. "Administrators often filled in 18 hours prior to the opening of school, and quite often two-thirds of the program was a waste—a little information and a lot of filler," said one veteran fifth-grade teacher. Teachers get frustrated, then angry that they just can't be left alone to get their classrooms ready for their new students.

Attendance is mandatory, so if a teacher decides his time is better spent on planning the first week's lessons, photocopying classroom rules, putting posters on the wall, arranging desks, or writing nametags, he gets charged a personal day.

The opinion seems to be that allowing teachers to have an unstructured work day is akin to giving them a day off. Part of the problem, of course, is the number of teachers who do goof off, but they are hardly the majority. If there is one message that administrators need to hear, it is: Trust teachers to manage their own time.

Educators love to latch onto a newfangled concept— and consultants know this too well. All one has to do is repackage a well-tried teaching concept, come up with a cute acronym, get a dynamic speaker, conduct nation-wide workshops and bingo! You've got yourself a trend in public education. Then incorporate a business that sells videotapes and binders and provides seminar support. Now that's the way to make real money in education.

Just because something is called by a new name doesn't make it wonderful. Anxious administrators search for instant solutions, and often fall victim to some new program that purports to have all the answers.

States and districts search continuously for the magic bullet that will improve student learning. Bringing in consultants and so-called experts makes public education look good to a public demanding to know what is being done "with all the money" to improve student learning.

This is the gestation of an education fad: Become frantic that you're not doing it; form a committee to devise a plan of action; bring in the "movement's" expert; buy materials; create staff development activities; have teachers write an objective about the "movement" in their evaluations; and make sure everyone is doing it.

Last year Georgia implemented statewide training for all middle school teachers in reading and writing. Even if an instructor had a Ph.D. and demonstrated mastery of teaching reading and writing, he had to take the eight days of training, which wasn't announced to many teachers in the state until nearly the end of the school year, creating havoc for those who had made summer plans.

Another mandatory training program, called "Georgia Framework for Integrating Technology" or "In Tech," tries to teach a wide spectrum of computer skills to all teachers in 50 hours without regard for their ability. It is a certification requirement, one that cannot be bypassed by demonstrating computer literacy. A Georgia teacher made this observation:

> Why not separate out those who are whizzes, those who are semi-literate and those who are novices, then offer separate break-out sessions for each ability level?
> It's like teaching a math class that's supposed to encompass the range of skills from basic arithmetic to calculus. The problem is that by attempting to teach you everything they end up teaching you nothing. They throw everything at you, but don't give you the opportunity to develop it for specific lesson plans. The whole process sours those who know it already and are bored—to them it's a complete waste of time—as well as those who know little and are intimidated—they end up going back to their classrooms continuing to use the computer only for record-keeping purposes. The course wasn't user-friendly, it was stressful, and it didn't need to be.

Teachers in one county also had to attend a two-day workshop, called "Making Schools Work," for which a consultant was paid $93,000. One teacher who attended the seminar said, "It was a major morale downer because nothing is coming out of this except to justify the 93 grand."

Districts could save themselves a lot of money and aggravation by relying on their expert teachers to help other teachers learn basic good teaching practices. It's not new, it's not sexy, it's not something that can be three-hole-punched into a glossy binder, but it's long-lasting and it is the least intrusive method to train a faculty. It provides a buy-in for teachers. They are more likely to use the work they develop themselves than work developed by others. But the people in power don't trust the teachers they employ.

Yet the prevailing district view is that if enough schools are using a program, then it's worth bringing in the experts. The assumption is that all staff members will take in the new concept hook, line, and sinker. So many times after a conference workshop or staff development session, I overhear teachers practically exclaiming, "Hallelujah," over how they have seen the light on how to teach reading or how to motivate at-risk students or whatever it may be. This frightening mob thinking runs counter to the philosophy of educators—to broaden and liberate the mind, not create schools of thought that put teachers in the position of "us versus them." God forbid the lone teacher who voices skepticism or opposition. Obviously, that teacher is not "with us."

Innovative teachers who think "outside the box" are punished. Creativity and divergent thinking, considered admirable traits in students, are not allowed to flourish. Complacent teachers thrive.

Meanwhile, lost in the sea of seminars are the wonderful teachers who produce terrific work in classroom after classroom. These are the people who should determine what their needs are and how best to meet them.

When full-day staff development occurs, the day is scheduled so tightly that teachers, even when given good ideas, have no time to implement them. Time needs to be built into staff development to allow teachers the chance to rewrite lessons using different strategies. Otherwise, what happens most often is that teachers find no time to use the new techniques so they fall back on what they normally do due to lack of preparation time.

What are the three most important characteristics of good staff development? A dynamic speaker to keep you awake; ideas that relate directly to the classroom that keep you engaged; and budgeted time to allow teachers to refine their lessons with whatever new information is dispensed. Teachers would like to have time to breathe, to reflect on what they are doing in the classroom.

Often, however, the routine workshop's agenda goes something like this:

1) Participants introduce themselves.
2) Have a cartoon with an education theme on the overhead.
3) Separate everyone into groups (keep treating them like children).
4) Write findings from each group on chart paper to give the aurally impaired (or desperately bored) a visual.
5) Each group chooses a spokesman to relay findings to the whole group (another student-like group behavior).
6) Allow a few people to complain and control most of the discussion.
7) Leave with a false sense that something was accomplished.

Some of the workshops that offer ready-made lesson plans may seem helpful, but if the presenter doesn't go through the lesson plans step-by-step, allowing the teacher to internalize the material, teachers leave that conference only with an armload of material (which most likely will weigh down a drawer in a filing cabinet, never to be used). When are teachers going to be given the time to look over it all and adapt it to their needs?

"It is unrealistic to expect that teachers will learn how to incorporate complicated practices into their repertoires on the basis of a few highly general workshops conducted after school in the auditorium by someone who doesn't know the field, the students, or the classroom contexts, and whom they are unlikely ever to see again" (Darling-Hammond, 1999, p. 2).

One of the few times staff development worked for me was when our principal had the chutzpah to tell teachers they had the whole day to do whatever each teacher deemed most important. As long as the teacher signed in at the beginning of the day, then signed out at the end, the assumption from the administration was, "we trust that whatever you do today will be productive" without watching over the teacher's shoulder. Sure, there were workshops that teachers could attend, but these were voluntary. If a teacher wanted to work in his room and tidy up, grade papers, look through professional journals, or simply contemplate the previous week's lessons and how they played out with the students, that was fine.

Sometimes just attending a conference outside the workplace can be extremely therapeutic for the teacher. It's almost like a vacation for the day because suddenly the teacher has the freedom to get a cup of coffee, go to the restroom, or get some fresh air. These are luxuries for teachers. Also, being away from the "office" gives teachers a new perspective on how they're teaching their students. That's why retreats have become so popular with companies. You can't hold the same conversation at the worksite and have the same outcome. Trapped in their classrooms, teachers need to break out a few times during the year; that's often the most beneficial part of attending any conference or workshop. Teachers feel reenergized just by being away from the classroom for a day.

With such a benefit, one would think districts would encourage their teachers to attend as many workshops and conferences as they can. However, by demanding that teachers use their own credit cards or write their

own checks to pay for conference fees up front, then provide reimbursement two months later, they in essence discourage many from expanding their knowledge. Registration fees can run up to $300 for a one-day workshop.

I'll never forget how surprised I was to discover how
differently public school teachers are treated from their
college counterparts. Early in my career I was on an
articulation committee of the local community college.
Since the college was in charge of the program, all teachers, college and high school, received the same compensation of $35 an hour, nearly double my district's rate.
Not only that, but the out-of-town conference I had to attend was prepaid, and a travel agent booked the flight
and hotel for me. I didn't have to fill out a single form except when I came back, for reimbursement of per diem.
This meant that teachers did not have to use their own
credit card or check to get registered. Also, the per diem
was so generous that we were shocked when our college
hosts suggested we eat out at a steakhouse. As a public
school teacher on a rare business trip, I'm used to watching every penny, choosing fast food over restaurant din-
ing.

True staff development must involve teachers being
given the time to talk, reflect, and find out from other
teachers what works and what doesn't. It cannot be
stressed enough how crucial this is to the future of public
education. Even doctors can talk to associates in their
own office.

But What about the Great Teacher Perks?

- Teachers get a lot of time off.
    True, but the vast majority of it is unpaid.
    Most teachers receive three weeks paid vacation,
    ten days personal time, and half a dozen holidays—
    quite average for most Americans. The often envied

summer vacation is more like ten weeks, not actually three full months, and it is without pay. This is how one Los Angeles–area educator explains it: "I immediately remind people that while in the summer we don't work, we also don't get paid. If we want money, we work summer school or find some other kind of work." Teachers must balance their monthly salary carefully, because for two months they have no income. Is there any wonder that some educators claim unemployment during the summer? While many states forbid this, as one Florida teacher puts it, what makes teachers different from resort personnel who can receive unemployment during the off-season? At least secondary teachers can fall back on teaching summer school.

- Teachers get to leave work at 3:00 P.M.

Sometimes. Perhaps if they had comfortable office space, more of them would stay at work longer. Just because teachers are no longer at work doesn't mean they have stopped working. On average, teachers work two extra hours a day, beyond school hours. Too, teachers might be motivated to stay later if the whole campus didn't start closing shop after the students leave. There is no hot food served after lunchtime, hallways are hosed down, doors are bolted. A school is not an inviting place to stay much later than 3:00 P.M., so many choose to work at home.

One high school Spanish teacher echoes how many others feel: "I don't think that as a teacher I am compensated properly for the job I do, or most teachers do, because I don't leave my work at school at 3:00; I take it home and work for another two to three hours. People can't understand this."

Plus, many are just plain drained. Teaching demands a high amount of stamina. Outside of surgeons, pilots, and stockbrokers, what other profession requires its workers to be fully alert and ready to work at 100 percent capacity as early as 7:00 A.M. and with only short breaks, for seven straight hours?

Also, the fact that teachers can't leave the workplace during school hours makes them want to leave as soon as possible. If someone locks you up in a room, the first thing you're going to do is dash off at the first opportune moment. Just look at how anxious kids are to leave school. You would think the district would encourage teachers to get out of their rooms during their preps and go off campus to get a bite to eat, as every other adult worker has a right to do, or go to Office Depot and buy supplies for the classroom, or go to a park, or take a walk. One is so much refreshed when taking such a break; you become a better teacher to your students when you take a breather.

Besides these two "perks," the only free things teachers receive are key chains, pens, pins, and PTA luncheons. One principal had a yearly holiday tradition of doling out coupons good for one hour of covering a class so that the teacher could savor a cup of coffee or simply take a stroll around the block. It may not seem like much, but to teachers who feel imprisoned most of the day, it was a generous gift.

In an industry that doesn't pay that much, where compliments from clients are rare, it's nice to be given treats once in a while. Unlike other equally educated professionals, teachers receive no end-of-the-year bonuses or holiday parties. Just a $5 gift certificate would pay dividends to teachers who are starved for appreciation. It would serve as an acknowledgment, a simple thank you, a pat on the back.

While my friends enjoy hotel-spread holiday parties and $10,000 bonuses, I face another year of having to pay $8 to attend a deli spread at a fellow teacher's house. Who wants to spend money on a holiday party the purpose of which is to celebrate a company's employees?

When we're talking about not having enough space to walk around the classroom, and insufficient materials for students, providing teachers with a Christmas party is definitely at the bottom of the list of what to do to change the teacher's work environment. But when all of this is added up and happens daily, it weighs heavily on serious-minded teachers who truly wish to make a difference and have a positive impact on their students so that they, in turn, positively affect society. These poor working conditions definitely deter smart young people from going into teaching.

Would newer buildings, more photocopiers, cleaner classrooms, and more constructive meetings increase test scores? Perhaps. Would these improvements increase student and teacher morale, instill pride in their workplace, and show the premium society places on their education? Absolutely.

PART 2

The Fight to Make Teaching a Full-Fledged Profession

As a way to recruit more teachers to the New York City schools, chancellor Harold O. Levy proposed up to three months of free housing to allow teachers time to find affordable permanent digs. In a city with a severe housing shortage, three months may not be long enough when one considers the salary requirements that landlords demand. A teacher earning $32,000 would only be considered for a $600 a month apartment—as common in Manhattan as a 10-cent phone call and a 25-cent newspaper.

When school districts offer housing assistance and states give tax credits because of what you do for a living, warning flags should go up.

As nice as it is to have Day of the Teacher and Teacher Appreciation Week proclamations, the fact that these Hallmark moments exist at all speaks volumes about the teaching profession's lack of prestige.

In his book, *In the Name of Excellence: The Struggle to Reform the Nation's Schools, Why It's Failing, and What Should Be Done,* Thomas Toch describes teaching as "an occupation marked by low pay, low standards, repetitious work, narrow career opportunities, little recognition of achievement, and a poor public image—characteristics of traditional assembly-line work" (p. 140). Instead it should have "tough entrance requirements, respectable salaries, collegiality, a serious intellectual environment, opportunities for leadership, rewards for achievement, a career path, and status—the hallmarks of professions such as law and medicine, and the characteristics of teaching itself in Japan and Germany" (Ibid.).

The National Commission on Teaching and America's Future (NCTAF) studied how other countries in Europe and Asia support high-quality teaching. Here's what they discovered:

- Teachers' salaries are in line with other professionals, such as engineers or civil servants, to avoid shortage of qualified personnel.

- Graduate-level preparation in addition to a bachelor's degree is either required or highly encouraged.
- Student teachers go through a year-long internship under the guidance of master teachers in a school that works closely with the university teacher education program.
- Examinations of subject matter and teaching knowledge are required before entry into the profession.
- Extensive time for learning and collaborative planning is included in teachers' schedules so that they can work together.

None of these conditions is true for American teachers.

A 1998 nationwide poll found that 90 percent of the public believes that a well-qualified teacher in every classroom is essential to improving student achievement, and more than half believe that the quality and caliber of teachers has the greatest influence on student learning—more than academic standards or standardized tests (*Essential Profession,* p. 7). And there are studies that prove that this is a fact, not just a belief.

When done well, teaching is a highly demanding, mentally exhausting, stamina-draining, energy-depleting activity. Teachers are performers working to engage their audience every minute of every day. It's all "live" with no TelePrompTers and hardly any time for rehearsal. And your audience changes frequently from hour to hour, requiring quick thinking on how best to capture—and keep—their attention.

How stressful is teaching? As Charlotte Danielson describes it in her book, *Enhancing Professional Practice: A Framework for Teaching,* "Planning for the productive activity of 30 or more individuals . . . and successfully executing those plans, all within the context of multiple . . . demands from the school, district, community, and state, leave many teachers—particularly novices—buffeted, confused, or discouraged" (p. 5).

A hard fact must be accepted: There simply are not enough talented people in today's teaching force to ensure that the vast majority of America's 53 million school children are receiving a quality education. However, that could change if steps are taken to elevate the professionalism of teaching to pull in higher-caliber people.

Whether looking at SAT scores, IQ results, or college GPAs, students with high scores and grades tend to avoid the teaching field. Why would school-smart people choose not to immerse themselves in an environment that has served them well? Better opportunities.

When's the last time you were handed a business card from a teacher? Have you ever seen a teacher's license hanging on the wall in a classroom? What prevents the teaching profession from attaining the same level of public respect as law and medicine?

First and foremost, teachers need to earn a professional wage. How much money is it worth to get better-qualified people into the classroom, especially for those children damaged daily by ineffective and ill-trained teachers? A six-figure salary shouldn't be out of the realm of possibility for an exceptional teacher. The key is *earn*— evaluated on criteria demonstrating exemplary teaching ability. Not all teachers deserve that kind of money; in fact, many deserve a pay cut. Polls have shown that taxpayers are willing to increase the salaries dramatically of those teachers whose performance merits it, so why has no action been taken to rectify the rapidly deteriorating quality drain in public education instruction? A 2001 poll conducted by Peter D. Hart and Robert M. Teeter (Hart and Teeter, 2001) found that 88 percent favor raising teacher salaries, and 81 percent strongly or somewhat favor "increasing the pay for most teachers, including doubling the pay for the top 20 percent of teachers, based on their performance and qualifications." However, the public needs assurances that higher-paid teachers are worth it. In fact, the public demands it.

While many people favor increasing education spending, they understandably want it linked to accountability. That's why strengthening teacher training and revamping the evaluation process is essential to revolutionizing the teaching profession. A "profession" is defined as an occupation requiring extensive education or special knowledge. This should be at the core of teacher education reform. So much more is expected from teachers in the twenty-first century that it makes it even more imperative that teachers entering the workforce are highly trained and skilled.

Also, career ladders need to be established to motivate teachers to better themselves, giving them opportunities to pursue higher salaries and prestige. Most teachers begin and end their careers as teachers because there exists no other positions for them to ascend to. This lack of upward mobility doesn't encourage people to work hard; it dampens their ambition.

Finally, teachers need control over their profession. Why shouldn't they be involved in designing their workspace or in structuring the school year? No longer can teachers remain in the subservient roles that the system has cast them in for more than a century and a half. They are down in the trenches and frequently have good ideas for winning the war against failing American education.

Linda Darling-Hammond, a prolific writer on education, wrote in her book, *The Right to Learn* (1997b, p. 298), "an occupation becomes a profession when it assumes responsibility for developing a shared knowledge base for all of its members and for transmitting that knowledge through professional education, licensing, and ongoing peer review." This hasn't happened yet with the teaching profession.

CHAPTER 3

A Professional Salary: How to Attract the Best and the Brightest

A person's worth is often judged by how much money he or she makes. With a good salary comes respect. How many municipalities pay more for firemen and police officers than teachers (both admirable jobs as demonstrated so vividly with the September 11th terrorist attacks) even though neither requires education beyond a high school diploma? In a society that pays city tree cutters $4,200 a month and starting teachers $2,500 a month, you can't expect the best public schools when the employees in charge of teaching earn the least of all equally educated professionals.

Seventy-five percent of new teachers polled by Public Agenda 2000 agreed with the statement, "I am seriously underpaid." And Americans recognize this as well, with 82 percent agreeing that teachers are not paid well (see figure 2).

With the ever-increasing strain on the existing teacher pool due to class-size reduction programs and impending retirements, finding people to fill two million positions in the next decade will take more than a public service announcement; it will take money.

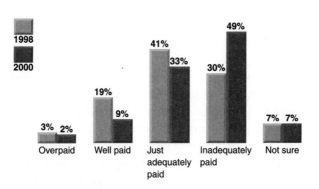

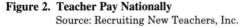

Figure 2. Teacher Pay Nationally
Source: Recruiting New Teachers, Inc.

Let's be realistic. If society as a whole, and parents in particular, want the United States to have an exemplary K–12 system, then money is going to have to be spent on hiring higher-quality teachers.

When educators ask for higher salaries, the public considers the image of teaching as a "noble" profession, a "calling" tarnished. No longer does "I'm there for the kids" sustain. Yes, by asking for more money, teachers become just like everyone else: hard workers who want to be compensated properly for the service they provide.

It is heartwarming to hear teachers say they are there for their students, but most probably they have a spouse who earns more than they do. "The world has long assumed that teachers, like preachers, should serve with selfless disregard for the circumstances of their work; that they should ignore the leaks in school roofs; tolerate salaries that fail to cover their bills; cope with lockstep schedules, large classes, and inadequate supplies" (Johnson, p. xiv). The public pins its hopes on the lofty ideal that there are still those willing to sacrifice money and respect to educate our country.

By chance, there are many good teachers who work extremely hard despite inadequate pay and less than optimal working conditions. That doesn't mean they should be perceived as martyrs, hoping that St. Peter will grant them entrance into heaven once "teacher" is stamped on their resume.

What's troubling is that teaching is not the chosen occupation of some of our brightest young people.

A 1999 Milken Family Foundation survey of college-bound high school students, who had a front-row view of teaching for 13 years, revealed that only one in ten expressed an interest in the teaching profession, citing low pay as a key concern, along with the poor image and lack of respect for teachers. Why is this?

Look at the following average beginning salaries and average salaries in figures 3a and b for teaching and other professions for 2000.

At a U.S. average starting salary of $27,989, freshly graduated college students are looking at a $20,000 difference between teaching and engineering in their first year on the job. That translates to a 40 percent decrease in earning power, quite an impact on one's standard of living. According to the American Federation of Teacher's *Survey and Analysis of Teacher Salary Trends 2000,* "Throughout

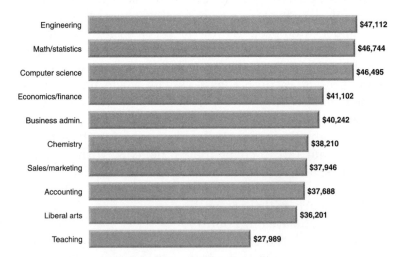

Engineering	$47,112
Math/statistics	$46,744
Computer science	$46,495
Economics/finance	$41,102
Business admin.	$40,242
Chemistry	$38,210
Sales/marketing	$37,946
Accounting	$37,688
Liberal arts	$36,201
Teaching	$27,989

Figure 3a. New Teacher Salaries Lag behind Beginning Salaries in Other Occupations
Source: *Survey & Analysis of Teacher Salary Trends 2000*

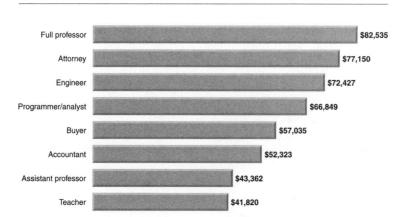

Figure 3b. Average Teacher Salary in 2000 Falls Short of Earnings in Other Professions
Source: *Survey & Analysis of Teacher Salary Trends 2000*

most of the 1990s, the percentage of college freshmen planning teaching careers hovered near 10 percent, down from the 1960s and early 1970s when more than 20 percent of college freshmen planned to pursue teaching careers."

As teachers progress through their careers, the earning gap worsens, with some jobs paying nearly double what teachers make.

All the professions illustrated in figure 3b earn more money than teaching does from the start, and all are fields from which potential teachers can come. Given the amount of education and experience of teachers, their salaries are lower, even when taking into account a ten-month work year.

Of course, teacher salaries, like those of other professions, vary according to the cost of living in different areas of the United States, as illustrated in figure 4.

The lowest starting salary in the country for the 1999–2000 school year was North Dakota, at $20,422, the last state to break the $20,000 barrier; the highest was Alaska, at $33,676. The lowest average salary was South Dakota, at $29,072; the highest average salary was Connecticut, at $52,410; thus, bringing the U.S. average teacher salary to $41,820.

Figure 4. Beginning and Average Teacher Salary in 1999–2000, Ranked by Average Salary within Region

State	Average Salary	Beginning Salary	State	Average Salary	Beginning Salary
NEW ENGLAND			**SOUTHEAST**		
Connecticut	$52,410	$30,466	Georgia	$41,122	$30,402
Rhode Island	48,138	27,286	North Carolina	39,404	27,968
Massachusetts	46,955	30,330	Virginia	38,992	26,783
New Hampshire	37,734	24,650	Florida	36,722	25,132
Vermont	36,402	25,791	Alabama	36,689	29,790
Maine	35,561	22,942	Tennessee	36,328	27,228
MIDEAST			Kentucky	36,255	24,753
New York	$51,020	$31,910	South Carolina	36,081	25,215
New Jersey	50,878	30,480	West Virginia	35,011	23,829
Pennsylvania	48,321	30,185	Arkansas	33,691	22,599
District of	48,304	30,850	Louisiana	33,109	25,738
Columbia			Mississippi	31,897	23,040
Delaware	44,435	30,945	**ROCKY MOUNTAINS**		
Maryland	43,720	28,612	Colorado	$39,073	$24,875
GREAT LAKES			Idaho	35,155	20,915
Michigan	$48,729	$28,545	Utah	34,946	23,273
Illinois	46,480	30,151	Wyoming	34,188	24,168
Indiana	41,855	26,553	Montana	32,121	20,969
Ohio	41,713	23,597	**FAR WEST**		
Minnesota	40,678	25,666	California	$47,680	$32,190
Wisconsin	39,897	25,344	Alaska	46,481	33,876
PLAINS			Oregon	45,103	29,733
Kansas	$36,282	$25,252	Nevada	43,083	28,734
Iowa	35,678	25,275	Hawaii	41,292	29,204
Missouri	35,660	25,977	Washington	41,047	26,514
Nebraska	33,237	22,923	**OUTLYING AREAS**		
North Dakota	29,863	20,422	Guam	$34,947	$26,917
South Dakota	29,072	21,889	Virgin Islands	34,784	22,751
SOUTHWEST			Puerto Rico	24,980	18,700
Texas	$37,567	$28,400	**U.S. AVERAGE**	$41,820	$27,989
Arizona	34,824	25,613			
New Mexico	32,713	25,042			
Oklahoma	29,525	24,025			

Source: *Survey & Analysis of Teacher Salary Trends, 2000*

When I first began my credential coursework in 1982, the beginning salary for a teacher in the Los Angeles Unified School District—the second largest school district in the nation after New York City—was $13,000. At the time I was earning $18,000 as a word processor while attending school full-time. I decided to stop my pursuit of a credential midstream because, with a 25 percent pay cut, I wouldn't have been able to pay my rent or other bills.

If Internet-savvy teenagers are offered starting positions in the $40,000 range without even a bachelor's degree, no wonder few smart young people choose teaching.

And when teachers have a master's degree, they fall even further behind their nonteacher counterparts (see figure 5).

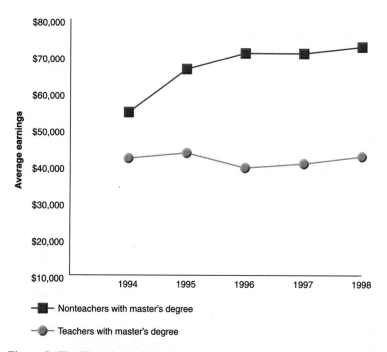

— Nonteachers with master's degree

— Teachers with master's degree

Figure 5. The High Cost of Teaching
Source: *Education Week, Quality Counts*
Note: All figures are represented in 1998 dollars to control for inflation.

Education Week, in its report, *Quality Counts 2000: Who Should Teach?* underscored the blatant salary gap that exists between teachers and nonteachers with equivalent education:

> In 1998, teachers ages 22 to 28 earned on average $7,894 less than other college graduates of the same age— $22,653 vs. $30,547 in pay. The salary gap was far worse for teachers ages 44 to 50. Among that group, the pay gap was $23,655—or $38,889 vs. $62,544.
>
> The difference was greatest among 44- to 50-year-olds with master's degrees. Teachers in that group earned $43,313 compared with $75,824 for nonteachers—a gap of $32,511.
>
> The booming economy of the late 1990s has made teaching even less attractive. The average salary for nonteachers with master's degrees increased by $17,505 from 1994 to 1998, after adjusting for inflation. The average salary for teachers with master's degrees rose by less than $200. (Olsen, pp. 8–9).

In a dismal showing, the United States ranks among the lowest of any industrialized nation in teacher pay per capita, while it ranks among the highest in number of hours of teaching. In other words, American teachers work harder and get paid less for it.

A report released by the Organization for Economic Cooperation and Development in 1998 discovered that teachers in Australia, France, and Britain earn above average pay among college graduates, whereas U.S. teachers are below average (Bromer). And a 1994 study by F. Howard Nelson on the International Comparison of Teacher Salaries and Conditions of Employment revealed that American primary teachers spend more than 30 hours a week teaching, compared to 20 hours by Japanese and German teachers. The report also showed that U.S. secondary teachers have the highest number of work hours and less training than their counterparts in other

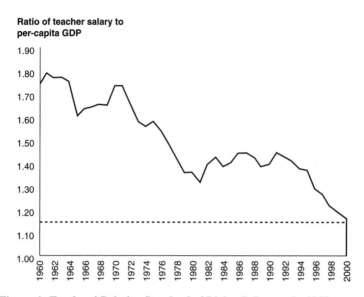

Figure 6. Teachers' Relative Standard of Living Is Lowest in 40 Years
Source: American Federation of Teachers, AFL-CIO

nations. "European countries . . . expect their high school teachers to have five or six years of training" (Nelson) and are paid more than primary teachers.

Figure 6 shows that a teacher's relative standard of living is the lowest it has been in 40 years.

Many teachers have to moonlight by tutoring, teaching at community colleges, or bagging groceries at a supermarket during the summer, or they have a spouse who also works. Nearly 40 percent of all teachers need to get a second job to make ends meet, according to an American Federation of Teachers survey (Olson, 2001a, p. 9).

Besides their annual salary, teachers can earn additional money in the form of extra hourly rates of compensation or stipends for specific types of work beyond their normal teaching duties. Typically, though, teachers get thrown bones to work even harder than they do.

How much is a good teacher worth? Very little in terms of dollars and cents. The usual going hourly rate is around $20. A person would be hard-pressed to find any white- or blue-collar worker to do any job for that kind of money. And stipends are usually less than that when broken down by the hour.

For example, a famous California university offers stipends for teachers to work in a variety of programs over the summer, from developing writing and reading strategies to ways of supporting other teachers. Without casting aspersions on the program itself (which is worthwhile), the stipend last summer was $1,200 for a minimum of 30 days at seven hours a day. That comes out to $5.71 an hour. To add insult to injury, teachers who participate in any of the programs cannot teach summer school, thus costing thousands of dollars in lost income to boot.

When huge grants are awarded to schools, many areas—supplies, outside consultants, district administrative fees—take big pieces of the pie, leaving crumbs to pay extra compensation to teachers. Teachers may be paid $500 for two weeks' worth of work. And then the work they do is not their own property, which means that other companies can make money off their hard work by conducting workshops and publishing materials. The teacher gets the measly stipend, and that's it. No credit, no royalties. The fairest solution would be to ensure that teachers receive the largest chunk of the pie. After all, they are the in-house experts.

The only other option for a teacher to earn more money is to become an administrator, a job that has little to do with teaching. (Who came up with the idea that teaching skills naturally transfer to administrative skills?)

Offering to pay a public school teacher $100,000 may shock some, but talented people want to be paid what they're worth, and too many have chosen other, more profitable professions. With the worst teacher shortage in public school history looming, isn't it about time that something dramatic is done to attract more and better people into teaching? How often do city officials say they need to "attract the best people" or "remain competitive with the private sector" when rationalizing six-figure salaries for their employees? Why don't the same standards apply to hiring top-notch teachers?

It should come as no surprise that when school districts offer dramatic pay increases, such as Oakland Unified School District's recent 23 percent raise over three years, they not only have more applicants flocking to them, but more qualified ones at that.

While the teachers unions deserve some of the credit for negotiating contracts that provide these double-digit raises, the unions are part of the problem. In their perpetual quest for fair salaries for all, they have created unfair lower salaries for the best. For the most part, they don't support programs that would pay more to those teachers who perform at a higher level of service and that would distinguish one teacher's abilities from another. Mainly, unions are out for the biggest pay raises they can get for their members, regardless of the members' talents to perform at a high level of achievement, and, therefore, with no guarantee (code name: accountability) to the students or their parents that they deserve those salaries.

If an employee feels that his special talents aren't rewarded financially or recognized by his superiors, he assumes a defeatist attitude. If no one acknowledges the effort shown, why continue working oneself into the ground? Such teachers either end up conserving their talents or leaving the profession for a business that does reward hard work.

You do the job expected of you; if little is expected, you will meet those minimum standards. This has much to do with the inconsistent quality among educators.

Would more money make a difference? "Definitely," a teacher from Pennsylvania said. "Several teachers would work hard if given more money."

As Martin L. Gross points out in his book, *Conspiracy of Ignorance: The Failure of American Public Schools,* teachers who do not hold high expectations of themselves cannot possibly demand greatness of their students, most of whom candidly clamor for stronger teachers.

Before discussing the current situation, it's necessary to review how the teaching profession has evolved, a definite look back into the future.

A Brief History of the Teaching Profession

Incredulously, the way teachers are paid has remained virtually unchanged throughout much of the twentieth century. The single-salary schedule first used in the 1920s, providing raises based on years of experience and number of college credits regardless of one's unique talents and job quality, has remained the same to this day.

The first way in which teachers were compensated in the early 1800s was through room and board. Since most families lived in rural areas, the teacher stayed with a student's family and thus was able to work around the farming schedule. Women who became teachers did so mainly as a way out of the house; then left teaching as soon as they married. The few male teachers taught to supplement their farming income or as a stepping-stone to public office. Most teachers at the time had little more than an elementary level of education. This "boarding 'round" compensation system allowed parents to monitor the teacher's lifestyle—the single most overriding concern at the time.

Schools that actually trained people to become teachers were developed in the late 1830s, spearheaded by Horace Mann in Massachusetts. For the first time, counties and states created standards for teachers and required training to get a license. These state-run institutions, known as "normal schools" (the Latin *norma* meaning conforming to a rule or model) were transformed into teachers and state colleges during the twentieth century. New York's Brockport Normal School in 1892 issued only 56 degrees to a class of 370, proving how difficult it was then to become a teacher—and to be paid the princely annual sum of $300.

Though teachers were predominantly female during public education's infancy, it wasn't until mass immigration between 1880 and 1925 when women began to dominate the teaching ranks. This was so because women were more likely than men to accept lower wages and to undergo the additional training now necessary for incremental pay raises.

In 1910, more than a third of all teachers had not completed high school, and only 5 percent had any college at all. High school teachers were the only public school teachers expected to have college degrees; that was the high esteem in which they were held.

As more states developed teacher certification guidelines and schools became four-year institutions, all teachers attained four-year degrees. Widely used during much of this time was a grade-based pay schedule that paid men more than women, higher grades more than lower grades, whites more than blacks.

This gave way to the single-salary schedule during the roaring '20s, which enabled teachers to receive raises by earning more college credit and working longer on the job—still the only two ways teachers can advance monetarily today.

The golden period for teachers was during the '20s, '30s, and '40s, when they were considered one of the most intelligent groups of workers in the country. However, as the number of college graduates grew during the years, as David F. Labaree describes it in *How to Succeed in School without Really Learning: The Credentials Race in American Education,* "teachers lost their education distinctiveness and slid back into the pack" (p. 140). Whereas, before they were part of a small group of college graduates, today they represent a small percentage of a significantly larger group of graduates.

As more states adopted teacher certification guidelines, and teachers became better educated themselves, their pay did not keep pace with their growing professionalism.

When Russia sent *Sputnik* into orbit in 1957, suddenly the spotlight was on strengthening math and science teaching in public schools. Teacher unions became more powerful during the 1960s and were able to command higher salary increases through collective bargaining agreements. Teaching was making a comeback.

But the profession would never be the same because of the women's liberation movement, which encouraged women to look beyond the home and their traditional professions of nursing and teaching. With the loss of bright women to other fields, it was clear by the end of the '70s that the quality of teachers had declined, and a shortage was beginning. The new opportunities for women transferred to new opportunities for minorities as well. A major reason why a disproportionate number of teachers today are nonminority—12 percent of teachers are minorities while nearly one-third of students are—has to do with minorities vying for more lucrative careers (Archer, p. 1).

The 1980s saw the arrival of the emergency teaching credential as districts sought teachers to fill classrooms. Without ever having been in front of young people, the emergency teacher stepped right into the classroom. For many this was and is a huge slap in the face to those who jumped through hoops to attain their license and put in their one-year unpaid student teacher stint. Imagine walking onto a theatrical stage and playing a dramatic role without ever having had an acting lesson; except with teaching, it's the students who are the audience.

By the '90s, the number of emergency certificates had exploded, as more undertrained and underprepared instructors were placed in classrooms. The main order of the day was to get warm bodies, not smart minds.

Into this turmoil landed three major federal reports that were highly critical of public education.

The first, 1983's "A Nation at Risk," suggested merit pay as the way to increase teacher effectiveness. Simply put, if a teacher was deemed to be doing a superior job, then he deserved more money. While a few districts tried this, most failed because standards of expert teaching practices were never established—what deemed a particular teacher "excellent" was more at the whim of an administrator.

The Fairfax County Public School District in Virginia enacted such a program in 1987, paying teachers an extra 9 percent of their salaries. Due to the lack of funding and union support, the program ceased after a few years. Tennessee and Florida also experimented with merit pay.

In 1986, the Carnegie Task Force on Teaching as a Profession released *A Nation Prepared: Teachers for the 21st Century*, and the Holmes Group (a consortium of college education deans) issued its study, *Tomorrow's Teachers*. Both promoted the often overlooked argument that "the quality of public education can improve only if schoolteaching is transformed into a full-fledged profession" (Labaree, p. 129), and both introduced true career ladder plans. Though different, the plans shared the idea that teachers need a reason to improve themselves as educators by aspiring to higher positions. Carnegie called for the creation of two teaching positions, teacher and lead teacher, while the Holmes group offered three: instructor, professional teacher, and career professional.

The quickest ways to bolster the status of teaching, thereby attracting more talented people, is to increase teacher salaries significantly and to offer a career ladder for those with strong ambition.

The One-Size-Fits-All Salary Schedule

Just like workers at an auto plant, teachers are paid by seniority. Individual performance has no bearing whatsoever on a teacher's salary.

Today, this one-size-fits-all compensation system remains in place for nearly all school districts in the nation. It's easy to see why teachers unions embrace it, since it eliminates administrators' subjective evaluation of a teacher's performance and treats all teachers indiscriminately, male or female, black or white, elementary or secondary, rural or urban. However, how can anyone with common sense pay all teachers the same amount of money regardless of individual performance? How can one justify paying a teacher $100,000 unless a threshold of achievement is in place?

Back in 1867 Pennsylvania superintendent Aaron Sheeley had an answer. He said that paying all teachers the same wages "offers a premium to mediocrity, if not to positive ignorance and incompetence. Inducements should always be held out to teachers to duly qualify themselves for their work" (Odden and Kelley, p. 36).

While both male and female workers receive equal pay for equal work in public schools, education is unequal to other professions because teaching is still labeled a female occupation. Nearly three-fourths of today's teaching workforce are women, further challenging the profession to gain the respect and pay it deserves in a male-dominated economy. And how rarely does the top administrative brass mirror the teaching rank and file? How many women are superintendents in a profession that is dominated by women?

Despite the large number of female teachers, the majority of high school principals and district superintendents remain male.

> Women should have equal pay for equal work and they should be considered equally eligible to the offices of principal and superintendent, professor and president. So you must insist that qualifications, not sex, shall govern appointments and salaries.—Susan B. Anthony, in a letter to the National Education Association, 1903

The Old Boy Network permeates education: Women traditionally are elementary school principals, while men are high school principals. I even had one female teacher tell me upon hearing that our next principal was to be a

Figure 7. Typical Single-Salary Schedule

Steps (years)	Class 1 BA	Class 2 BA + 15	Class 3 BA + 30	Class 4 MA	Class 5 MA + 30	Class 6 Doctorate
1	$25,000	$25,250	$25,500	$26,000	$26,500	$27,500
2	25,250	25,500	25,750	26,500	27,000	28,500
3	25,500	25,750	26,000	27,000	27,500	29,500
4	25,750	26,000	26,250	27,500	28,000	31,000
5	26,000	26,500	27,000	28,500	29,000	32,500
6	26,250	27,000	27,750	29,500	30,000	34,000
7	26,500	27,500	28,500	30,500	31,000	35,500
8	26,750	28,000	29,250	31,500	32,500	37,000
9	27,000	28,500	30,000	32,500	34,000	38,500
10	27,250	29,000	30,750	33,500	35,500	40,500
12	28,000	30,000	32,000	35,500	37,500	43,000
16	30,000	32,000	34,000	38,500	40,500	46,000
20			36,000	41,500	43,500	49,000
24					46,000	52,000

woman that she did not want a female in charge of a high school; she was only comfortable working for a man.

While variations exist from district to district and from state to state, figure 7 presents the most common characteristics of a typical single-salary schedule for teachers based on the average beginning pay of $25,000.

The "Steps" column shows the number of years teaching, and the "Class" columns are based on college credits beyond a bachelor of arts degree as well as advanced degrees. Some districts add more credits for the last column and pay teachers with doctorates a stipend instead.

This schedule tells teachers:

1) exactly what their salary will be each year;
2) how to earn more money: stay on the job and attend more college classes; and
3) quality does not matter—thanks to unions, they are guaranteed these salaries.

The best thing that can be said about the long-standing salary schedule is that it creates a totally objective measure, eliminating any political whims on the part of administrators. The worst thing is that it renders all of a teacher's individual traits and talents meaningless.

Teachers' ambitions are curbed by salary ceilings. The best teachers can expect to do is to double their beginning salary during the course of their career *if* they have an advanced degree. They know exactly how much they will earn as they progress through the salary schedule, and as they progress, the raises dry up, leaving one to wonder: Why would teachers work harder knowing that as they become more experienced their salary remains frozen? Try recruiting prospective attorneys with a starting salary of $20,000 and a ceiling of $60,000. Let's find out which doctors truly believe in the Hippocratic oath if a single physician couldn't earn more than $50,000. When people contemplate which career to follow, a key ingredient is the earning potential for that particular job much more than the initial salary earned.

A California teacher feels this way: "Pay increases start drying up after 10–15 years. I think that this is terrible. As the years go by, teaching children becomes more and more difficult, and the materials become less readily available, and it is the classroom teacher that has to deal with this, usually out of his or her pocket. How are we to supply our students with the materials they need if we don't have the money, and the school doesn't supply the material?"

It's understandable why half of the country's teachers have advanced degrees: they are paid more. Unfortunately, most of these master of art degrees are in education, not nearly as challenging or relevant as an M.A. in one's teaching area. Advanced degrees in education are big business for colleges. They are relatively easy to get since there seems to be a tacit understanding between districts and colleges that all teachers are trying to do is to earn more money, not necessarily expand their knowledge. It is doubtful that teachers would even seek advanced degrees if it weren't for the financial incentives offered by school districts.

Encouraging teachers to continue attending college hinders them from becoming more effective instructors, especially new teachers who are more motivated to move quickly along the salary schedule. Novice teachers, who should be conserving their energy and developing their craft, are the most tired and least likely to reflect on their practice because they take college classes in the late afternoon or evening hours right after teaching all day, or on weekends, when they should be recuperating. And these college classes are usually not paid for by the districts, unlike many professions that encourage their employees to expand their knowledge by covering tuition.

Notice that a teacher with no additional college coursework will never see a pay raise after 16 years on the job. Of course, all teachers do receive an increase in pay whenever a new contract is signed with a district. Still, the idea of no regular pay raises after teachers are potentially one-third of the way through their careers sends a terrible message. What would be for most people the most productive time of their careers, the second and third decades, is dead wood for these teachers. Where's the enticement to make teaching a lifelong career?

A 30-year veteran teacher from New York feels for the ten- to 12-year teachers "who are really hurting. Many are rethinking their careers. Our district is finally paying for master's degrees, and they should, since it is required in order to teach in New York State."

The idea of a teacher leaving for another district is fiscally unfeasible because districts commonly don't give teachers credit beyond the first seven or eight years of their teaching experience. This discourages teachers from leaving a district later in their careers, practically institutionalizing them.

Here's an example of education's seven-year itch. Let's say Sally, a 25-year veteran with an M.A. and 30 college credits moves ten miles to another school district. On the sample pay schedule, Sally earns $46,000. When she switches jobs, however, she will be placed on step 7 in the new district's salary schedule, and take a $15,000 pay cut. In addition, Sally has little chance of ever maximizing her salary in the new district because of how close she is to retirement. A teacher next door to her with 18 fewer years of experience earns the same amount of money. Yet, Sally is teaching the same number of kids, creating the same number of lesson plans, grading the same number of papers, and working as hard as ever. It's like asking a doctor who moves to another city to take a pay cut. Obviously, districts wish to prevent their most experienced instructors from abandoning ship. Yet, at the same time, they are blocking magnificent educators from coming on board.

A real-life example of a teacher who wanted to make a lateral move was depicted in Lynn Olson's *Education Week* article, "Finding and Keeping Competent Teachers":

> Rachel had been teaching for seven years in Massachusetts when she decided to move to New York City to be near her family. That's when the problems began. Although the 34-year-old educator was fully licensed to teach in Massachusetts, with master's degrees in both teaching and public policy, she had to sit through 12 hours of testing to earn her professional license in New York state. She also had to submit a videotape of her classroom performance and, to work in the city, complete a course on how to recognize child abuse. All that to take a $17,000 pay cut—from $58,000 to $41,000—to teach in the New York City schools.
>
> "I know plenty of people go through it," Rachel said, "but I wasn't a 25-year-old teacher anymore. I was a person in my mid-30s with a lot of experience. And it really made me angry."

How can a salary schedule like this motivate teachers to continue enriching their teaching practices when there is no financial incentive to do so? What reason is there for a teacher to *volunteer* to take on more responsibilities, such as serving on a committee or as a club adviser, especially when fellow colleagues do as little as possible yet earn the same pay? Eighty-nine percent of Americans in the RNT poll believe that teachers should be able to transfer easily to other districts and other states without losing pay (Hasselkorn and Harris, p. 21).

A More Complex but Fairer Way to Pay Teachers

Even if a teacher is paid based on performance rather than years of experience or number of college credits, a single salary schedule still wouldn't reflect the variety of teacher talent properly. Teachers should be placed on varying salary schedules according to different factors, the four most important being grade level taught, subject area, workload, and location of employment.

1) Secondary teachers should be paid more than elementary teachers.

Until the 1970s, this used to be true. Elementary school teachers and administrators were paid less than their secondary-level counterparts. We need to return to that pay differential. The number of students, length of the school day, expert knowledge in one particular field required, and severity of student behavior problems are all reasons why teaching at the secondary level is more demanding than teaching elementary school. Additionally, today's high school is more like precollege, with its stronger-than-ever emphasis that all students be prepared to go to a postsecondary institution.

That is not to say that elementary school teachers should be underpaid. An outstanding first-grade teacher is certainly worth more than $50,000. However, just as in medicine, the specialists—oncologists, neurosurgeons—make more money than general practitioners or doctors in less specialized fields, such as dermatology and podiatry, it should be harder to find an exceptional history teacher than an exceptional third-grade teacher. Such exclusivity should be rewarded.

Myron Lieberman, who wrote *Public Education: An Autopsy,* explains it this way. "[In colleges] those who teach doctoral courses are typically paid more than those who teach freshmen. The supply and demand for people who can do the work . . . is the most critical factor in setting salaries" (p. 58).

Here are my suggested starting salaries for teachers in metropolitan areas at the elementary, middle, and high school level:

K–5 $40,000
6–8 $45,000
9–12 $50,000

   2) Teachers in high-demand fields such as math and science should be paid more if they majored in those areas.

Only 55 percent of math teachers have majored in their field, so it is critical that more mathematicians and scientists enter teaching. Since more job opportunities await math and science majors than history and foreign language majors, the teaching profession has to reach out to those individuals who could help students. Chicago has done just that with its Global Educators Outreach program to recruit math and science teachers from around the world. Utah offers a one-time $20,000 bonus for new math teachers if they agree to a four-year commitment.

   3) Teachers who have more paperwork should be paid more.

In the business world, it makes sense that if one sees more clients during the day, one should earn more money. However, in education, what also needs to be taken into account is the type of student work produced. An English teacher who teaches five composition classes spends several more hours grading papers than a business teacher, though both may have the same number of pupils.

4) Teachers working at hard-to-staff schools should be paid more.

Many studies show that at low-performing schools, especially those serving poor and minority children, more of the teachers are noncredentialed. The schools that need the best teachers end up with those who are least experienced. Since many unions forbid mandatory transfers, principals can't move quality teachers where they are needed most. Not that such transfers should happen quid pro quo. Why have in place an adversarial relationship full of anxiety where teachers don't know where they will teach from year to year? Instead, offering more money would motivate excellent teachers to work at facilities that need them. The New York City schools have a Teachers of Tomorrow Program that grants financial rewards up to $3,400 for those who work at hard-to-staff schools. Teachers who already work at these schools can receive the same amount of compensation in the form of reimbursement for coursework toward the required master's degree. And Detroit pays an extra $3,000 to teachers working in high-need subjects.

As it stands now, suburbs generally pay more than inner cities and offer a better work environment. "In 1994, the best-paid teachers in low-poverty schools earned over 35% more than those in high-poverty schools" (Darling-Hammond 1997a, p. 20). With that kind of extreme salary differential between large urban school districts and their suburban counterparts, it is difficult to staff low-performing schools with quality teachers.

A New York teacher who works at one of these schools explains that "some of our wonderful, intelligent teachers with seven to ten years' experience are being pirated by suburban districts."

While one-time bonuses are a good start, if districts really want teachers knocking on the doors of schools desperate for outstanding instructors, significantly higher salaries need to be offered. For example, $50,000 may be a beginning salary at a suburban high school, but at an urban one, the salary should start at $60,000.

Additionally, it should be possible for teachers to earn more money than their principals. There has always been a distinct gap between the highest-paid teacher and the lowest-paid administrator. This salary barrier needs to be shattered. It is the expert teacher who has the greatest impact on a student's learning, who handles the delivery system of education to the student. And those who deliver the goods deserve just compensation.

Therefore, it is time to recognize the prime importance of teachers. Stop the lip service and pay them a professional salary, and celebrate the tremendous job many of them do with young people.

This is what American Federation of Teachers President Sandra Feldman had to say in a May 2001 press release about increasing teacher pay:

> Given the continuing teacher shortage and heightened pressure for better student performance, it's startling that school districts aren't tearing out a page from corporate handbooks. When teachers are paid as the professionals they are, the "Help Wanted" signs will come down. Until then, salaries must at least become competitive to attract and keep quality teachers.

Once a teacher is placed on the appropriate schedule, that teacher can be evaluated according to competencies and job tasks.

CHAPTER 4

Accountability:
How to Earn $100,000

Have you ever heard of a teacher losing his license because he didn't:

- have lesson plans
- assign homework
- return student work
- know how to teach geometry
- know the periodical tables
- know grammar

Of course not; yet there are teachers working today who fit such a description.

Incompetence is rarely grounds for dismissal. The few teachers who do lose their jobs do so because of criminal activity such as sexual abuse of students. But the abuse of students' minds goes unpunished.

When one teacher was an aide, she consistently called students "stupid, stupid." Soon thereafter, she became a full-time teacher who still complains about how dumb the kids are. This person clearly has no business working with young people.

Teaching is a good gig, and those who wish to take advantage of its weaknesses can do so throughout their careers. Your immediate boss is hardly ever around watching you do your job; you receive only periodic job evaluations based on prearranged visits from your boss; and, if you keep a low profile and don't make waves, you can have the job for the rest of your life.

Administrators have so much on their plate that observing every teacher on a regular basis is impossible, especially at a large high school. Often a teacher can work an entire year without a performance evaluation. Even when an observation is conducted, it is very possible to fool someone with a couple of gloriously constructed lesson plans showcasing the teaching methodologies du jour, thus covering up major weaknesses apparent only to the students who sit in that class all year long. And when teachers are evaluated, the results have no bearing on how much money they earn or whether they keep their jobs.

Such single-day observations provide "too narrow a snapshot of an educator's performance" and "little opportunity for new teachers to learn from the experience" (Archer, 2001b, p. 6). Think how much of a learning experience it would be to videotape a teacher's performance, then have a master teacher sit down with the teacher to view and analyze it together. The master teacher could also learn from such encounters.

It's as if some secret deal had been made decades ago that teachers wouldn't be bothered that much with being held accountable in exchange for a lifetime low-paying job.

Teachers don't make much money, but they do have job security. In other words, no matter the lousy job one performs, once tenured (after two or three years of teaching), one is in it for life. Relax, copy the same lesson plans year after year, dust off the same yellowed tests from the filing cabinet, and hold on until retirement. Happily, this description does not fit many teachers, but it does fit too many.

Once teachers are tenured, they are guaranteed a certain amount of money and a lifetime job. There is very little a district can do to rid itself of an incompetent instructor because of union contracts. Firing a teacher requires such a long paper trail and huge time investment that districts tend not to go after bad teachers, making it essential that administrators maintain high standards when evaluating new teachers who have yet been tenured. The New York School Boards Association, in its document, "A Blueprint for the Professionalization of Teaching," reported that it "takes an average of fifteen months and $177,000 to fire a teacher," $317,000 if the case is appealed (Gross, p. 220). The future of student learning depends on strict principals holding the line on weak instructors, principals who are not willing to accept an "OK" or "average" or "fair" performance from teachers, despite today's high-pressure climate of hiring anybody who walks through the door to fill the many vacancies.

Once administrators decide to retain a teacher after the first few years, that's it. The district has that teacher for life—and so do the students.

Well, the gig is up.

Concessions must take place for teachers to gain the respectability they have longed for. Teachers need to trade job security for professional integrity. They need to open the door to their classroom, welcome any administrator, show off their strengths as an educator, and get the big bucks if they are deemed worthy. There needs to be a real threat to teachers that they may lose their jobs if they don't meet minimum standards. The union's protection of the most incompetent taints the public perception of teachers, making taxpayers more resistant to higher teacher salaries. In the 2001 Hart/Teeter poll, 89 percent of people want incompetent teachers to be fired more easily. Americans feel that poor teachers should be given a chance to better themselves; however, once additional training has been tried, if no improvement is shown, then those teachers need to be shown the door.

Accountability is the latest buzzword in education, and many teachers perceive it as a vicious bee sting. When politicians first began uttering the word a few years ago, the idea was to hold teachers accountable for their students' performance—not necessarily a bad thing.

But accountability has mushroomed into standardized testing for one, standardized testing for all. Since unions balked at the idea of holding individual teachers responsible, what has developed in many states is a schoolwide accountability system. Texas's Successful Schools Award System (TSSAS) and California's Public Schools Accountability Act (PSAA) are just two state programs that offer financial rewards when schools meet a certain threshold of success based on standardized test results. This watered-down version of accountability does little to ensure that all teachers are doing an excellent job. A school could have a mix of very good and very bad teachers, yet still earn bonuses for everyone on campus. That means even more money for the incompetent instructor for doing a lousy job.

The American public wants to see results and is willing to pay higher taxes for better public schools, so what's the problem? If the teachers say, "Show me the money," the people say, "Show me the learning." There's nothing wrong with that. In the private sector, earning $100,000 takes much effort. In the same regard, teachers need to prove that they are good by having their teaching skills evaluated authentically.

Many good teachers are willing to be evaluated more than twice every two years and held accountable for their teaching abilities if there is a carrot in front of them—the carrot of professional wages and career opportunities.

Taxpayers should expect a link between pay and performance. However, common sense dictates that a teacher, no matter how gifted, can't possibly be held fully accountable for an individual student's performance. There are too many variables in students' lives, such as home environment and individual health, that cannot be controlled by a teacher.

Instead, the accountability of the teacher should revolve around his ability to perform spelled-out teaching standards at a certain level of competency.

Most unions oppose performance-based evaluations for fear of hurting the collegial atmosphere and creating

divisiveness among the faculty. First of all, little collegiality currently exists on school campuses. Teachers are
isolated in their classrooms; such solitary confinement
does not promote teachers working with each other. Especially at the secondary level, teachers are not a tightly
woven, closely bonded group of workers. And why would
jealousy erupt if the whole purpose in recognizing
higher-performing teachers is to raise the level of student
achievement?

Every teacher should be evaluated every year, with a
minimum of two observations. However, for the first few
years before tenure sets in and for every five years after
that, a teacher should receive a much more comprehensive five-year review that could include the following:

- minimum of two formal observations (one
  videotaped) with prior notification;
- minimum of four informal observations without
  prior notification;
- student portfolios; and
- teacher portfolio.

Such a review can be an integral part of a teacher's
license renewal every five years, something required in
almost every state. While time-consuming for both the
evaluator and the teacher, this substantive review (which
a few districts around the country are trying out) is the
only way to ensure that teachers are doing their jobs.
This means that principals need to get out of their offices
more often and visit classrooms regularly. Plus, under
peer review programs (discussed later), expert teachers
would help out with the evaluations so that the burden
wouldn't be entirely on principals. These evaluations,
done by a team of seasoned teachers and administrators,
would be used to determine if a particular teacher should
be promoted to a higher teaching position and, in turn,
which ones should be demoted.

Training on how to use the rubrics is essential, not
only for those doing the evaluating but for the teachers
themselves. Teachers should be trained en route toward

licensing what areas they will be evaluated on so they can receive proper preparation. The scoring guides could become the professional standards teachers are held responsible for demonstrating in the classroom.

Teachers must be in on the ground level in creating the criteria by which their colleagues can be measured and assessed. Teachers must take responsibility for creating these competencies and their assessment system; otherwise, they are not taking control of their profession and are very unlikely to accept such a system.

Establishing Evaluation Criteria

In her book, *Enhancing Professional Practice: A Framework for Teaching,* Charlotte Danielson develops 22 components organized under four domains (see figure 8) as a way "to define what teachers should know and be able to do in the exercise of their profession" (p. 1).

Many of these components have been used for Educational Testing Service's PRAXIS III, a competency test for teachers that assesses teaching skills and classroom performance; they are also similar to the criteria set by the National Board for Professional Teaching Standards (NBPTS).

By using a rubric—a scoring guide that establishes steps of competency—this framework could be used to evaluate a teacher's performance. And, in fact, such rubrics have been used as the blueprint for some of the progressive districts that have replaced the single salary schedule with a competency-based one.

Figure 9 shows an example of the rubric for Component 3C, Engaging Students in Learning, from Domain 3: Instruction. This could be used by an evaluator during an observation to determine a teacher's ability level.

Notice the four levels of the rubric: unsatisfactory, basic, proficient, and distinguished. By spelling out carefully what each level of performance represents, it de-

Figure 8. Components of Professional Practice

Domain 1: Planning and Preparation	**Domain 2: The Classroom Environment**

Domain 1: Planning and Preparation

Component 1a: *Demonstrating Knowledge of Content and Pedagogy*
Knowledge of content
Knowledge of prerequisite relationships
Knowledge of content-related pedagogy

Component 1b: *Demonstrating Knowledge of Students*
Knowledge of characteristics of age group
Knowledge of students' varied approaches to learning
Knowledge of students' skills and knowledge
Knowledge of students' interests and cultural heritage

Component 1c: *Selecting Instructional Goals*
Value
Clarity
Suitability for diverse students
Balance

Component 1d: *Demonstrating Knowledge of Resources*
Resources for teaching
Resources for students

Component 1e: *Designing Coherent Instruction*
Learning activities
Instructional materials and resources
Instructional groups
Lesson and unit structure

Component 1f: *Assessing Student Learning*
Congruence with instructional goals
Criteria and standards
Use for planning

Domain 2: The Classroom Environment

Component 2a: *Creating an Environment of Respect and Rapport*
Teacher interaction with students
Student interaction

Component 2b: *Establishing a Culture for Learning*
Importance of the content
Student pride in work
Expectations for learning and achievement

Component 2c: *Managing Classroom Procedures*
Management of instructional groups
Management of transitions
Management of materials and supplies
Performance of noninstructional duties
Supervision of volunteers and paraprofessionals

Component 2d: *Managing Student Behavior*
Expectations
Monitoring of student behavior
Response to student misbehavior

Component 2e: *Organizing Physical Space*
Safety and arrangement of furniture
Accessibility to learning and use of physical resources

continued

Figure 8. *Continued*

Domain 3: Instruction

Component 3a: *Communicating Clearly and Accurately*
Directions and procedures
Oral and written language

Component 3b: *Using Questioning and Discussion Techniques*
Quality of questions
Discussion techniques
Student participation

Component 3c: *Engaging Students in Learning*
Representation of content
Activities and assignments
Grouping of students
Instructional materials and resources
Structure and pacing

Component 3d: *Providing Feedback to Students*
Quality: accurate, substantive, constructive, and specific
Timeliness

Component 3e: *Demonstrating Flexibility and Responsiveness*
Lesson adjustment
Response to students
Persistence

Domain 4: Professional Responsibilities

Component 4a: *Reflecting on Teaching*
Accuracy
Use in future teaching

Component 4b: *Maintaining Accurate Records*
Student completion of assignments
Student progress in learning
Noninstructional records

Component 4c: *Communicating with Families*
Information about the instructional program
Information about individual students
Engagement of families in the instructional program

Component 4d: *Contributing to the School and District*
Relationships with colleagues
Service to the school
Participation in school and district projects

Component 4e: *Growing and Developing Professionally*
Enhancement of content knowledge and pedagogical skill
Service to the profession

Component 4f: *Showing Professionalism*
Service to students
Advocacy
Decision making

Source: Danielson, p. 3–4

Figure 9. Domain 3: Instruction
Component 3c: Engaging Students in Learning

Level of Performance

Element	Unsatisfactory	Basic	Proficient	Distinguished
Representation of Content	Representation of content is inappropriate and unclear or uses poor examples and analogies.	Representation of content is inconsistent in quality: Some is done skillfully, with good examples; other portions are difficult to follow.	Representation of content is appropriate and links well with students' knowledge and experience.	Representation of content is appropriate and links well with students' knowledge and experience. Students contribute to representation of content.
Activities and Assignments	Activities and assignments are inappropriate for students in terms of their age or backgrounds. Students are not engaged mentally.	Some activities and assignments are appropriate to students and engage them mentally, but others do not.	Most activities and assignments are appropriate to students. Almost all students are cognitively engaged in them.	All students are cognitively engaged in the activities and assignments in their exploration of content. Students initiate or adapt activities and projects to enhance understanding.
Grouping of Students	Instructional groups are inappropriate to the students or to the instructional goals.	Instructional groups are only partially appropriate to the students or only moderately successful in advancing the instructional goals of a lesson.	Instructional groups are productive and fully appropriate to the students or to the instructional goals of a lesson.	Instructional groups are productive and fully appropriate to the instructional goals of a lesson. Students take the initiative to influence instructional groups to advance their understanding.

continued

Figure 9. *Continued*

	Level of Performance			
Element	Unsatisfactory	Basic	Proficient	Distinguished
Instructional Materials and Resources	Instructional materials and resources are unsuitable to the instructional goals or do not engage students mentally.	Instructional materials and resources are partially suitable to the instructional goals, or students' level of mental engagement is moderate.	Instructional materials and resources are suitable to the instructional goals and engage students mentally.	Instructional materials and resources are suitable to the instructional goals and engage students mentally. Students initiate the choice, adaptation, or creation of materials to enhance their own purposes.
Structure and Pacing	The lesson has no clearly defined structure, or the pacing of the lesson is top slow or rushed, or both.	The lesson has a recognizable structure, although it is not uniformly maintained throughout the lesson. Pacing of the lesson is inconsistent.	The lesson has a clearly defined structure around which the activities are organized. Pacing of the lesson is consistent.	The lesson's structure is highly coherent, allowing for reflection and closure as appropriate. Pacing of the lesson is appropriate for all students.

Source: Danielson, p. 98–99

mystifies teaching skills in addition to removing as much subjectivity as possible for the evaluator. Teachers then would be paid according to their level of proficiency in each of these areas.

Despite the long-held belief that one cannot evaluate a teacher objectively, this proves that measurable qualities can be developed.

National Board for Professional Teaching Standards (NBPTS)

Just within the last few years, thousands of teachers from across the country have voluntarily undergone the most demanding evaluative process available via the NBPTS. Established in 1987 with teachers comprising the majority of its board members (a rather obvious idea other national education groups should model), the organization's mission is to transform "teaching into a true, dynamic profession," according to President Betty Castor. Here are its five core propositions:

- Teachers are committed to students and their learning.
- Teachers know the subjects they teach and how to teach those subjects to students.
- Teachers are responsible for managing and monitoring student learning.
- Teachers think systematically about their practice and learn from experience.
- Teachers are members of learning committees.

These propositions are good, commonsense qualities all teachers should embody, yet no one has written them down before and fleshed out specifically what they mean and how to demonstrate them.

This program is proving the naysayers wrong when it comes to codifying and evaluating those specific teaching skills that constitute high competency among instructors. The long-standing myth that you can't measure good teaching skills has finally been debunked. With a less than 50 percent pass rate, NBPTS holds teachers accountable to a high level of mastery. While completely voluntary, the NBPTS process should be the standard for teacher certification all across the country.

As of this writing, more than 16,000 teachers nationwide are national board certified, representing one-half of 1 percent of all of the teachers in America. The goal of NBPTS is to have 100,000 board-certified teachers by 2006. With each passing year, more teachers apply for national certification. Obviously, the financial rewards and prestige are two of the main reasons why teachers submit to such a grueling process. It also shows how ambitious and self-motivated teachers can be when given a carrot. What would happen to the quality of public schools if all teachers had extrinsic as well as intrinsic reasons to work harder?

Some may find the NBPTS elitist; however, what is wrong in identifying and rewarding instructors who do a far better job than most of their colleagues? Is it so terrible to hold up a teacher to others and say, "Here's a teacher for others to model themselves after"?

To obtain certification, a teacher needs to pay a $2,300 application fee. Some states and districts help subsidize the cost, though subsidies generally are limited to a fixed number of candidates. North Carolina has stepped forward and offers to pay the whole cost for any teacher in the state willing to put himself through the rigorous process, which NBPTS recommends taking two years to complete, though some finish in one year.

There are two main components to the NBPTS process: the portfolio and the assessment. A box is mailed to each candidate containing preprinted labels, envelopes, the NBPTS Standards booklet for the candidate's specific field (e.g., Adolescence Language Arts), verification forms, and dozens of pages of instructions for completing the portfolio. Streamlined just recently, the portfolio is made up of four entries: two 20-minute unedited video segments of the candidate teaching, and two detailed analyses of student work. Shortly after the due date of the portfolio in mid-April, candidates sign up for the assessment tests, which occur several weeks later. For this, teachers receive materials with which to prepare. Six hours of testing is performed.

A growing number of school districts also offer bonuses to their certified teachers. Again, North Carolina offers the most aggressive support. Because it pays the full fee for all teachers, increases pay by 12 percent, provides three days of paid release time to work on the portfolio, and offers seminar support using teachers with national certification, the state leads the nation in board-certified teachers, with more than 36,000, or nearly 25 percent of the country's total.

California offers a one-time $10,000 bonus to every teacher in the state who earns certification, Delaware increases a teacher's salary by 12 percent, and Virginia authorizes out-of-state teachers who are board certified without further licensing requirements, promoting the idea that a nationally board-certified teacher has proven abilities transferable anywhere.

Still, some districts require additional hours of work for the board-certified teacher to receive any stipend. What a shame that teachers must prove themselves further after achieving national board status instead of simply receiving a bonus for already putting in their own time and money.

If teachers become nationally certified, that is more of a guarantee that their students will receive high quality teaching. A 2000 study done by the University of North Carolina at Greensboro, "Accomplished Teaching: A Validation of National Board Certification," revealed that NBPTS-certified teachers "outperform their peers . . . on 11 of 13 key dimensions of teaching expertise." When comparing student work samples from both certified and noncertified teachers, those students taught by certified instructors "differ in profound and important ways."

Unfortunately, the report found that board-certified teachers' expertise was not being used by school districts. This could be due to a lack of understanding of what

NBPTS is all about, or a refusal by districts to relinquish control of curriculum and methodology to a bunch of teachers. In either case, until enough teachers become board certified and unite into a persuasive bargaining unit, the future of real teacher reform will remain unrealized. Imagine student achievement results if a contingent of these exceptional instructors entered low-performing schools.

If superlative teachers got paid what they're worth and got the recognition they deserve, there wouldn't be a need for an organization like NBPTS. All teachers in the profession should have to be board certified to receive pay raises and promotions.

Performance Pay

The most common alternative to the single salary schedule that has been tried in a few districts is performance-based, or skills-based, compensation. Instead of just assuming that more years on the job automatically makes one a better teacher, a performance-based pay system takes into account how teachers do their job.

Replacing education units and years on the job with specific competencies ensures a more direct link between what the teacher knows and the effect it has on the students. Just because teachers have a master's degree in education does not necessarily mean their students learn more effectively. Some districts have retained the college and experience credits as the teacher's base salary, then have added performance incentives for those teachers wishing to earn more money.

The Consortium for Policy Research in Education (CPRE), headquartered at the University of Wisconsin–Madison, joins four other research institutions (University of Pennsylvania, Harvard University, Stanford University, University of Michigan) in conducting extensive studies on alternative ways to compensate teachers in place of the traditional single salary schedule. Often the

CPRE is called in to help work with states, districts, and teachers unions to devise a new system of compensation.

Douglas County, Colorado

In 1993, a committee was formed in Douglas County, Colorado, to explore a new pay system for teachers. The group consisted of 20 people appointed by the teachers union and ten people appointed by the school district. This ensured an immediate buy-in by teachers of whatever resulted from this committee. When finally implemented in the 1994–95 school year, the plan had one of its main objectives to "attract, retain and motivate the highest qualified teachers while competing in the employment market." As stated in CPRE's report, *Douglas County Colorado Performance Pay Plan:*

> The Douglas County, Colorado School District . . . became one of the first school districts in the country to implement a compensation plan that incorporated elements of knowledge and skills-based pay and group-based performance pay into the salary structure. The plan maintained the educational credits and degrees portion of the single salary schedule, linked pay for years of experience to teacher evaluations, and added several new elements, including . . . knowledge and skill-based pay, group-based performance pay. . . . While these new elements redirected only a small proportion of teacher pay, they appear to have made a significant contribution to focusing and enhancing the human resource management system in the district. [CPRE, p. 2]

Single Salary Schedule	*Douglas County's Performance Pay Plan*
base pay	base pay
+ educational units and degrees	+ educational units and degrees
+ years of experience	+ years of experience
+ specific responsibilities	+ specific responsibilities
	+ skill-based pay
= total salary	+ responsibility pay
	+ group incentive pay
	+ outstanding teacher bonus award
	= total salary
Courtesy: CPRE	

Skill-based pay: Bonuses for teachers who master a skill that the district deems meaningful, such as knowledge of a computer software program.

Responsibility pay: Bonuses for teachers who do mentoring or work on committees.

Group incentive pay: Bonuses go to a group of teachers who work together on a specific student learning objective such as working with at-risk students.

Outstanding Teacher Bonus Award: For instructors to receive the teacher bonus award, they first need to volunteer for it, then provide a portfolio demonstrating their achievement. What's important is that the award is criterion-based—that is, "any teacher judged to be outstanding will receive the bonus" eliminating "competition among teachers for a limited number of awards."

Each year, between 240 and 280 teachers have submitted outstanding teacher portfolios, and about 230 have been approved as outstanding. . . . Teachers reported that the process of developing portfolios for the . . . award promoted (in many cases for the first time) meaningful, high-level discussions about professional practice among teachers.

[Positive results of the plan have included] improvements in student achievement as a result of the group incentive pay plan, particularly for targeted at-risk student groups; enhanced teacher skills as a result of participation in skill-based pay; enhanced school culture related to rewarding teachers for their work through site responsibility pay; and an enhanced focus on teaching practice for teachers participating in the outstanding teacher award. . . . Teachers have reported that tying pay increases to the teacher evaluation process resulted in principals and teachers taking the evaluation more seriously. [CPRE, p. 13–14]

With so many benefits, it's amazing that hundreds of districts haven't switched over to a performance-pay system.

Some performance-based systems pay teachers more money as they go, similar to professional baseball players earning additional compensation when they meet certain performance thresholds. The Vaughn Next Century Learning Center in Los Angeles is in its third year of

performance-based pay, offering a menu of incentives
that can add up to $20,000 to a teacher's annual pay. Be-
ing a charter school (which unions, for the most part, do
not support), it can offer more innovative ways to evaluate teachers. Voluntary for veteran teachers, but mandatory for new ones, the salary system in its first year saw 20
of the school's 66 teachers participate. Fifty participated
the following year, reflecting the positive effect the system had on teachers.

"This is a more accurate reflection of what I am doing," Louise Larson told *Education Week*. Added Paul
Johnson, "I felt proud about myself because I knew I'd
earned it." An ancillary benefit to paying teachers what
they are worth is that those who work hard and earn rewards feel better about their jobs and, in turn, are more
effective instructors for their students.

Yvonne Chan, the school's charismatic principal, allows her staff to evaluate her as well. "I have to go on performance pay. If I don't go, no one goes."

Teachers at the Robbinsdale Area Schools in Minnesota can earn up to $15,000 annually in skill-based pay.
There are eight performance categories in which teachers
can earn compensation added to their base salary; they
include national board certification, classroom observation, portfolio demonstrating student learning, work on
district task forces, and, most interesting, customer satis-
faction for which data are collected via student and parent surveys.

A Teacher's Career Ladder

Nearly every teacher who does not become an administrator usually begins and ends his career as a classroom
teacher. A teacher is locked into that job title for life;
there is no other position to aspire to. The Protestant
work ethic does not exist for teachers. Such a lack of

qualitative evaluation allows below-average teachers to have a lifetime job.

The two groups that leave teaching the soonest are the beginning teachers and the brightest teachers. It's easy to figure out why novice teachers who can't quickly engage with their students tend to leave the profession first. What they perceived as a relatively stress-free job with plenty of free time turns out to be the exact opposite. Often left alone to fend for themselves, they quickly become discouraged and exit quickly.

As for the smartest who leave, they recognize a raw deal when they see one. They have little tolerance for dysfunctional structures that offer little support. They come to the conclusion that other opportunities await them, so why waste their talents in an arena that doesn't appreciate their unique qualities? According to Myron Lieberman, "Because teaching offers so few opportunities for risk takers and entrepreneurs, individuals who can raise the productivity level of the education industry enter other occupations" (1997, p. 214). So bright, ambitious people leave.

Additionally, scores of schools have 20-, 30-, even 40-year veterans who have no vehicle through which to pass on their acquired and accumulated knowledge. They are not viewed as a resource. Instead, veteran teachers, especially when they reach a certain age past 60, are no longer seen as viable, but rather as educators to be shunned for their outmoded ways of thinking. A large reason for this is the fact that they have been doing the same job in the same position since they began their careers. If teachers have no more challenges ahead of them in terms of earning more money, even if they work harder or do other kinds of work related to teaching, their minds begin to atrophy and they are no longer interested in what they're doing. It's like a Broadway actor who performs the same role thousands of times. Sooner or later, you're going to get stale, and your audience, in this case students, will not be interested either.

A Proposal

The quickest way to attract more people to teaching is by raising starting salaries to the level of comparable jobs: but the surest way to retain the best instructors is by creating a career ladder for teachers.

Salaries would vary according to the region, urban versus rural, as well as the cost of living for a particular area. For simplicity purposes, here is a basic five-step career ladder for secondary teachers in metropolitan areas; in other words, the highest starting salaries for teachers in the country:

Sample Pay Scale

Position	Teaching Experience	Starting Salary
Instructor	training	$ 50,000
Teacher	2 years	55,000
Facilitator	5 years	60,000
Mentor	10 years	75,000
Master	15 years	100,000

On top of this salary, annual bonuses are added as described earlier for high-demand fields, for courses with more paperwork, and for working at hard-to-staff schools. Also, salary would vary, depending on an individual teacher's job performance; it may be higher than the above example, or it may be lower.

This sample has two important improvements over traditional schedules: 1) it pays a professional salary of $50,000 right from the start, thus attracting more college graduates, and 2) it encourages teachers to stay for the long haul by offering significantly more money the longer they stay in the profession and the more responsibilities they take on.

Having a single salary schedule is a disservice to a particular school and its unique student achievement level. Principals should have the authority to offer a signing bonus to attract teachers they need.

Each position would have its own evaluation rubric. The actual dollar amounts would vary, depending on an area's cost of living. For example, in Sioux Falls, South Dakota, salaries would begin at $35,000, while in Miami Beach, Florida, they would begin at $45,000.

The specific amounts aren't as significant as the separation between positions. If a board-certified teacher earns an extra $2,000 annually, that may not serve as a strong enough incentive for teachers to pursue such a time-intensive endeavor.

Teachers earning advanced degrees would still earn more money, but those with M.A.s and Ph.D.s in their subject field would receive higher increases. Nationally certified teachers should command the highest salaries because of the intensity of the work and its relevance to student learning. Highly trained skills in technology, administrative/leadership skills, training/mentoring other teachers, coordinating/conducting staff development, budgeting, and curriculum development are all areas that could be used to create various teaching positions and appropriate salary schedules.

Instructor Position

All beginning teachers would start here. After a two-year probationary period, a teacher can aspire to the position of Teacher. If at any time during the two years, evaluations are poor, that teacher would be fired.

Instructors would be assigned a Mentor teacher who would work closely with them for their first year.

The ideal schedule for an Instructor would be teaching half-days, then working with the Mentor the rest of the day analyzing work done with the students. A game plan would be devised jointly to be tried each following morning.

Teacher Position

All third-year teachers who receive positive evaluations would move on to this position, which would represent their first pay raise. Teachers would remain in their positions if they maintain good evaluations, with minor salary adjustments along the way, depending on the performance evaluation. If evaluations are mediocre, they would be demoted to the position of Instructor. And if there is no improvement after one year the teacher would be fired.

Facilitator Position

After serving successfully as a Teacher for at least three years, these teachers could apply to become Facilitators, exceptional instructors who have mastered teaching methodologies. They would earn more money because they would have greater responsibilities.

Facilitators would hold department chair positions; thus, they would teach one less class per day to free up time for department business.

As long as they maintain positive evaluations, Facilitators would remain at this level, with higher raises for those receiving top marks. Otherwise, they would be demoted.

The majority of current teachers most likely would become Teachers and Facilitators.

Mentor Position

Facilitators who have exemplary evaluations for five straight years could apply for Mentor positions. Mentors would have half the typical teaching load of Teachers, Instructors, and Facilitators. The rest of their day would consist of working one-on-one with probationary Instructors and demoted teachers, observing their classes and helping them to improve their methodology.

Ideally, Mentors would teach a balance of the best classes and the worst—the two most difficult classes.

That's another reason why they would be paid a higher salary.

Mentors would remain in their positions as long as they received positive evaluations.

Master Position

This would be the ultimate level a teacher could attain after serving as a Mentor teacher. Each would have a minimum of 15 years of exemplary teaching experience. It is crucial that Master teachers be the highest-paid employees on campus, including the principal, to underscore the importance of their job and because they would be responsible for many of the things principals now handle.

The Masters would coordinate the Mentor teachers, assist in evaluating all teachers, and conduct staff development workshops throughout the school district, yet remain in the classroom one period a day to practice new techniques. After all, why would the absolute top teachers be taken away completely from the job they do so well?

They would also participate in hiring; site decision making, such as purchasing books and supplies; coordinating teacher support services; and scheduling.

Additionally, Masters would work with college credential programs to bridge the training from school to work; some might even teach courses at local colleges.

Master teachers would remain in their positions indefinitely if they receive positive evaluations.

One teacher with nearly 30 years' experience sees a Master teacher as one who would "facilitate discussions to talk about how to better group our students" and other pertinent issues that teachers don't have the time to talk about.

All of these levels, with the exception of the Master teacher, would be evaluated by an on-site panel of administrators and Masters. Master teachers would be evaluated by a panel of on-site administrators and off-site Masters.

In determining annual raises, teachers would maintain a yearlong working portfolio of student work, lesson plans, reflection journal, and videotapes of lessons based on a set of goals for themselves. In other words, it would be up to individual teachers to put as much time into the portfolio as they deem necessary to earn as much as they desire.

The Rochester Experiment

In 1987, the Rochester Teachers Association and its New York district agreed to a landmark contract adopting many recommendations from the 1986 Carnegie report, including:

- salaries up to $70,000, the highest in the country at the time,
- a career ladder,
- mentors for first-year teachers,
- shared decision making at all schools, and
- more teacher/parent involvement.

Teachers reaching the upper rung of the career ladder spent "half their time in the classroom and half in leadership roles," such as mentoring or peer review. These teachers were awarded "adjunct professorships in the teacher-education program at the University of Rochester" (Toch, p. 146).

Adam Urbanski, in his eleventh consecutive two-year term as head of the Rochester Teachers Association, was able to convince the rank and file to accept peer review, an essential component of evaluating teachers more authentically in performance-pay systems.

Under peer review, mentor teachers help new teachers and struggling veterans. This opens the door to a new realm for teachers—policing their own, an important step toward gaining control over their profession.

"In Rochester, where mentors recommend whether first-year teachers should be reemployed, 10 percent of all new teachers have not been rehired, a far higher percentage than in the past" (Toch, p. 195). According to Dr. Urbanski, "Mentor teachers are tougher than administrators."

One Rochester educator with twenty years of experience had this to say about her experience as a mentor teacher:

> Being a mentor has kept me engaged professionally. At this point in my career, I am enjoying the challenge of working with adults new to the profession as well as still being able to teach my students half the day. I find the work fulfilling, the stipend is helpful, and I believe I am able to contribute more to the district without having to become an administrator.

Many of the original Rochester contract provisions remain in place nearly 15 years later.

"Most programs are still intact, and some are thriving, such as the mentor-intern and school-based planning programs," said Dr. Urbanski. "And the substantial salary increases had no adverse impact on district programs," referring to a common reason why districts can't provide higher pay to teachers.

The most recent Rochester agreement "guarantees that the district will pay tuition for education for its teachers, meetings are voluntary, and there is no dismissal time for teachers."

While initially leery of such a concept, unions are slowly embracing peer review programs so they can control as much of each one as they can. Districts like it because they get state funding for implementing the program. In a 1997 American Federation of Teachers (AFT) survey, 77 percent said that they support peer review for new teachers, and 63 percent support it for poorly evaluated tenured teachers.

It may surprise people how many teachers are interested in evaluating other teachers' classroom performances. But isn't that a primary reason a person goes into teaching: the desire to help others? What better way to help than with one's own colleagues? Plus, teachers police their own profession.

"Peer evaluation within career ladders has fostered greater collegiality among veteran teachers. It has brought teachers from different disciplines together and encouraged a sharing of ideas among them" (Toch, p. 195).

In Ohio, the Toledo Public School system removed an average of 9.4 percent of its new teachers between 1988 and 1998 through its peer review program, "The Intern Program," again showing how much tougher teachers are on their own colleagues.

Cincinnati Teacher Evaluation and Compensation System

In September 2000, the Cincinnati Federation of Teachers (CFT), an affiliate of the American Federation of Teachers, the more visionary national teacher organization compared to the National Education Association, reached a groundbreaking agreement with Cincinnati Public Schools for a new pay-for-performance evaluation system by a 55 percent vote, shattering the long-established seniority pay scale. Teachers are evaluated several times a year based on 16 standards of good teaching in four domains and can ascend a career ladder in positions from apprentice to accomplished.

"The Cincinnati Teacher Evaluation and Compensation System provides a fast track to higher salaries for very able teachers who are early in their careers," according to Rick Beck, CFT president. "We believe this, along with new hiring standards, will attract some of the best and most highly qualified new teachers in the area to Cincinnati Public Schools."

Teachers helped to plan the program, which is why it enjoys widespread support. Costs for paying higher salaries will be offset from those teachers earning less. The plan will be implemented fully in the 2002–03 school year.

"This is the first move off the single salary schedule for any district in the country since 1921," University of Wisconsin–Madison education professor Allan Odden said in an *Education Week* article about the system he helped create.

The standards developed (figure 10) were based on those established by the NBPTS, the Interstate New Teacher Assessment and Support Consortium (INTASC), the PRAXIS III assessment administered by the Educational Testing Service (ETS), and the Association for Supervision and Curriculum Development (ASCD).

Teachers are evaluated on how well they do in each of these domains, on a rubric scale of one to four, four being the highest. A balance was struck to accommodate different teaching approaches that occur at elementary and secondary levels.

How well teachers do on the scale determines their placement on the Career Level salary chart (figure 11).

In effect, if teachers do not demonstrate Career Teacher skills by their eighth year of teaching, they no longer have a job. The expectation is that most people will need up to five years to accomplish the first three steps, with the majority of teachers remaining at the Career level.

The Cincinnati career ladder also encourages teachers to earn more money by teaching in a shortage area such as science, or by earning advanced degrees in their field or national board certification.

The missing piece in this well-crafted compensation plan is the development of different teaching positions as mentioned earlier, a truer career ladder for those teachers performing different responsibilities such as mentoring. It is essential that those who do more not only are given additional money, but have a lighter teaching workload to do their job effectively.

Cincinnati Public Schools implemented tougher hiring standards in 2001 as well. All new teachers must have a 3.0 GPA in college and an extensive classroom internship.

Figure 10. Standards of Good Teaching—CPS

1. Planning and Preparing for Student Learning	2. Creating an Environment for Learning	3. Teaching for Learning	4. Professionalism
The teacher will:	The teacher will:	The teacher will:	The teacher will:
1.1 acquire and use knowledge about students as individual learners in preparing lessons which consider the student's cultural heritage, interests, and community.	2.1 create an inclusive and caring environment in which each individual is respected and valued.	3.1 know the content, content-specific pedagogy, and the knowledge and skills students need prior to learning new concepts.	4.1 track student progress toward Promotion/Credit Granting Standards, maintain records to show how decisions are made about rubric scores and grades, and keep accurate noninstructional records.
1.2 write clear instructional objectives that will enable all students to meet or exceed Promotion/Credit Granting standards, establish high expectations, address individual learning needs, and make connections within and among disciplines.	2.2 establish a classroom culture where high expectations for learning and achievement are communicated to students, and all students are invited and encouraged to participate.	3.2 communicate learning objectives, performance standards for those objectives, directions, procedures, and assessments effectively.	4.2 inform families about the academic and social progress of their child and events in the classroom and encourage parental involvement in child's education.
1.3 design lessons and use clearly defined assessments aligned with standards, and select/adapt instructional resources appropriate for the developmental levels of students.	2.3 establish, maintain, and manage a safe and orderly environment in which time is used to maximize student learning.	3.3 pose thought-provoking questions, foster classroom discussion, and provide opportunities for each student to listen and speak for many purposes.	4.3 establish and maintain a professional relationship with peers/teams, function as a member of an instructional team, department, or level, and participate in school and district initiatives.

continued

Figure 10. *Continued*

1. Planning and Preparing for Student Learning	2. Creating an Environment for Learning	3. Teaching for Learning	4. Professionalism
		3.4 engage all students in learning activities that encourage conceptual understanding and connections, challenge student thinking, and address real-life situations.	4.4 improve content knowledge and pedagogical skills by participating in professional development activities and applying what is learned.
		3.5 provide timely, constructive information on student performance through a variety of assessment strategies.	
		3.6 reflect upon and adjust instruction to respond to differences in student knowledge, experiences, cultural heritage, and traditions, and persist in finding effective instructional strategies to meet individual needs.	

Source: Cincinnati Public Schools

Figure 11. Career Levels—CPS

Apprentice	Novice	Career	Advanced	Accomplished
New teachers	Must have 2s or better in all domains	Must have 3s or better in all domains	Must have a 4 in Teaching for Learning domain and at least one other domain; must have at least 3s in other domains	Must have 4s in all domains
May have temporary teaching license nonrenewed at end of year 2 if Novice status is not attained	Must pass Ohio's teacher licensing test (PRAXIS 3) nonrenewed/terminated at end of year 5 as a Novice if Career status is not attained	May remain in category throughout career	May remain in category throughout career	May remain in category throughout career
Salary: $30,000 Bachelor's degree	Salary range: $32,000–35,750 Bachelor's degree	Salary range: $38,750–$49,250 Bachelor's degree	Salary range: $52,500–55,000 Bachelor's degree	Salary range: $60,000–$62,500 Bachelor's degree

Source: Cincinnati Public Schools

"It may narrow the pool of applicants initially, but it will be worth it," said Deborah Heater, CPS's director of human resources.

Elsewhere across the country, performance-pay or competency-pay salary schedules and career ladders for teachers are emerging: Iowa, Kentucky, Indiana, Minnesota, Wisconsin, Tennessee, Utah, Missouri, Montana, Nebraska, New Mexico, Washington, and Georgia.

North Carolina's Charlotte-Mecklenburg school system created a six-step career ladder that generated enthusiasm among teachers and administrators. During the process, teachers became closer to one another, not more adversarial as so many unions claim would happen. Some teachers commented that it was "a shot of adrenaline," "you get a sense of achievement, and there is recognition . . . it has prestige." One principal said, "Teachers are working very hard at being better teachers." The career ladder system attracted the right type of people who want to be compensated for how hard and how well they work.

As Toch explains it, "The discontent that the career ladder did foster was generally confined to teachers not participating in the program. That has been true of other teacher-incentive programs as well" (p. 192).

Many administrators might scoff at the idea of doing this type of in-depth evaluation for each teacher, considering the amount of work they now do. However, this evaluative process not only gives more regular feedback to the teacher, it forces the administrator to return to the classroom to see how certain policies are executed. Observations are key to ensuring that teachers are doing a good job.

Bonuses

The only time the word "bonus" comes up in a teacher's life is when discussing a room addition to a house. Increasingly, though, more states and districts are considering or offering bonuses to attract talent:

- Houston offers bonuses and stipends for high-demand areas.
- Baltimore gives teachers housing allowances.
- Signing bonuses are offered in Dallas and Detroit and Utah and Massachusetts. Massachusett's offer of 60 $20,000 signing bonuses for a four-year teaching commitment attracted 800 applicants from around the country.
- Unions have agreed to bonuses in Boston and Columbus, Ohio.

This last item is very significant because most unions oppose bonuses, since many are used to attracting individuals who bypass the normal certification process. And they have a point. Bonuses should be given to those individuals who have demonstrated skills above and beyond the average teacher. Giving extra money to unproven novice teachers is like awarding your 16-year-old son with a brand-new car in the hope that he will do well in high school. Now that he has already been rewarded, what is his motivation to get good grades? The carrot needs to be given after a trick has been completed, not before.

Bonuses should entice the best teachers to leave the friendly confines of their suburban middle-class schools to work at low-performing urban campuses. Besides, inner-city schools are already overrun with new teachers. "If you put a beginning teacher in a low-performing school building that you already know does not have the capacity to support beginning teachers, you have done a disservice," said JoAnn Norris who administers North Carolina's Teaching Fellows program. "Those schools already have a high proportion of beginning teachers. So I would suggest that is not good public policy."

When administered properly, however, bonuses can help attract qualified instructors to schools at which they otherwise would not work. As stated in *Education Week's Quality Counts* report, "The New York City schools offered a 15 percent raise to employees . . . who agreed to work in schools that were on the state's academic watch list. . . . As a result of the salary increase, 233 educators transferred into the city's low-performing schools in 1999–2000, including 190 senior teachers and 43 who were not yet fully licensed."

What needs to be done, then, is to develop standards for the teaching profession for which real evaluation tools can be developed. Hold teachers accountable, then pay those with excellent evaluations more money, and fire those with poor performance reviews.

As stated earlier, teachers must be at the forefront of developing these assessment systems; otherwise, they won't buy into them. They must be teacher-driven.

Offering more-qualified teachers higher salaries is not greedy in terms of personal wealth; rather, it's greedy in offering the children opportunities to reach their maximum potential. As the next chapter shows, better teachers mean better student results.

Yes, taxpayers should expect a link between pay and performance, but teachers should demand it; it's their quickest ticket out of the professional ghetto.

CHAPTER 5

===============

Rigorous Training:
Teacher Interns

"If education leaders want to close the achievement gap, they must focus, first and foremost, on developing qualified teachers."—Kati Haycock, director of the Education Trust

The perception is that those who go into the teaching profession are at the bottom of the academic barrel: Those who can do, those who can't teach.

For too long the education establishment has been willing to accept less than stellar talent. This is reflected in teacher evaluation forms that give principals only two options to check: "satisfactory" or "unsatisfactory," "does meet expectations" or "does not meet expectations." No other options are available, not "outstanding" or "*exceeds* expectations," which is precisely the point. If the system does not expect its most important employee group to excel, then what should students expect? It's as if schools breathe a sigh of relief if their teachers merely meet expectations; it's simply serendipity if a teacher goes beyond that.

How comforting is it to know that there are people working in America who say that if their current careers go sour they can always "fall back" on teaching. Instead of teaching being a career of choice and stature, it's usually a last resort for many. Do you ever hear people talking about falling back on engineering? What other professions do people go into after getting laid off? Do they suddenly decide to become orthopedic surgeons?

Becoming a teacher is too easy, and remaining one is even easier. It's as if teaching is the one profession everyone can do. You can't walk into an operating room and perform an operation, you can't appear before a judge and jury and try a case, you can't be on a construction site and pore over blueprints, but, with very little training, you can enter a classroom. Teaching 30 impressionable students is no problem.

Teaching well is not, nor should it be, easy. Here are merely a handful of skills expected of today's teachers:

- effective instructional strategies;
- exceptional organizational and time management skills;
- knowledge of local, state, and national academic standards;
- effective assessment techniques;
- curriculum development;
- ongoing staff development, keeping abreast of current research;
- leadership qualities;
- ultimate decision maker, hundreds of times a day;
- knowledge of budgets and how to allocate them for classroom use;
- psychologist; and
- performer.

Attorneys and doctors thrive on the challenge of passing the bar exam and completing internships. Why not put teachers through more rigorous training? With the prospect of excellent salaries in front of them, people would push themselves hard to do well. Once teaching is perceived to be more prestigious, college students who otherwise might not consider teaching will line up.

At a time when the focus needs to be on increasing instructional quality, the nation's purely quantitative needs over the next several years do not bode well for the professionalism of teaching, a workforce whose quality is already in question.

The danger is that, as the teaching shortage increases, standards, qualifications, and requirements will fall, allowing more and more unqualified people into America's classrooms.

This is the wrong direction for public education. Becoming a teacher should be harder than it is now, not easier. Teachers are going to have to be trained in a body of knowledge specific only to the teaching field so that, like law and medicine, teaching evolves into a highly selective, specialized field that the majority of people are not capable of succeeding in.

Qualifications to enter teacher education programs need to be raised, coursework needs to reflect relevancy to classroom work, student teachers need to get into classrooms sooner during their study and for longer periods of time, competency tests need to be strengthened, and extra care and time needs to be taken with first-year teachers to combat the horrendous attrition rate.

Of course, one could argue, so you pay teachers $100,000, get smarter people into the profession, train them more effectively and for a longer period of time, and then what? Bottom line, does it make any difference in making students smarter?

The Impact of Good Teachers on Student Achievement

Ask any parent who the best kindergarten teacher is at a particular school, and you won't have difficulty eliciting strong opinions. Parents know who the best teachers are, and so do the students. And even if they aren't sure who's the best, they know that having their children taught by the best can only benefit the learning curve of their sons and daughters.

It's only common sense that a skilled teacher makes a difference in how well students learn. But where's the proof? Is there a direct link between a high-quality teacher and improved student learning?

Studies show "that teacher expertise is one of the most important factors in determining student achievement . . . teachers who know a lot about teaching and learning and who work in environments that allow them to know students well are the critical elements of successful learning" (Darling-Hammond, 1997a, p. 8).

> [A] study of high- and low-achieving schools with similar student populations in New York City found that differences in teacher qualifications accounted for more than 90% of the variation in student achievement in reading and mathematics at all grade levels tested. Research using national data and studies in Georgia, Michigan, and Virginia have found that students achieve at higher levels and are less likely to drop out when they are taught by teachers with certification in their teaching field, by those with master's degrees, and by teachers enrolled in graduate studies [Ibid., p. 9].

Harvard researcher Ronald Ferguson examined the impact of qualified teachers on student performance in his study, "Paying for Public Education: New Evidence of How and Why Money Matters" published in the *Harvard Journal on Legislation* in 1991. After studying 900 Texas school districts, he discovered that nothing—books, computers, workbooks, videos—has the same impact on student learning as a highly competent instructor, accounting for a 40 percent variation in achievement.

Ferguson also studied this subject in Alabama. He found "a significant positive relationship [existed] between teacher test scores . . . and student test scores . . . with higher scoring teachers more likely to produce significant gains in student achievement than their lower scoring counterparts." And math and science teachers who majored in their respective fields got "higher student performance than teachers who did not" (Haycock, p. 6).

North Carolina and Connecticut have dedicated themselves to improving the quality of their teachers over the past decade by offering higher salaries and other financial incentives, and their schools have shown higher student achievement.

> North Carolina has posted among the largest student achievement gains in mathematics and reading of any state in the nation, now scoring well above the national average in 4th grade reading and mathematics, although it entered the 1990s near the bottom of the state rankings. Connecticut has also posted significant gains, becoming one of the top scoring states in the nation in mathematics and reading [Darling-Hammond, 1997a, p.11].

There are also studies showing that bad teachers hinder student learning.

Economist Eric Hanushek of the University of Rochester discovered in his study, "The Trade-Off Between Child Quantity and Quality," that "the difference between a good and bad teacher can be a full level of achievement in a single school year" (Haycock, p. 3).

William L. Sanders and Joan C. Rivers published a study in 1996, entitled "Cumulative and Residual Effects of Teachers on Future Student Academic Achievement," based on their research in Tennessee schools. "Elementary school students who are assigned to ineffective teachers for three years in a row score significantly lower on achievement tests than those assigned to the most effective teachers over the same period of time" (Ibid., pp. 9–10).

A study of the Dallas Independent School District reveals how the caliber of teaching has a direct influence on student ability:

A group of beginning third-graders in Dallas who
averaged around the 55th percentile in mathematics
scored around the 76th percentile at the end of fifth
grade after being assigned to three highly effective
teachers in a row. By contrast, a slightly higher
achieving group of third graders—averaging around
the 57th percentile—were consecutively taught by three
of the least effective teachers. By the conclusion of
fifth grade, the second group's percentile ranking had
fallen to 27th. This time the youngsters, who had scored
nearly the same as beginning third-graders, were
separated by a full 50 percentile points just three years
later [Haycock, p. 5].

An examination of the Boston Public Schools by Bain
and Company found that "the students with teachers
from the bottom third showed virtually no growth" in
reading and math, leading one headmaster to declare,
"About one-third of my teachers should not be teaching."
The most effective teachers in the study produced "six
times the learning seen in the bottom third" (Ibid.).

Kati Haycock, director of the Education Trust, a
Washington-based group focusing on ways to improve student learning among poor and minority children, wrote in
her article, "Good Teaching Matters . . . A Lot," that the
achievement gap between higher-economic and lower-economic children would disappear "if we . . . assigned our
best teachers to the students who most need them" (p. 2).

That's why parents take an active if sometimes aggressive role in getting their children into certain teachers' classrooms. This activism tends to fade as the child
ascends through the upper grades in public schools. After
all, everyone agrees how crucial it is to establish a good
education foundation in the early years. However, there
is only a limited number of superlative teachers to go
around. Not all children get the best teachers. Not all
children have parents who fight for the best for their chil-

dren. Yet, why should parents have to work so hard in the first place? Why can't the vast majority of teachers be truly outstanding?

If teaching students at a higher level with greater expectations is the rallying cry in public education, then public education needs professionals who can meet the challenge. Patte Barth, senior associate at the Education Trust, said, "We've got to make sure that our kids have teachers who can bring them to those high standards."

Education of the Educator

Each year four million school children receive math instruction from a teacher whose last math class was in high school.

A majority of math and science teachers did not major in their respective fields.

And the children who need the best teachers possible are more likely to be taught by these unqualified instructors.

Liping Ma's book, *Knowing and Teaching Elementary Mathematics: Teachers' Understanding of Fundamental Mathematics in China and the United States,* revealed that American math teachers performed dreadfully on simple tests, compared with their Chinese counterparts. When "asked to divide $1\frac{3}{4}$ by $\frac{1}{2}$, only nine [of 23 seasoned] teachers got the correct answer of $3\frac{1}{2}$" while all 72 in China answered correctly. She also tested their ability to create effective lessons. For the above example she asked them "to use pizza or cookies to illustrate" it. Only one American teacher was able to come up with anything, while 90 percent of the Chinese teachers suggested many examples (Colvin, Aug 11, 1999).

The problem with public education isn't so much that Johnny can't read, but that Johnny's teacher can't teach reading.

How shameful is it that so many teachers do not know the subject that they teach? What could be more basic than that?

The National Center for Education Statistics reveals that while 66 percent of high school teachers majored in the field they teach, only 44 percent of middle school teachers fall into that category. This means that millions of schoolchildren have teachers, supposed experts in their subject matter, who never majored in that field.

And it's worse for students in high-poverty areas. According to the National Commission on Teaching and America's Future's report, *Doing What Matters Most: Investing in Quality Teaching,* in "schools with the highest minority enrollments, students had less than a 50% chance of getting a science or mathematics teacher who held a license and a degree in the field he or she taught" (Darling-Hammond, 1997a, p. 2). If anything, these students should be taught by the best instructors, not the worst.

Too many teachers are from the bottom rung of college graduates. The average SAT and GRE scores of teachers are lower than for other professions. Some colleges allow candidates with GPAs as low as a C- to enter teacher preparation programs.

Figure 12, from AFT's *Quality Counts* report, compares the percentages in the top quartile on the SAT or ACT exam among three groups: those who trained as teachers in college and those who did not; those teachers who actually taught; those who finished their training but never went into the field; and those teachers who stayed versus those who left.

In each of the three cases, the further along a person went toward becoming a teacher and staying, the lower his or her score on the SAT or ACT.

"College graduates with high test scores are less likely to become teachers, licensed teachers with high test scores are less likely to take teaching jobs, employed teachers with high test scores are less likely to stay, and

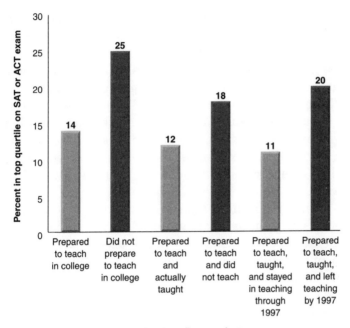

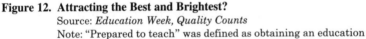

Figure 12. Attracting the Best and Brightest?
Source: *Education Week, Quality Counts*
Note: "Prepared to teach" was defined as obtaining an education
degree, student-teaching, or both.

former teachers with high test scores are less likely to return" (Murnane et al., p. 10).

The notion that people who are less academically in-
clined go into teaching is reflected in the direction some
states and districts have taken. Adopting direct instruction reading programs with materials that spell out for
the instructor what to do and, in some cases, what to say,
shows a complete lack of confidence in teachers' skills.

In big-city districts like Chicago and Los Angeles,
curriculum is structured so stringently that it sucks dry
any input from individual teachers, leading them by the
hand day-to-day by telling them what lessons to teach and
what homework to assign. Here is where the trite saying,
"We all need to be on the same page," is actually true.

Such verbatim step-by-step lessons may be a godsend to clueless teachers, but it's a straightjacket for qualified instructors who feel they have the professional know-how to teach a subject. You might as well sit students down in front of a computer and have them go through a tutorial.

Teaching-by-the-numbers reading programs, such as Open Court and Success for All, rob teachers of all creativity and innovation. All of the lessons are scripted, like instructions for administering standardized tests, including acting directions such as, "read slowly, with expression."

"Teachers are not given a choice to use the program, plus it is an exhausting amount of work," said a veteran elementary school teacher who has used it.

Donna Moffett, a teacher who participated in the New York City schools alternate route program, New York City Teaching Fellows, and who was highlighted throughout the 2000–01 school year in a series of articles in the *New York Times,* worked with the Success for All reading curriculum. Once when she was reading from a scripted story having to do with a mischievous boy, she improvised a statement that the boy was "just like some students in here," using a clever teaching technique to connect the material to the students. Unfortunately, her mentor teacher observing her that day became upset, later admonishing Moffett never to do it again. Was she a "bad" teacher for veering away from the word-for-word instructions?

The fact that such programs exist at all says more about the lack of faith education publishers and the entire education bureaucracy have in the ability of teachers to teach than it does about low-level readers.

If this trend continues, more good teachers will leave, refusing to be dictated to about what they can teach in their classrooms, leaving the less-qualified to multiply.

In fact, the longer I've been in education, the more I've seen the basics indoctrinated, prescribed, and required— becoming part of a teacher's evaluation. It crushes the best teachers at the expense of the worst ones. Instead of retraining only the struggling teachers, the good get punished and their creativity stifled. Teachers have no choice in whether to use the program. This is quite typical of the bureaucratic mentality: if a few are having trouble, then all will be forced to attend staff development sessions on new materials. It's difficult to think of one "innovation" that provides more freedom of thought or rewards thinking "out of the box." The reason for this is that many educators do not follow the general curriculum that has led to such encroaching control on the teacher's day-to-day operations. No trust exists that says, "You're the professional—you can handle it."

If this is what teaching is becoming, then the whole problem of enticing top talent to enter the profession becomes moot; all one would need then is someone with the ability to read the script—an actor (whom children view more as a role model anyway). That is why content standards have been developed all around the country: to ensure quality control.

Therefore, the whole path to a teaching credential needs to be strengthened, from higher GPAs to more difficult competency tests. In short, future teachers need to:

- major in the field they will be teaching (elementary teachers major in liberal arts);
- have a minimum 3.0 GPA instead of 2.75 to get into any teacher training program;
- be classified as "pre-ed" during the last two years of their bachelor's program so job shadowing and introductory classes can occur;
- enroll in a one-year intern program for elementary education or a two-year intern program for secondary education;
- be paid a minimum salary (living wage) as interns to work in a school during the day alongside a mentor teacher; and
- turn in a portfolio of sample lessons plans and assessment strategies, and pass a rigorous standards

exam (such as the NBPTS process) before receiving a teacher's license.

Smarter teachers entering the profession will bring fresher approaches to student learning pathways and know their subject matter better so they can feel they are the experts in their field, and, therefore, will be able to handle student inquiries more effectively.

As Martin Gross says in *The Conspiracy of Ignorance,* "If we want students to be more scholarly . . . then we must have more scholarly teachers in public school" (p. 52). If we want teachers to have high standards for their students, then the teachers themselves need to have strong academic backgrounds.

Having a higher IQ does not necessarily translate to being an effective instructor. Observations of university professors bear that out. Yet how many excellent teachers were awful students? I'm not saying to raise the bar a foot—just a few inches higher would help. Membership in MENSA doesn't have to be a requirement. Of course, having smarter teachers could mean more independent teachers—something possibly to be feared by unions and school districts.

The Lowly Status of Teacher Colleges and Credential Programs

John Silber, former chairman of the Massachusetts Board of Education, once declared that "education programs have a reputation as a place for dum-dums . . . the laughing stock by serious scholars."

Studies of the college education of teachers reveal that they end up taking fewer units in their majors than those who go into nonteaching fields—that is, teachers are put on easier tracks toward their degrees. After studying 91 teacher training programs, Eugene Hickok, former Pennsylvania state secretary of education, concluded in an article in *Policy Review* (September–October 1998), "Few teacher-education programs had meaningful admission standards. . . ." Math majors going into teaching were allowed to take easier courses to earn their degrees than those not intending to go into education. This means courses in differential equations and advanced calculus could be avoided (Gross, p. 46).

Too many middle school teachers lack subject-specific coursework for the classes they teach. One 1998 study conducted by the Southern Regional Education Board in Atlanta found that a third of all middle school teachers in 16 states had only elementary school certificates. In one state, 70 percent of eighth-grade English classes were taught by instructors holding licenses in either elementary education or home economics. Why was this? Because obtaining an elementary education license was far easier than obtaining a single-subject one.

Anti-intellectual curricula dominate teachers colleges and credential programs, offering little substance or relevance. Courses like "The Culturally Diverse Classroom," "Lettering, Posters, and Displays in the School Program," and "Standard First Aid and Personal Safety" frequently make up the coursework (Toch, p. 157). As mentioned earlier, the state of New York requires completion of a two-hour seminar in child abuse recognition and reporting before granting a teaching license, making one wonder if the state is issuing certificates for teachers or social workers.

Instead of taking classes on children's health habits and multiculturalism, student teachers need to be in the classroom with a mentor teacher, interacting with real children. Instead of espousing the virtues of Piaget, universities should have drama instructors and vocal coaches show teachers how to keep their students' attention without overly straining their voices.

About a decade ago, Rita Kramer spent a year visiting credential programs and teachers colleges across the country. Her conclusion, in her book, *Ed School Follies: The Miseducation of America's Teachers,* was that "among teacher-educators today, the goal of schooling is not considered to be instructional, let alone intellectual, but political. The aim is not to produce individuals capable of effort and mastering, but to make sure everyone gets a passing grade." She goes on to say that "what matters is not whether or not anyone has learned anything, but that no one [fails] . . . in the schooling of teachers as well as in the schools in which they will teach" (p. 209–11).

If more than one-third of college students in teacher training programs opt out of becoming teachers, then something is wrong.

Kramer offers this dim view: "The worst of the ed schools are certification mills where the minimally qualified instruct the barely literate in a parody of learning. Prospective teachers leave no more prepared to impart knowledge or inspire learning than when they entered" (p. 220).

The 1986 Holmes report found that "teacher education long has been intellectually weak . . . an underpaid and overworked occupation, making it difficult for universities to recruit good students to teacher education or to take it as seriously as they have taken education for more prestigious professions" (Laboree, p. 141).

Unlike other fields, where the training is transferable to other professions, "this is not the case with programs of teacher education. If you do not become a teacher, teacher training is largely a waste" (Lieberman, 1997, p. 216).

In writing about teachers' experiences with credential classes, Christine Baron in her *Los Angeles Times* column found that "young teachers feel that the education courses they took in college did not begin to prepare them for the reality of public schools," offering them "a lot of irrelevance and busywork that has little to do with becoming an effective teacher."

Here's how one California instructor described her education classes:

My credential coursework had little to do with what I do in the classroom today.

I learned most of what I do by working with other teachers as an assistant in the classroom. Teacher training programs need more hands-on opportunities for entering teachers. This would allow them to see how things really are and at a variety of schools and districts. Universities should also have elementary and high school teachers come on campus and tell student teachers what they do or show them what to do. Give them ideas.

One of the problems with the lack of legitimacy of education as a profession is its lack of specific knowledge; that is, education deals with all areas of academic pursuit—science, math, history, etc.—so what unique body of knowledge comprises education? There needs to be a science of teaching.

Another reason why brighter people don't enter teaching is the lack of interest shown by most major universities in training teachers. Departments of education represent the lowest level of academia. It seems that no department rates lower in prestige except campus food services. Even professors of education earn on average $11,000 less than their counterparts, according to the National Center for Education Statistics.

Currently, the University of California (UC) trains only about 4 percent of all its state's teachers, though that number used to be in the double digits. Richard C. Atkinson, president of the nine-campus UC said, "For the last 30 or 40 years, schools of education have been going downhill in their position in the university" (Atkinson and Reed). The university's education departments prefer to focus on doctoral candidates and research projects, and especially staff development (some $70 million worth), and leave the training of teachers to the state university system, which does just that for 62 percent of the state's teachers. "The preparation of teachers is just as important in our society as the preparation of doctors and lawyers," according to Charles B. Reed, chancellor of the 22-campus Cal State University (Ibid.).

What's interesting is that the most influential researchers in education, whose work often is the basis of reforms, come from institutions such as Harvard and UC–Berkeley, which are not known for training new teachers.

The *New York Times* reports that, "unlike medical or law schools, education programs are . . . not required to be certified or accredited by a professional board." This is borne out when only 40 percent of the 1,200 education departments in the country are accredited by the National Council for Accreditation of Teacher Education, according to Gross (p. 54).

Slowly, states are beginning to demand more accountability from education schools and credential programs. Alabama is the only state that puts out a report card on how well the state's colleges are preparing new teachers, rating them as Clear, Caution, or Alert. Texas also examines its teacher-training programs. Last year, ten of the 87 accredited programs fell short. It's almost as if states are afraid to be too demanding in requirements for fear of getting fewer qualified candidates. But you can't have it both ways. You can't demand higher-quality teachers while streamlining the training process. You can't demand higher student achievement when more and more unqualified teachers or teachers with minimum training are teaching in the nation's classrooms. Yet both sides is exactly how states are playing the game. Have stricter requirements on one end, but at the other, allow anyone without a criminal record to fill the slots.

What would be very helpful is to enlist currently working teachers to teach teacher interns at colleges, similar to doctors who teach in university hospitals. This would be the role of the Master teacher: to be a liaison in the higher ed partnership, bringing to the teacher interns real classroom lessons.

Teachers colleges and university credential programs should be the birthplace of the teacher revolution. To reform teaching, teacher training needs to gain status. The quality of teachers will not improve unless the quality of teacher education improves first.

Pre-Ed and Teacher Interns

Teachers need to follow the example of the medical and legal professions: More training should be required, more knowledge should be gained, then more money would be justified.

Education students should enroll first in medical school–like internships and residencies, giving prospective teachers more hands-on experience. Texas is one state doing just that, while at the same time diminishing the number of irrelevant educational psychology classes, which have long been the backbone of teacher training in this country. Having Mentors teach hands-on classes at colleges would provide a more reality-based experience for student teachers.

The term, "student teacher," which refers to a college student teaching in a school setting toward the end of his credential work, is derogatory. The seeds of inferiority have already been planted. Are medical students referred to as student doctors or interns? While interns and residents are paid little (and very few states pay teachers when they student teach—it's mainly a year's worth of free labor), at least they know financial security awaits them. This is not so for teachers. While they, too, sacrifice as other students do by quitting their jobs and living at home with their parents, or depending on a spouse's salary for an entire year, many feel that those sacrifices do not justify the end result, which discourages many from getting a credential—unless they are clever enough to get an emergency certificate, thus circumventing the whole process.

Teacher candidates should major in the field they will be teaching, declare themselves "pre-ed" as undergraduates, then study the science of teaching as graduate students in teaching schools (like teaching hospitals), leading to a master's degree—a level at which all teachers should start (Labaree, p. 129).

Graduate students in training to become teachers need to go into the classroom as soon as possible. Except for meeting a particular course's requisite observational hours, the long-standing tradition of teacher training has been to wait until the last half of the process before having students teach actual lessons in front of schoolchildren. Such a "too little, too late" practice needs to stop. Have them conduct lessons during the first part of the day, then go back to the university later that same day to discuss the strengths and weaknesses of those lessons with their mentor teacher. The students then would return to the classroom the following day to try out new approaches, as mentioned earlier.

According to a teacher who finished her training only four years ago, "There definitely needs to be a longer internship. That way the student can get more ideas from his mentor teachers. It would also help to observe as many grades as you can and to get both a city and rural experience."

Having some kind of preparation, regardless of its quality, is beneficial to teacher interns as well as the students. *Doing What Matters Most* found that "not only does teacher education matter, but more teacher education appears to be better than less—particularly when it includes carefully planned clinical experiences that are interwoven with coursework on learning and teaching." Programs that require a fifth year of study "find their graduates are more successful and more likely to enter and remain in teaching than graduates of traditional undergraduate programs" (Darling-Hammond, 1997a, p. 10).

The University of Cincinnati, in collaboration with Cincinnati Public Schools, has a five-year teacher education program in which all candidates end up with a master's degree; engage in ongoing clinical experiences in professional practice schools; tutor in their second year; and complete a full-year internship in year five that combines half-time teaching responsibilities with coordinated seminars under the joint supervision of school and university faculty. During this fifth year they have a consulting teacher who, after the year is up, determines whether that candidate should continue. Only then do the candidates become professional teachers.

Exclusivity: Not More Teachers, Better Ones

What makes doctors and attorneys different from teachers as a professional group is their length of training and the fact that only a minority of the workforce can perform such specialized work. This is not the case with teaching.

One of the challenges teaching has to overcome in its pursuit of professional equality is that we need ten times more teachers than doctors, thus limiting how exclusive the profession can be. The necessity for three million teachers requires a lower threshold of who is qualified to teach: all the more reason for the profession to demand a reasonably high level of competency.

How curious that at a time when high standards are being implemented, when standardized test results determine which schools are good and which are not, when the stakes for public education are as high as they have ever been, it has never been easier to become a teacher.

Reducing class size, as wonderful an idea as it may be, means hiring more noncredentialed teachers. While it's true that teacher training curriculum leaves much to be desired at least licensed teachers have stepped into a classroom before being hired. It's like a disease epidemic where there aren't enough doctors to care for the sick so medical boards toss out much of the medical training needed to increase the number of doctors to aid the ill. That's reminiscent of the Old West when the sheriff needed to round up a posse and deputized any man willing to join, no matter his skill. Well, such myopic procedures may stop the hemorrhaging, but the patients —the students—are going to end up intellectually crippled.

Teacher Tests

Teachers unions have always been opposed to teacher competency tests since their inception 20 years ago, primarily the National Education Association (NEA). The NEA must be afraid that if its teachers are tested for competency in the subject they teach, many would be found to lack the knowledge they have been licensed to pass on to students. For once, the NEA is right.

In the spring of 1998, Massachusetts administered its first statewide test for teachers. The result: 59 percent of the 1,800 teacher candidates flunked. Another 2,100 took the test in July: 47 percent failed. As with all state licensing exams (and 43 states require future educators to take and pass one before being issued a certificate), candidates are allowed to retake any portion of the test as many times as necessary to pass—that's how desperate states are to certify teachers.

Toch aptly concludes that "the tests are keeping only the most grossly incompetent teachers out of the nation's classrooms" (p. 163). Not only are the tests easy, but the passing score for them is so abysmally low that nearly everyone receives certificates. In Georgia, candidates can get teaching certificates even if they answer half of the math questions incorrectly. This is the only way to get enough people to fill positions.

The Educational Testing Service has the most widely used tests, PRAXIS I, a basic skills test, and PRAXIS II, a subject matter test. As stated in *Education Week's Quality Counts* report, "Of the eight states that required the PRAXIS II professional-knowledge test, only Florida set its passing score above the 25th percentile" (Bradley, p. 8). Ironically, when schools have student scores that low they are considered failing institutions.

Such a low passage rate is not to be condemned if the test itself is truly challenging. After all, one-third of all lawyers-to-be fail the bar exam the first time. But with a scarcity of personnel, states and districts can't afford to turn away anyone who can fill out a job application properly.

Some states, like Florida, allow people to teach in a classroom for up to two years without having to pass a competency test. What about the children who are in the classrooms of these "untested" instructors?

Of the states requiring passage of a test before teaching, only 29 require tests in the subjects candidates will teach, and only 14 go beyond a multiple-choice test to include an essay, an assessment many believe reveals the depth of someone's knowledge.

In addition, some states face lawsuits from those claiming that these tests are discriminatory. The California Basic Educational Skills Test (CBEST) deleted many questions on algebra and geometry because of such a lawsuit, so the state no longer tests future math teachers to see if they "know the difference between a median, a mode and a mean" (Colvin, 1999a).

Math passages for high school teachers are considered to be at the ninth-grade level. Here's a sample question:

> The Mills Library has 1,007,199 books. The Springvale Library has 907,082 books. Which of the following is the best estimate of how many more books the Mills Library has than the Springvale Library?
>
> A. 100,000 books
> B. 80,000 books
> C. 10,000 books
> D.   8,000 books
> E.   1,000 books
>
> [correct is A]

Reading passages on the test for elementary teachers have been described as "written on the level of *National Geographic*" (Colvin, 1999a). And still, last year, California gave 1,000 new teachers waivers from the CBEST.

Here's where a rigorous test is needed before a credential is handed out. These tests cannot be watered down. Many teachers, especially in science and math, currently enroll in subject matter summer sessions, two-week intensive courses where they learn about what they are teaching. Sounds like something they should have gotten *before* receiving a credential.

In a report for the Education Trust, entitled "How Teacher Licensing Tests Fall Short," authors Ruth Mitchell and Patte Barth examined the content of credential programs and teacher tests and found that:

- State licensing requirements place more emphasis on prospective teachers' pedagogical knowledge than on their content knowledge.
- There is no indication that the content learned in college courses is at all relevant to what prospective teachers will need to teach.
- The majority of tests examined were dominated by high-school level material.
- Passing a licensing exam can mean nothing more than a high school diploma.
- The subject area tests examined are too weak to guarantee that teachers have the content they need to teach students to high standards.
- Because licensing exams are reported only on a pass-fail basis, there is no way of knowing if successful candidates score high or just barely make the cut.

What so-called teacher tests fail to assess is the skills working teachers must have, such as classroom management ability, lesson plan writing, and assessment of knowledge gained by students. This can't be shown in a multiple-choice test setting; it requires observation by a master teacher and compiling a portfolio.

Of course, some candidates, just like some students, are not good test takers. That is why it is important to use a competency test as just one measure of an intern's ability to teach, not as a go-for-broke tool. Just as standardized tests for students should not be the sole standard of a student's knowledge, nor should teacher tests be the sole indicator if a person is ready to teach.

Here is where a portfolio would be beneficial. Just as national board candidates have to do, teacher interns should compile a portfolio as they go through their internship, reflecting how their teaching practices have progressed. The meetings with their Master teacher would be a part of this portfolio. Videotapes of the candidate in various settings, from talking to the whole class to working with students in small groups, can be an extremely useful tool to analyze with the Master teacher. Teacher interns can use the theory and research they learn and apply it to real classroom lessons, each day reflecting on the strengths and weaknesses of the lesson plans. The portfolio would also include sample student work, along with the candidate's detailed analysis of it. Through the portfolio a candidate can begin not only to think of interesting activities, but also to connect classroom work to research with reasoning behind the decisions made. After teachers have worked for one or two years in a classroom, their portfolios, along with their competency tests, would be evaluated by the university or the state. No doubt, evaluating a portfolio is a time-consuming process that will cost more money to accomplish, but it's the best way to determine if someone is ready to enter the classroom.

This is a much more well-rounded approach to assessing someone's skills than just a paper test. Nevertheless, a teacher test should remain one piece of a candidate's performance and not be discredited as meaningless.

The whole reflecting process—having lessons videotaped, discussing practices with a Master teacher—would continue on in the new teacher's first year on the job. A side benefit to being observed so frequently by the Master teacher is that teachers would feel more comfortable having visitors in their classrooms once they are on the job. Veteran teachers become very protective of their "class-world" and sometimes feel threatened when being observed. By starting this process from the onset of training, teachers would accept frequent observations more readily.

The University of Connecticut has one of the toughest licensing programs in the nation, yet it has no trouble attracting highly qualified people because it pays teachers one of the highest salary levels in the country.

Teacher candidates have to 1) major in an academic subject not in education, 2) maintain a 3.0 GPA in college, 3) pass a basic skills and a subject area test, and 4) renew their license every five years. Not too long ago the common practice was to issue lifetime licenses to teachers. Many states now require renewal every five years by taking additional coursework and/or staff development training. This is like doctors who have to go through board certification every ten years.

The students in this program must complete portfolios. "In a series of written summaries, logs, and reflections, the teachers must describe how they carried out specific lessons, and what they would do differently in the future. Along with the portfolios, they must submit videotapes of themselves in action" (Archer, p. 4). The Connecticut Department of Education trains teachers to do the evaluation on a scale of 1 to 4. "Those who score a 2 or better receive a provisional license; the rest are given a third year to redo the entire portfolio and videotaping process. Teachers who do not receive at least a 2 on the second try are denied a license, and may no longer teach in the state's public schools" (Archer, p. 4).

And what have the results been? "About 13 percent of those who submitted math portfolios in 1999 failed to receive a score of 2 or above, as did 18 percent of those who completed one in science. Though they still have one more year to submit portfolios, it already appears that the process will weed out more new teachers than the observation-based assessment, which in recent years failed only about 2 percent of teacher-candidates at the end of three years" (Archer, p. 7).

The AFT's *Quality Counts* study reports that "applications to the University of Connecticut's school of education . . . [have] tripled" since implementation of these stricter standards, which many people predicted would dissuade people from becoming teachers. Additionally, the "students' GPAs rank, on average, higher than those of 10 of the 11 other schools on campus, including engineering, business, and nursing."

"When you raise standards, you get more interest, because people are willing to work hard for something they think is valuable," said Richard L. Schwab, the school's dean.

After successfully submitting a portfolio and passing a competency test, a final step should be added to earning a teacher's license. As a professional way to culminate the process, all future teachers should take a Socratic oath, similar in spirit to physicians' Hippocratic oath, pledging allegiance to helping the uneducated.

With the added training and stricter testing, new teachers would earn a license and with it a title. Doctors have Dr., attorneys have Esq., and teachers should have Ed. following their names.

Teaching without a License

A college student who has just graduated and is thinking about teaching has two options these days: continue a fifth year of taking courses and student teaching to obtain a credential, or get an immediate job on an emergency permit. Who would choose to spend one's own money on tuition for an additional year in college without a salary to earn a license over a full-time teaching position where one can learn on the job and receive free training that leads to the same license? Plus, the person continuing on

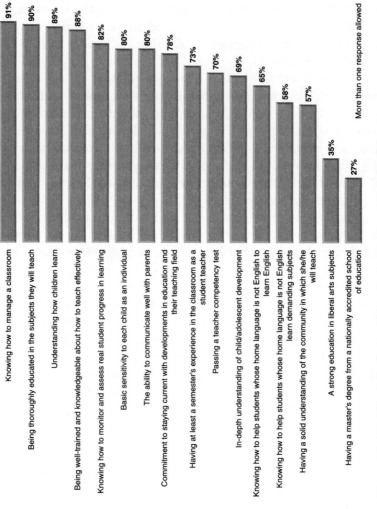

Figure 13. Qualifications Deemed Very Important for an Excellent Teacher
Source: Recruiting New Teachers, Inc.

Knowing how to manage a classroom — 91%

Being thoroughly educated in the subjects they will teach — 90%

Understanding how children learn — 89%

Being well-trained and knowledgeable about how to teach effectively — 88%

Knowing how to monitor and assess real student progress in learning — 82%

Basic sensitivity to each child as an individual — 80%

The ability to communicate well with parents — 80%

Commitment to staying current with developments in education and their teaching field — 78%

Having at least a semester's experience in the classroom as a student teacher — 73%

Passing a teacher competency test — 70%

In-depth understanding of child/adolescent development — 69%

Knowing how to help students whose home language is not English to learn English — 65%

Knowing how to help students whose home language is not English learn demanding subjects — 58%

Having a solid understanding of the community in which she/he will teach — 57%

A strong education in liberal arts subjects — 35%

Having a master's degree from a nationally accredited school of education — 27%

More than one response allowed

in college enters the workforce giving up one year of seniority to the unqualified person already on the job.

The public expects a variety of qualifications from its teachers, as illustrated in RNT's survey (see figure 13).

A large number of working teachers do not have four of the top five qualifications listed by more than 80 percent of the people—"being thoroughly educated in the subjects they will teach," "understanding how children learn," "being well-trained and knowledgeable about how to teach effectively," and "knowing how to monitor and assess real student progress in learning."

Hiring people who haven't taken one course in teaching methodology, or delivered one lesson to real students, makes a mockery of all those teachers who have taken all those courses and delivered all those lessons. Additionally, there are no financial incentives to motivate those interested in teaching to complete a licensing program, just as there are no penalties for those who wish to bypass one. What does this say about the hiring practices of states and districts? They'll take just about anyone.

If states continue to allow unlicensed people into the profession, why even demand that one needs a license in the first place? Can an individual open up a beauty salon and cut someone's hair without a license? Absolutely not. The state forbids it. But it is perfectly okay to be completely unprepared and untried and to "try teaching" with impressionable young minds. Parents who would not put up with such a disgrace don't— they are the ones who usually have their children attend schools with mainly licensed instructors. It is the disadvantaged parents who have a host of issues besides education to deal with, and who don't have the time or energy to combat a sorrowful situation at their neighborhood schools that are littered with unqualified instructors.

How many of the emergency-certified people choose their pathway to teaching, not because they were lazy and didn't want to earn a license, but because they viewed teacher training as a waste of time. In a way you can't blame them. Do people look on the training an engineer undertakes as useless, irrelevant, and a waste of time? Making teacher training programs more relevant and helpful would eliminate this mindset. If it's proven that the training really does make you a better worker, and that by being a better worker you will be compensated appropriately, who wouldn't want to be better prepared? Of course, states and districts must be ready to hire only those teachers with permits. For the last 20 years, that has not been the case, and the future looks bleak in holding the line on that.

Think of the mixed message states send teacher candidates about their own licensing requirements. By adding additional courses to take and staff development hours to earn, states give the impression that they are making it tougher to become a teacher. Yet, due to the tremendous shortage of teacher talent, anyone off the street walking through the district's human resources door with a college degree has a very good likelihood of landing a job. So much for states' stringent prerequisites. Such hypocrisy is why many decide to teach with an emergency credential.

According to Sherry Posnick-Goodwin, "Some districts may actually choose to hire uncredentialed teachers. Without job security, teachers may agree to take difficult assignments that no one else wants. They are afraid to complain or become politically active, which makes them desirable employees in some administrators' minds" (2001).

Stanley O. Ikenberry, president of the American Council on Education, calls unqualified teachers a "reprehensible form of public sanctioned malpractice." While some states apply a term limit on emergency permits, others have allowed teachers to retire on them and complete a full career without ever having earned a certificate to teach.

The public recognizes the importance of properly trained teachers as well. In an RNT survey, 82 percent of the people polled oppose lowering state standards to abate the teacher shortage, 88 percent would actually prefer eliminating hiring unqualified teachers altogether, and 76 percent are in favor of strengthening the licensing standards for teachers (Haselkorn and Harris, p. 21).

States, are you listening?

Basically there are two ways to get around the traditional process of earning a teaching license: emergency credentials and provisional programs. Emergency certificates are the quickest way to get a body into the classroom. People with no prior teaching experience immediately begin to teach young people. If they're lucky, they are assigned a mentor teacher who will help them throughout their first year. Otherwise, these rookie teachers are completely on their own. Most districts have certain timetables up to two years long by which emergency teachers need to complete downsized licensing coursework.

According to the National Commission on Teaching & America's Future, 27 percent of new teachers do not have all the necessary requirements fulfilled for state licensure: 15 percent have emergency permits and 12 percent have nothing at all.

Currently, California has 40,000 noncredentialed teachers, according to the Center for the Future of Teaching and Learning's report, *The Status of the Teaching Profession, Update 2000.* That amounts to one in every seven teachers. And in urban areas that average goes up. In 1999–2000, 20 percent of teachers in urban schools, one out of every five, lack credentials; the number decreases to 9 percent in the more affluent suburban schools.

So the students who need the most experienced teachers are getting the least experienced ones instead, many without a license to teach.

"Minority and poor youngsters—the very youngsters who are most dependent on their teachers for content knowledge—are systematically taught by teachers with the least content knowledge," said Kati Haycock of the Education Trust. "Students in high-minority secondary schools are more likely to be taught by teachers without a college major in the subject they are teaching. . . . As a nation, we have deprived out neediest students of the very ingredient most important to learning: a highly qualified teacher."

In the second-largest school district in the country, Los Angeles Unified School District, 21 percent of the 36,000 teachers are on emergency credentials, down from a high of 27 percent a year before. The decrease had to do with a new contract signed in 2001 giving teachers a 15.3 percent pay raise. The district's director of teacher recruitment, Antonio Garcia, told the *Los Angeles Daily News* that "the (higher) salaries have [had] an impact" in attracting people with credentials. If, however, a true accountability system is not in place at the time of a huge salary increase such as this one, then it could have negative effects in the long run for the profession, because no real evaluation system will weed out the weaker teachers. And without a strong quality teaching force, student achievement will not improve, making public support for double-digit raises more unlikely. The smarter move would have been to offer a 15 percent raise to those teachers who demonstrated exemplary skills. If I'm incompetent, I just got a present from the Los Angeles School Board. It's like high-priced athletes with guaranteed contracts, regardless of their performance. How do you know these people are worth this kind of money?

New York state issued more than 10,000 temporary licenses in 1998–99; however, a new policy prohibiting nonlicensed teachers to work in New York schools begins in September 2003. In Texas, more than 40,000 out of 250,000 teachers are not fully certified. At least state law requires districts to notify parents if their child has an unlicensed instructor. Eight out of ten Americans agree with the policy that parents should be informed about the qualifications of a child's teacher (Haselkorn and Harris, p. 18).

Back in 1985, New Jersey did away with emergency permits except for special education. However, the state with the strictest prohibitions against unqualified teachers is Connecticut, where only 100 out of 38,000 teachers are unlicensed.

National Education Association President Bob Chase said, "We entrust the education of our children to teachers without adequate licensure. Such a lack of quality control would be considered criminally negligent in any other profession" (Olson 2001a, p. 6).

Even when teachers do have a license to teach, that's no guarantee that they are teaching only those courses for which they have been certified. One-third of teachers teach at least one class not in their licensed area.

Does any school track to see how many unlicensed teachers individual students get? Are there any safeguards in place to protect them from having an entire slate of emergency-permit teachers?

Provisional teachers (and they number about 80,000) end up having to do more than emergency teachers. Some 44 states provide for some form of alternative certification. In many cases, they need to have 30 college credits in their teaching area and pass the appropriate National Teacher Examination (NTE).

New Jersey boasts a quite popular nontraditional program that produces nearly one-quarter of the state's new teachers. On the positive side, it has helped to decrease emergency permits. Still, those teachers are coming into the classroom with only a crash course on teaching.

There are four main findings about provisional routes, according to *Education Week's Quality Counts:*

1) they attract a higher proportion of math, science, and minority candidates;
2) candidates perform as well on state licensing exams as students taking traditional routes toward licensing;
3) candidates are more willing to teach in urban settings; and
4) candidates are more likely to stay in the districts that train them.

"After six years . . . 87 percent of the graduates of California's 'teacher internship' programs are still teaching—88 percent in the schools where they began." However, "few studies have examined whether alternative-route teachers perform better in the classroom or produce higher student achievement" (Olson, 2001c, p. 2). Linda Darling-Hammond, who views alternate certification as "education malpractice," makes a valid point that practically all these teachers get jobs at poor urban schools. "If this was really such a good idea, to have people come into teaching who don't really know about teaching, then why aren't those affluent schools beating down the door to get teachers like that?" (Ibid., p. 3).

Teachers placed on the fast track to a credential must take classes right after a full day of teaching, and they are teaching for the very first time. That in itself is exhausting.

Due to so many poor emergency candidates, New Jersey implemented the Provisional Teacher Program in 1985 as a way to eliminate emergency credentials. Alternate-route candidates must pass the NTE and participate in extensive training and evaluation before being granted credentials. They also receive on-the-job support during their first year of teaching.

According to New Jersey's department of education, teachers who take the alternative-certification path have higher scores on the NTEs than those who chose the traditional teacher-training program (Toch, p. 160). The teaching internship needs to be added, however, to strengthen their knowledge of teaching.

To attract more teachers, New York City schools chancellor Harold O. Levy helped to develop the New York Fellows program, an accelerated-certification program that costs $25,000 to train each teacher (Philadelphia, p. 68). Teachers who go through the process agree to work at the lowest-performing schools. Is this fostering high-quality education?

"People who take an accelerated path to earn a credential usually can't survive in the profession and don't do a good job while they are in the classroom," said a high school teacher.

A large percentage of new teachers nowadays are career switchers, people in mid-life who have become disenchanted with their original choice of employment or have been laid off or have retired early. Some are successful as teachers, others find it exhausting work and end up returning to their previous occupations.

Whenever stories surface about these people, who represent 5 percent of the teaching population, they tend to be former judges, engineers, and entertainment agents (Philadelphia, p. 67). In other words, all who, after having made substantial money, now feel they want "to give something back."

About one-fourth of all universities have programs specifically designed for second-career individuals. Some programs require less than two months' training. Imagine if an engineer wanted to switch into law and learned everything he needed to know in eight weeks. It makes a mockery of the three years of law school, and what those students went through to get where they are. Putting people through intensive MTV-ized training will not produce better teachers. In fact, it could have the opposite effect, because they may feel that's all they need to know about their craft.

While helpful for filling positions in the short term, such minimal training programs damage the integrity of the profession. Offering a Cliff's Notes approach to a credential diminishes what it takes to become a skilled instructor making it look like anyone can become a teacher. And that is just dead wrong.

If a NASA scientist wants to teach physics in a public high school, the route to make the switch shouldn't be paved with speed bumps. He shouldn't have to start from scratch, like a first-year pre-ed student. His job experience should count for something. He and other professionals like him can bring a real-world component into the classroom, like teaching kids the science that helps the space shuttle take off. On the other hand, he still needs to go through an internship or residency before receiving a license. He needs to practice delivering lessons to students to determine if he can transfer his knowledge to others. We shouldn't be pushing these people through a classroom door, regardless of the level of their subject matter knowledge.

Ultimately, as the saying goes, drastic times demand drastic measures. Instead of handing out teaching licenses like driver's licenses, credential programs need to get their act together and hold the line on hiring only fully licensed instructors for the nation's children. The students' minds are at stake.

There are a variety of teacher recruitment programs available to stem the enormous teacher shortage:

- Teach for America, a ten-year-old nonprofit organization begun by Wendy Kopp, has placed thousands of college graduates in America's worst-performing schools for two-year stints.
- Troops to Teachers takes military veterans and places them in the classroom, simplifying the certification process.
- Project TEACH (Teachers of Excellence for All Children) began in 1985 to bring more minorities into the teaching profession; it offers an accelerated one-year program.

What these programs have in common is a convenience store approach to becoming a teacher. You go in quickly, do what you got to do, then leave. They perceive the teaching profession as a paid Peace Corps—everyone should put in a two- to four-year stint—in other words, glorified community service.

Some programs offer one-year accelerated programs, crash courses, that confer teacher credentials *and* master's degrees. It's like summer school for teachers, where only about half of the curriculum can be covered compared to the full year of study.

While run by honorable individuals who mean well, this approach is wrong-headed in terms of elevating the teaching profession. There's no such thing as an emergency license to cut someone's hair, so why should there be shortcuts to educating a child?

As Labaree rightfully points out, both law and medical schools have established themselves "as the only door through which a person can gain entry to the profession. And each has made it difficult to get through this door by instituting restrictive admissions and rigorous programs of study" (p. 23).

The Lot of the First-Year Teacher

Most seasoned teachers look back on their first year teaching in amazement. How could they have inflicted that much punishment on their students? Too few teachers have a smooth transition from training to their first year in the classroom. For the vast majority of novice teachers, that first year is baptism by fire. But it doesn't have to be that way if induction programs are made available to new teachers, offering them Mentor teachers and workshops to smooth out the lumps during the first year.

The first lump the newly minted teacher encounters is going through the application process.

The Application Process

Seeing the human resource departments of school districts is like walking into a Social Security or unemployment office. If you didn't know you were about to be a public employee, you do now. It has the cold feeling of institution. You get an immediate sense of being just anybody who is looking for a job, rather than an educated professional whom the district has a vested interest in hiring.

The application process itself can sometimes be more challenging than getting the teacher's license. Fairfax County, Virginia, streamlined "what had been a 62-step hiring process that took months to complete into a computerized, carefully managed two-week process" (Darling-Hammond, 1997a, p. 18).

The way districts hire teachers needs overhauling. "Many school systems, particularly in big cities, are slow to respond to inquiries. Too often, they rely on a centralized hiring process, and cannot tell candidates whether they've been hired or where they will teach until late in the summer or even after the start of the school year" *(Quality Counts)*. This was very true for me.

When I first applied for a teaching job in April for a September position, I followed all the rules of Los Angeles Unified School District. I drove to downtown Los Angeles to the uninviting pale pink central office—which hasn't changed in the 13 years since I was first there, except for the addition of a small banner near the main entrance declaring, "Welcome Teachers," as if that makes everything else that's depressing there acceptable. During my all-day application process, I had five interviews, signed up for the new teacher in-service, showed them copies of my fingerprints (mandated by state law), and, most important, had my credential. One of the women who interviewed me was a former teacher herself. When I asked her why she left teaching for a desk job, she told me that eight years of teaching had burned her out. She would come home and collapse on her couch. Yet, there she was, screening new teachers. Everything seemed in order—or so I thought.

Imagine my surprise when July came and August came and I still hadn't received a call from the main office. Sure, I made a couple of calls during the summer inquiring about my situation and was told not to worry. But I knew how desperate they were for qualified teachers, and that even if

I didn't have a credential, I probably would have been given a job.

Still, I had no clue where I would teach, or what grade level or English courses it would be. I wanted to prepare lessons in advance while I had time. I wanted to become acclimated to my new surroundings and find out how to get books and supplies.

Finally, in late August, my worst fear came true: my application folder had been misfiled under candidates *without* credentials. But, not to worry, I would have a job.

A couple of days before the start of school, I got a call to go to Marshall High School. Great! It was close to where I lived and was considered one of the best high schools. I attended the morning "welcome back" faculty meeting very excited. Sure, I didn't have all the preparation time I needed, but I was eager and willing to tackle anything. When I went into the main office after the meeting, the principal pulled me aside to tell me that instead of teaching at Marshall, the district office had placed me at Garfield High (the Jamie Escalante *Stand and Deliver* school). Okay. So I drove to East Los Angeles and went to my new new worksite. What an introduction to the world of teaching!

Surviving on One's Own

New teachers typically are given the worst classes at the worst schools at the lowest pay, despite studies that show when experienced teachers are at these schools, student reading scores go up.

New teachers are saddled with schedules that veteran teachers would have difficulty handling: teaching courses in two different departments, having three or four different courses each requiring separate preparation, having the lowest-ability students, having 35–40 students. First-year teachers are foolishly considered fully prepared and are plunged immediately into the working schedule of a ten-year veteran teacher—like throwing a first-time swimmer into the English Channel. The system does not provide a way to ease into teaching.

In the *Los Angeles Times,* Richard Lee Colvin describes a teacher who, without a teaching credential and only five days of training (sample topic: how to take attendance), found a job in the Los Angeles Unified School District. She was given no teacher manual, had ten books for 40 students, and once taught with blood on the floor from an in-class fight while waiting for a janitor (1999c).

Why have the most inexperienced faculty members handle the most struggling students? It just doesn't make any sense. One would think that districts know how fast new teachers leave the profession and would do everything possible to stem the tide by cushioning their first few years. Instead, the Master teacher should teach these young people.

The first two years are the most critical for a beginning teacher, so, a new teacher should be given a schedule that includes a balance of easy and challenging classes; teach half the normal schedule of an experienced teacher to allow for reflection; go through an induction program involving workshops; and receive ongoing observation and instruction from a Mentor or Master teacher.

Some states, like North Carolina, prevent new teachers from taking on additional job duties, such as cheerleading adviser, during their first three years without permission. This policy allows them to concentrate fully on teaching students, giving them a chance to establish themselves and gain some experience before tackling extracurricular jobs. Unfortunately, these jobs are tempting for the new teacher for two main reasons. First, taking on additional responsibilities pays them stipends. If they are fresh out of college, new teachers may be overeager to pay off any college loans. Second, they tend to be eager beaver types, idealistic and high-energy. Many principals love to tap into that energy, especially when dealing with some veteran teachers who show no interest in being a club adviser. However, principals would do new teachers a tremendous favor by holding out for the first few years. Considering the high teacher attrition rate, retaining good new ones should be a top priority for schools. These teachers don't know what they are getting themselves into and are likely to take on more than they can handle as a way of pleasing their principals.

New teachers need support, even when they don't think they need it. There is a prevailing attitude among new teachers that they already know everything about teaching because they have their teaching credentials. Not even 20-year veterans should have such an attitude. Teachers are in the business of learning, and good teachers learn constantly from their students and want to find the key to unlock that particular batch of kids' minds to maximize their learning potential. This is why assigning new teachers to Mentor or Master teachers would pay dividends, not only by offering overall support, but in retaining teachers. If new teachers feel welcome and will be given a hand whenever they need it, they are more likely to have a positive attitude towards their job and, therefore, more likely to stay longer. Often, new teachers become frustrated quickly, and when there is no one to turn to, they just leave. Why put up with bad classes, unruly students, too few books, paying for their own photocopying, and being treated like a child, all for a low salary and poor working conditions?

This is why it is crucial that all first-year teachers receive as much support as they can. *Quality Counts* found, "those who did not go through an induction program were roughly twice as likely to give up as those who had support" (Olson 2001a, p. 11). Currently, only 19 states offer mandated mentoring for new teachers, but states cannot afford to let promising young teachers falter on their own and leave in a couple of years.

California offers a two-year induction program, called the California Formative Assessment and Support System for Teachers (CFASST). It is absorbing and offers many helpful activities that require new teachers to reflect on what they're doing in the classroom. Teachers must develop instructional plans, collect student evidence, and analyze how well the results reflect the plans. Besides being trained extensively in how to do this process, they also work closely with their Mentor teachers. The work required from both the beginning teacher and the Mentor teacher is demanding but worthwhile. The problem with this program (as is true with so many meaningful ideas in public education) is that no time is budgeted to do the work. New teachers may be given a few days throughout the year by their districts for such activities. But to make this experience truly beneficial requires *daily* commitment to it. New teachers should be permitted to teach less than a full schedule so they can go through an induction process properly. This would keep teachers from feeling burned out so soon and perhaps like the process enough to continue doing it on their own after completing the program.

In most states and districts, however, the type of mentoring that goes on with new teachers consists of their attending several meetings, mostly after school hours. This is very impractical because this "support" adds more time demands on already stressed out, time-deficient new teachers, some of whom are still taking credential coursework immediately following the end of the school day, some who are already feeling burnout because of the energy teaching demands, and are simply too tired to stick around work for another hour or so. As a mentor, I found it challenging to get new teachers to come to my monthly meetings. Most would not show up and, with few exceptions, wouldn't even let me know that they weren't going to show up. The district had them attend so many meetings as it was, they were "meeting-ed out." The problem is that all of these meetings, aimed at helping new teachers, in the end add more stress because of the extra time commitment or the missed days from the classroom that this system of support requires. If new elementary teachers were to teach only half a day and secondary teachers were only to teach three classes instead of five, they would have less work to do in terms of grading papers (90 kids versus 150), and would still have a reserve of energy for the rest of their workday for reflection and mentoring by another teacher.

A veteran teacher with 26 years' experience has seen dedication decrease over the years "especially among the newer teachers, because they don't look at teaching as a profession. They have a more lax attitude about teaching. They don't seem to take it as seriously. Commonly heard from today's student teachers is, 'I don't do lesson plans.'"

With nearly half of all new teachers leaving the profession within their first five years, the days of giving the new kid on the block the worst schedule of classes need to cease. New teachers need a strong support system, be it a mentor teacher or other classroom veteran. And Mentors who would only be teaching two or three classes themselves would have enough energy left to work with these new teachers.

How It's Done in Japan

Whenever international comparisons are made between public school systems, Japanese schools are usually held up as a paragon of the way it should be here in the United States. With that in mind, let's look at what is done in Japan and why its educational system attracts higher-quality people than ours does.

First of all, in Japan, the teaching profession is a highly attractive one to enter, with five qualified applicants vying for every job opening, so schools can afford to be very selective. A major reason for the profession's popularity is that salaries for beginning teachers are higher than for engineers, pharmacists, and other public employees. Teachers can also earn much more money as they progress through their careers. Instead of the 1:2 ratio in the United States, from starting salary to ending, Japanese teachers can triple their salary over the years.

The process of becoming a teacher is harder in Japan. Teachers go through a year of residency in which they spend 60 hours a week in training sessions. Then they take a tough comprehensive exam that only one in six passes.

Supporting first-year teachers is an important feature of the Japanese education system. All new teachers work under a master teacher. They "receive at least twenty days of in-service training during their first year on the job and sixty days of professional development," according to *Right to Learn: A Blueprint for Creating Schools That Work* (Darling-Hammond, 1997b, p. 324). New teachers watch "other teachers at length, discussing problems of practice, presenting and critiquing demonstration lessons, and with groups of colleagues, imagining and acting out how students might respond to certain presentations of material."

Everything Japanese teachers do with one another fosters collegiality and teamwork. Each morning teachers gather around 8:30 for a 15-minute meeting promoting a congenial and collegial atmosphere. The desks in the teachers' workroom face one another, encouraging teachers to talk with each other. Teachers control staff development and propose ideas for training. One common method is for teachers to demonstrate a lesson for other teachers. James Stigler and Harold Stevenson researched Japanese math teachers and discovered that "there is a very systematic effort to pass on the accumulated wisdom of teaching practice to each new generation of teachers and to keep perfecting that practice by providing teachers the opportunities to continually learn from each other" (Darling-Hammond, 1997b, p. 324).

Japanese educators teach 15–20 hours per week instead of 25–30 for U.S. instructors. In fact, this country leads the world in that category. For every 20 hours they teach, Japanese teachers receive 25 hours of prep time, compared to less than three for American teachers. This work schedule allows teachers time to interact with one another and share strategies, something not available in the American system. Students benefit from this as well because lessons used have been massaged and tweaked for maximum result.

While Japanese teachers actually teach fewer hours, their work year is longer than American teachers'. Less time with students means more time with colleagues. When they aren't teaching, they're working with their colleagues. They also take on more of a role as a counselor for students and meet more often with parents.

Japanese students attend about three more weeks of school than American children. However, their 195-day school year consists of complete days without the interruptions of field trips, festivals, or assemblies. Those activities occur outside the school calendar. By the time Japanese students have graduated from high school, they have received a full year more of schooling than American pupils (*Japanese Education Today*, p. 8). It has also been estimated that Japanese students spend one-third more time learning because they are more attentive and have fewer behavior problems.

And parents pay tuition at the senior high school level ensuring a more vested interest in the schooling of their children.

All the prerequisites and preparation and practice ultimately affects students and their learning. It is plain to see that the better the teacher, the better the student, and the better the workforce.

As Education Trust Director Kati Haycock put it, "If education leaders want to close the achievement gap, they must focus, first and foremost, on developing qualified teachers" (p. 12).

At the turn of the twentieth century, doctors were more like the teachers of today: undertrained, with much less stringent entrance requirements for medical school. Except for a few teaching hospitals, most physicians only had a few months of training.

In 1910, a headmaster from Louisville, Kentucky, Abraham Flexner, came out with a report for the Carnegie Foundation for the Advancement of Teaching deploring the poor quality of America's medical schools. "He found that most medical schools were 'diploma mills' with little emphasis on science, producing doctors of insufficient skill and learning" (Gross, p. 67). The report called for these institutions to become an integral part of universities, and for students to perform more clinical work. Suddenly, the majority of these "mills" were shut down. The old medical schools transformed themselves into legitimate training grounds for future doctors, establishing more rigorous standards and a higher level of excellence and quality control. Medicine became a postgraduate calling and one of the most highly regarded professions in the country.

Another revolution took place early last century at the college level when professors wrested control from their college presidents, forming the American Association of University Professors.

Unlike physicians, public school educators remain a group of people whose training and practices are consistent. Unlike their college counterparts, K–12 teachers remain hirelings with no control over their faculty and curriculum.

It's going to take a monumental effort to raise the teaching profession to the level of law and medicine. Where is the Abraham Flexner for education?

Sure, the main distinction that separates teachers from doctors and attorneys is that they are publicly paid employees who do not charge their clients. However, the argument is not that teachers should earn the same exact salary as these other professions; rather, that their pay and stature be commensurate with their education.

The professional salary, accountability, and rigorous training are all "small steps" toward making teaching a full-fledged profession; the "giant leap" is having the teachers be in control.

CHAPTER 6

Empowerment: The Final Frontier

"Teachers are telling us the kinds of support that they need and want—more peer collaboration, team teaching, common planning periods. If we don't listen to them, we will shortchange our children and our teachers by hanging onto comfortable but self-defeating practices."—Former U.S. Education Secretary Richard W. Riley, 1998

Second only to "accountability," the term most bandied about in education circles today is "empowerment." Everyone needs to be empowered. Students need to feel empowered that they have what it takes to accomplish a task, teachers have to feel empowered that they have control over what they teach, and custodians have to feel empowered that they can make decisions on their own, too.

Well, true empowerment would be for teachers to have full control over their own profession. Otherwise the term remains just an overused word having no meaning.

Ironically, educators use words to miscommunicate. Here are some examples:

a "win-win" situation—The administration gets what it wants, and there aren't any complaints from teachers (really a "lose-lose").

on the same page—Everyone agrees with the state's
way of educating children.

facilitate—Don't lecture to students; in other words, do
not impart knowledge. Gently guide them to learning—
empower them.

facilitator—A person who facilitates (see above).

accountability—Give the appearance that all teachers
are highly competent by holding the entire school
responsible for test scores. Any individual
responsibility does not exist.

empowerment—Giving teachers the *feeling* that they
have power, that what they say matters.

In addition to euphemistic terminology, the hard-
working teacher struggles upstream against public education hypocrisy constantly:

- *States and districts want to raise standards
  through more rigorous curriculum.*

Yet at the same time, they want to improve standardized
test scores by having students practice test-taking skills,
skills that are purely artificial and nontransferable to
real-world abilities and serve only to improve scores on
those tests.

- *States and districts want to increase student
  connectedness by personalizing the high school
  experience for the student—that is, by giving
  students a sense of belonging to their school for
  them to have more of an involvement in their
  learning.*

Yet at the same time, they implement block scheduling
(classes meet every other day), which eliminates daily
contact with all teachers.

- *States and districts want teachers to be
  hyperorganized with agendas written on boards,
  lesson plans thought out, syllabuses ready before
  the first day of school.*

Yet at the same time, school administrators consistently demonstrate the opposite of those skills demanded, giving teachers last-minute notices of anything happening at school.

- *States and districts want more students in advanced placement classes, regardless of whether they meet prerequisites, to show how inclusive they are in opening all courses to all students.*

Yet at the same time, they get upset if AP test scores go down and wonder what's wrong with the teachers.

- *States and districts expect teachers to squeeze maximum use out of every instructional minute, having students do quiet activities, then group activities, then writing activities.*

Yet at the same time, their classroom environment gets bombarded incessantly with P.A. announcements, student messengers, false fire drills, and phone calls.

None of this doublespeak would happen if teachers were in charge or even asked for their input, because there would no longer be a need to convince teachers to do something against their better judgment.

During the past 15 years, some teachers associations have managed to get districts to agree to site-based management teams. The original intent of such management was to provide an avenue for teachers to have a say about how schools were run. However, it was never intended to allow teachers to be in charge; it only gave the appearance that teachers' voices were heard. About all these teams accomplish is to decide hours of operation for the photocopier and have contentious battles over the school's budget.

Taking that crucial next step of placing teachers at the forefront of education policy has yet to happen. Teachers may be given the steering wheel in driving education, but actually they are just passengers. For the most part, the town has already been planned; they're just being asked where to place the road markers.

The majority of teachers do not perceive themselves as having a say about what is taught and how to teach it. Teachers themselves recognize what is best for students, but they lack the power to implement real change. It's as if teachers' only reason for existing is to follow marching orders.

Everybody who has a hand in the education cookie jar has encroached on what limited control remains for a teacher, and what remains are only crumbs. More and more teachers are told what to write on their boards, and in what order and with what color markers, when to be on a certain page in a certain book, how to evaluate student work, and what test to use.

Sure, schools have a token teacher—along with a parent and a student—on committees. For the most part, this is symbolic, and most decisions coming from such committees are inconsequential and have nothing to do with the nuts and bolts of teaching. The appearance is one of an administration listening to teachers' concerns, whereas major final decisions never come from these groups. Teachers have no veto power.

Even when suggestions and feedback are provided, it is rarely followed up, making teachers feel, "what is the point?", resigned to the fact that their opinions matter little and are hardly valued at all.

When teachers realize that their voices fall on deaf ears, they recede into their classrooms, never to be heard from again. They just decide that it's not worth the time and energy to serve on committees or offer suggestions. The people in charge will do what they want to anyway, so why waste one's time, especially when that time can be better spent on evaluating student work or developing lesson plans.

This disenfranchised feeling sometimes develops into anger, making many veteran teachers bitter after decades of service.

Such a brooding sense of powerlessness infects the spirit of the educator. What role, then, do they play? What use is their license if, over and over again, they need "development"? The subliminal message isn't so subliminal after awhile.

"When they are told they now *must* teach reading by a new method, *must* cover certain topics by the end of the year, *must* learn to use the computer . . . no one should be surprised if they become resentful and look for ways to return to old and tired procedures with which they are familiar" (Berliner and Biddle, p. 337).

Teachers must be involved heavily in the education process, from designing schools to designing curriculum. It's the only way to have a buy-in by the faculty at-large. When teachers are in on the process, they are more likely to accept an unpopular decision and to take advantage of what these people in the field know rather than something from the top that is imposed upon them.

Teachers need to have not just a seat on education panels and committees, but to be in charge of developing local and state standards, creating standardized tests, and adopting textbooks. Why do politicians and university personnel wield the power on these boards that determine what the classroom teacher should be doing in K–12?

As Susan Moore Johnson stated in *Teachers at Work,* "Teachers will not be recognized as professionals until they have more say in how children are educated and how schools are run" (p. 180).

They must be in charge of something other than what they do within the walls of their classroom. Imagine a physician who can treat a patient to the best of his knowledge while that patient is in the examination room, but instead of the office personnel supporting his work, they oversee what the doctor does: the receptionist becomes the principal, the office manager becomes the superintendent.

Additionally, teachers need greater involvement in hiring teachers and allocating budgets.

Empowering teachers means that the public education system relinquishes control so that educators can:

1) collaborate, getting out of their classroom shell and sharing their experiences with their colleagues;
2) have a reasonable workload to participate in this collaboration;
3) redesign the school year for maximum teacher-to-student contact and teacher-to-teacher contact; and
4) help design their workspaces.

Collaboration: Breaking through a Teacher's Classworld

The best studies on how to teach kids effectively are right under the noses of teachers every day—in their colleagues' classrooms. Yet much of this vast knowledge never gets passed on from teacher to teacher. When career instructors retire, there is no system in place to pass down their knowledge. It just evaporates. Perhaps a few lesson plans may be left in the filing cabinet, but paper is lifeless, unlike observing a real teacher in action.

Why should a teacher's knowledge of how to teach something not be shared with his co-workers? The answer lies in the strictly controlled environment of the public education system. Teachers who do work together make a concerted effort on their own time to do so. Why are teachers hesitant to share lesson plans or work together? The answer is simple: they aren't used to doing that. Nothing in the daily work schedule provides or fosters such collaboration. And schools contain no conference rooms for such interaction. What ends up happening is that teachers remain cocooned in their classworld, with only student results offering feedback on lessons.

In a 1998 U.S. Department of Education report on teacher quality, only 6 percent of teachers surveyed said that they had regular contact with colleagues teaching the same subject at their school, despite the vast majority desiring it and perceiving it as highly beneficial. Unlike many other countries, American teachers do not interact regularly.

In countries like Japan and China, "teachers routinely work with their colleagues on developing curriculum, polishing lessons, observing each other's teaching, participating in study groups, and conducting research on teaching." Teachers have "regular time to compare notes about particular lessons and problems, conduct demonstration lessons for one another, discuss how their students respond to specific tasks, and develop plans together" [Darling-Hammond, 1997a, p. 3].

None of this exists in the United States. Ask any veteran teachers if they've ever seen a colleague at their school site teach. The almost unanimous answer would be no. Teachers remain boxed in.

In America, it is a "you don't come into my classroom and I don't come into yours" world, according to Eugene C. Schaffer of the University of North Carolina–Charlotte. Like Californians, who stubbornly cling to their solo driving practices, teachers are protective of their classworld, an extension of American individualism.

Teachers in Japan and Taiwan have their offices bunched together, which fosters working together. In America, teachers have no offices—their desk in the classroom becomes one by default.

Teachers need time to work with and learn from one another. "We need to create a culture in which teachers examine the way they teach," said UCLA Professor James W. Stigler.

Of course, even if there was a way for collaboration to happen, some teachers might not be willing to open their doors so readily.

A form of paranoia and possessiveness breeds in the teacher's isolated work environment. Sharing a lesson, let alone inviting fellow teachers to sit in on a class, is a frightening proposition for some. "Maybe I'm not teaching something I should" or "Maybe I don't know what

I'm doing" are common thoughts of the doubtful teacher, stemming from not having anyone to observe them regularly except for the infrequent administrator/observer. It is much more comforting and safer for teachers to keep everything in their classworld, the door acting as a bulwark against outside interference.

That is the quirkiness of the education profession. The employees work in isolation with their clients, only getting together formally for monthly meetings.

It takes a tremendous effort for teachers to get to know other teachers, and the higher the grade level, the more removed the teachers are, forming cliques among departments. Some of the more successful school environments have faculty clubs, picnics, and car pooling to certain school events. Events like softball team matches need to be organized so that teachers from other disciplines or areas of the campus can get to know one another.

However, if the process of collaboration began in earnest during the credential years, teachers wouldn't feel the need to shield their work from their peers, veteran teachers would be open to the idea of sharing, and new teachers would come to expect a support system.

Not just specific lessons would be discussed. "Discussing individual students and their issues, such as acting out in class, would be an advantage to collaboration," said a high school biology teacher.

But, unfortunately, teaching does not build in such collaboration, so new teachers founder year after year, and only those with persistence, those who make the effort to get help independently, survive.

Of course, for the instructor who has a high level of self-discipline, is well organized, and has a strong sense of purpose, teaching alone can be attractive. But it can be an equally appealing setting to a person who can't get along with people, one who is eccentric, power hungry, and domineering. There is little in place to protect students from this type of teacher.

"Some of my colleagues are just antisocial and never come to department meetings, while others feel they are the best and deserve only high-level classes and then go on to insult everyone," said a high school teacher.

There are schools that do foster teachers working alongside one another. Team teaching, where a social science and English teacher plan a connected curriculum and teach to the same group of students, is an excellent first step toward establishing a collegial work environment. Still, teachers have to be given common prep periods to accomplish this, and this isn't always easy to do. Additionally, the effort to work with someone, plus conduct other individual business, cannot be completed in only one hour a day. Teachers need to be given additional regularly scheduled time during the school/workday to collaborate properly.

Such time deficiencies are common among many worthy programs in education. No matter how well-thought out the idea may be, not enough time is budgeted to do the work needed. The most glaring example of this is the current standards movement. While a worthwhile concept, with the time needed to write down exactly what teachers should be doing and what students should be learning (discussed further in chapter 9), even the most dedicated teacher could not possibly teach to all of the standards in the 180-day school calendar.

One of my best experiences with collaboration was when the district allowed all the English department heads from the secondary schools to plan their own all-day meeting at the beginning of the school year. The first thing we agreed on was that the meeting would last no longer than noon to provide a completely free afternoon for teachers to get their rooms ready. Then we decided on the most pressing issues facing English teachers and met in grade-level groups. Here is staff development at its best, teachers discussing their practices with others in their fields. This form of interaction needs to occur weekly rather than once a year.

Think of the wonderful exchanges that could occur on school campuses across the country:

- Primary grade teachers could find out from one another which reading strategies work best.
- A Spanish teacher discovers that her worst student is the top of his class in algebra, so he isn't a "bad" student after all.
- A history teacher and a science teacher realize that the same students are cheating in both classes.
- After realizing they both happen to administer tests on Fridays, the music teacher and the business teacher agree to stagger test days so their students aren't overwhelmed.
- Teachers agree to teach other classes based on certain strengths. For example, a fifth-grade teacher, who is an expert in grammar, "trades" with another fifth-grade teacher, who is gifted in storytelling.
- All math teachers create a common final exam for each course.
- All English teachers examine together writing portfolios of students to observe common writing problems and, together, devise strategies to help students improve their skills.

All of these enriching learning exchanges could happen regularly if the teachers' workday allowed time for them to happen.

With collaboration, burnout would diminish, and teachers would actually do what every other worker in America does—work with fellow employees.

Parateachers

For teachers to collaborate, they must be relieved of teaching time. With the widespread increase in staff development and pulling teachers out of the classroom, a more permanent solution to the absence of the educator is needed. Some teachers miss up to three weeks of instructional time because of conferences and meetings.

What is needed is a much broader network of teacher assistants who require more training than they currently do, but less training than a teacher. Lawyers have paralegals. Teachers need parateachers.

These people would be responsible for much of the paperwork and the mundane tasks—taking attendance, filling out forms, bubbling in report cards, grading some homework and in-class assignments—that need to be done, yet distract teachers from focusing more on the business of teaching students.

Parateachers would be better trained than adult instructional aides, the current group of nonteacher workers in classrooms.

Parateachers can act in the same capacity as graduate students who work for professors at the college level. Teachers would hand over the student work with an attached rubric that spells out exactly the elements that should be contained in the assignment, making sure the parateacher understands how to grade the work, then be free to work on other lessons.

In elementary schools, parateachers can help with handing out and collecting materials, even yard supervision. Elementary teachers would be relieved in the afternoon hours to meet with colleagues, while secondary teachers would be relieved on Mondays under the four-day workweek plan discussed later in this chapter. Parateachers could help tutor students as well.

Another advantage to parateachers is that they could replace substitute teachers entirely. Long the bane of both good teachers and good students, substitutes should be done away with. A complete stranger cannot do the work of a professional educator, so why even try? When your regular doctor is unavailable, you end up seeing a colleague, not a substitute doctor who never attended medical school. Colleges simply cancel classes when professors don't show up, but public schools need to house the students for financial reasons (schools receive funding based on daily attendance) and to fulfill their role as day-care centers.

One of the main problems of substitutes is the wild variance in requirements from state to state. In parts of the country, a bachelor's degree is required; elsewhere all a person needs to do is attend a one-day seminar.

Ask teachers how they feel whenever they miss a day of work, especially if it's beyond their control, to attend a conference or meeting that requires their presence. Their one overriding concern is who will be in the classroom. When meetings are held at work, some teachers frantically rush back to their room during breaks to make sure nothing is topsy-turvy. The anxiety substitutes generate is enough to wipe out any benefits to teachers spending a day away from their stressful teaching environment. Returning to the room to find out that lesson plans, no matter how well spelled out, were not followed, that gum—which never was a problem—suddenly is stuck under desks, and that there's graffiti all over the desks does not give instructors a secure feeling that when they're away everything will run smoothly.

Every teacher has a substitute horror story. One of the worst is a sub allowing students to use the teacher's computer to change grades.

"One lady has to be in her 80s. She falls asleep behind the desk, the students run out on her, and other teachers have to come and control the class for her. Is this how desperate we are for subs?" asked a California Spanish teacher.

Here's a New York story:

Kids were allowed free time all day, none of my plans were touched, and the woman gave a vivid talk about Monica Lewinsky and President Clinton to my fourth-grade students. Many of my students didn't understand what she was telling them but some did.

We had some backlash from that day, and she was banned from the building. Previously, she had already had teacher complaints after calling one third grader an asshole.

This is how parateachers could be a boon to the education environment. If the teacher were absent, the parateacher would take over, knowing the class and the students and the work being done. And if on occasion both the parateacher and teacher were absent, a parateacher from another room could fill in.

"A parateacher could help me set up labs," said a Pennsylvania science teacher. "That would save me a lot of time. We do two to three labs a week, and each takes one and a half to two hours to set up."

A Los Angeles high school instructor said, "A parateacher would be great because, even if you were out, she could continue with the lesson because she would know exactly where you left off and what the next lesson would be. The students would also be more receptive because she would be someone they knew."

When a teacher does find a reliable substitute, that sub is often in such demand, that he usually ends up getting his own teacher's license, thus creating a void in the sub pool.

All across the country districts are experiencing a second shortage crisis, that of substitute teachers. "More than 86 percent of the nation's school districts have problems finding subs," according to Barbara Kantrowitz and Pat Wingert's article "Teacher Wanted" in *Newsweek*. The Chicago Public Schools Substitute Teacher Center places more than 2,000 subs a day. Instead of a pool of 10,000 subs, it has just 3,000.

The sub pool will continue to go wanting as long as subs are paid as low as $40 a day to dodge spitballs.

If you were to add up all the days students have substitute teachers over the course of their public education, they would total a full year of not being taught by a real teacher. While students would miss having "free time" when the teacher is away, parateachers would ensure that kids are still learning.

Workload

College professors are usually stunned when they realize that secondary teachers teach five classes a day, five days a week. It's a breathless, mind-numbing work environment.

How can teachers be effective when they spend all their scheduled work time teaching, with little time to digest what they are doing and how their lessons are playing with their audience, the students? It's funny how teachers are trained how to use reflection as a learning tool with students, yet they have little time themselves to reflect on what they are doing day to day, period to period.

This explains why once teachers create a lesson, that lesson frequently has a life expectancy of the teachers' career. Instructors feel satisfied that at the very least they have a lesson. Who cares whether the lesson works or not, whether it is effective for different learning styles? Just having a lesson plan is considered enough of an accomplishment.

While some may see this as outright laziness, it is simply a realistic survival strategy for teachers. Each work day they go through their lessons, collect student work, grade it, return it, and move on to the next lesson. There is no stopping. Like an automatic walkway that waits for no one to get on or get off, teachers go from bell to bell, flailing their arms and legs in a whirlpool of instruction, struggling to survive until the next Saturday or holiday. For new teachers, this sink-or-swim analogy is especially true. Many times first-year teachers are lucky enough to be developing lessons the night before they present them to the students, and they are sometimes only pages ahead of their classes in the textbook. Such daily stress builds up, explaining why so many leave the profession in the first few years—they are never able to stay ahead of the students. After a while, their batteries run dry. For those who survive with their year's worth of lessons, what reason do they have to put themselves through such a grind to revise those plans? It's easy to just use the same assignments, year after year; good for the teacher, but bad for the student.

To ease the workload for teachers and, thereby, increase the effectiveness of student learning, here are three plans that should be considered, especially for the secondary grades.

Plan 1: Cap Class Sizes at 25 Students for Certain Courses

If teachers had to teach four or even five classes, but they were guaranteed no more than 25 in each class, it would go a long way toward relieving the pressures of teaching 40 students in each class, five times a day. Teaching 125 students versus 200 is an enormous difference. If the goal is to teach rather than simply house students, this is the way to go.

While reducing class size has taken hold in many primary grades across the country, usually limiting 20 pupils to a room, the vast majority of grades 4–12 still push the limits of seating capacity for students, especially in large urban areas.

For years, teachers have cried out for smaller class sizes. And who can argue? It seems pretty sensible that if an American literature teacher has 42 students rather than 22, their writing will suffer. The tendency would be to write fewer comments on the students' papers and assign less work. If nothing else, smaller class sizes would relieve stress for teachers and enable them to get to know the abilities of each student more precisely.

Despite the clear benefits of smaller classes, the reality is that there may not be enough talented people to fill these teaching positions or enough space to house the additional classes.

Many schools have already scraped the bottom of the barrel to fill positions. Some schools have resorted to placing a second teacher in an overcrowded classroom, thus meeting the legal definition of a 20:1 student:teacher ratio. Sometimes teachers teach out of their major. How beneficial is it for the students if their English teacher is really a math teacher who has never taught the course before? Teachers could be teaching to five kids, but if they don't know what they're doing, then a smaller class size has negligent impact on student learning. In fact, it could cause harm.

Finding space to hold the extra classes also presents problems. Computer labs, music rooms, libraries, auditorium stages, faculty lounges, even storage rooms have been turned into makeshift classrooms. What good is a small class if it's held in a basement shelter with no windows or adequate heating?

While studies have shown mixed results in terms of student learning, smaller classes do help to cut down discipline problems and increase one-on-one interaction. But both could be accomplished with a parateacher in the room. Certainly, when balanced against the two main disadvantages, less qualified teachers and less classroom space, smaller class size isn't so attractive. And, again, poorer schools suffer more. The number of noncredentialed teachers in those schools has increased tenfold in California since the introduction of class size reduction (Kerr).

In an ideal world, teaching ten students would be heaven. But when a country offers free education for 13 straight years to more than 50 million children, it's not going to happen. Therefore, a compromise needs to be reached allowing for some larger class sizes. It's better that children not write as often as they should, but be exposed to a first-rate master teacher than for them to do more work with an instructor who is teaching from a manual. This means, of course, larger classes instead of smaller ones, a difficult concept for an English teacher whose classes number 40 or more students each. However, if it means more qualified instructors are reaching more students, then larger classes are needed.

This is why the second best alternative would be to select those grades and courses where smaller class size would have the greatest impact: early grades, English-as-a-second-language courses, classes with at-risk students, and honors and AP classes.

Districts use a formula to determine the average number of students in a class, and it's strictly arbitrary. Many factors should be taken into consideration when it comes to numbers of students in a class. Actually, the thinking should be about the number of students for a course.

For the early grades, especially kindergarten through fourth, children are still assimilating to school life and finding their educational footing. These are the most crucial years to build an educational foundation. Students who begin having academic problems at this stage will continue to struggle later on. For these classes, 25:1 makes sense.

Classes with non-English-speaking children should have a cap of 25 students. It's very easy for a child new to this country to feel lost in a large classroom. In a smaller class, that child will receive more individual attention from the teacher.

Classes with predominantly lower-achieving students should remain capped at 25 as well. Struggling students are more likely to fall through the cracks in a larger class than a smaller one, and they would benefit a great deal from increased one-on-one attention. And some academically weak pupils often have behavior problems, stemming from their frustration. Such behavior is less likely to happen in smaller class settings, where they have a smaller audience.

Finally, honors and AP classes also should have no more than 25 students. Teachers who have never taught these classes before view those who do as having an advantage. While it's true the advanced students are more motivated to learn (which is half of the battle in teaching young people—getting them interested in what you're doing), it's also true that most of them turn in their work. In a regular class of 35, a teacher may expect attendance in the 20s, whereas honors students rarely miss class. The teacher of a regular class of 35 may receive homework from 20–25 students, while the AP teacher can count on a full house of work coming in. Besides the increase in the paperload, advanced classes demand more from the teacher in terms of challenging lessons and assignments to stimulate gifted minds. Teachers of advanced students are more likely to be intellectually spent at the end of the day than instructors who have nonadvanced pupils.

Caseload is more important than class size. Several teachers who complain about how large their classes are go ahead and take on an additional class to earn extra money. How effective can that teacher be with 200 students?

Plan 2: Teachers Have No More than Four Classes

Under the best of circumstances, asking professional educators to teach more than three hours a day is asking for a compromised learning environment. If teachers could teach half of their workday, then spend the rest of the time analyzing what they're doing, students would benefit in addition to the teachers. Students would have instructors who wouldn't communicate their stress to the class, and the lessons would be well-thought-out and student work well assessed. In today's teacher shortage, teaching only three classes is not feasible. However, four classes are possible, though that would mean opening more teaching positions.

Some school districts already have this policy for English teachers, recognizing the amount of paperwork literature classes generate. With four classes, teachers would have time to develop research methods, use their classrooms to collect data on teaching practices, thereby further establishing the legitimacy of teaching as a true profession.

Much stress builds up throughout the day when teachers aren't able to act on what they need to, call that parent, make that copy, get that overhead pen. All business beyond the teaching of students—and that load keeps getting heavier with each new government-imposed task that is added—must be organized efficiently into 50-some minute prep periods where sorting out student portfolios, filling out forms, returning calls, and catching one's breath is about all that gets accomplished. If people think teachers can do half the things they need to in less than an hour a day, forget it. That's why four classes a day, providing two scheduled hours of nonteaching time, would be optimal to allow teachers time to work on lessons and with other teachers.

Plan 3: A Four-Day Workweek

While the most radical of these plans in terms of altering the traditional school workweek, this plan would offer the most benefit in terms of professionalizing teachers by formally scheduling regular time, one day a week, for teachers to work with one another. It would be less wearisome for a teacher to teach to 200 students a day, but only four times a week, than teaching fewer students a day every day. Even if plans 1 and 2 were not used—that is, teachers continued to teach five classes with 40 students each, this plan would still be beneficial.

All studies show that for staff development to be effective, it has to be integrated into the regular workday, such as purposely scheduling planning time into the weekly schedule so that all teachers can discuss what works and what doesn't week after week. Some elementary schools do this by scheduling weekly 30- to 45-minute grade-level meetings. A good start, but not enough time to allow collaboration to flourish. Not only will this produce better teachers, but better students as well who will benefit from lessons that have been reviewed by more than one teacher.

Teachers would not be in the classroom on Mondays. Parateachers would be in charge of the students, so that teachers could undertake a variety of activities to strengthen their instructional time with the students.

A Los Angeles teacher said, "A four-day week would be great, especially around grading period. Sometimes a teacher just needs one day to catch up on paperwork. It would be so much better to have that Monday than to use a sick day."

Fortunately, some schools are trying out different ways of structuring the teacher's work week.

In an analysis by K. H. Miles, for his *Educational Evaluation and Policy Analysis* article, "Freeing Resources for Improving Schools: A Case Study of Teacher Allocation in Boston Public Schools," teachers at Hefferan Elementary School in Chicago "teach four full days of academic classes each week and spend the fifth full day planning together with their multi-grade teams and pursuing professional development. Meanwhile, their students rotate to 'resource' classes in music, fine arts, computer lab, physical education, library science, and science lab" (Darling-Hammond, 1999, p. 4).

At New York City schools' International High, "teachers on interdisciplinary teams share 70 minutes of planning time daily, and have a half day each week for staff-planned professional development while students are in clubs. This amounts to nearly nine hours of shared time each week." Does it benefit students? "Virtually all of International's students—who enter 9th grade unable to speak English—graduate from high school and go on to collage" (Ibid., p. 4).

Monday is the most logical day to have teachers work collaboratively for several reasons. Many schools have pupil-free days or minimum days on Mondays. Look at a high school's bell schedule, and you can find several different ones, depending on what is going on at the school: a regular schedule; a banking schedule, which has shorter classes to enable teachers to meet once a month; a minimum day schedule; an assembly schedule; and so on. Instead of 180 days of instruction, with 10 percent of them half-days, four-day workweeks would be made up solely of full days.

Having minimum days for students is not educationally sound. The not-so-subtle message these days send to students is that while education is important, other things are even more so, to the detriment of instructional time.

Minimum days equal minimum effort by some teachers. They simply write off these days offering students "free" time. This is another reason to eliminate minimum days.

For example, where I work, the big football game between rival high schools provides the school with its best opportunity to get new students involved in the spirit of their school. That's fine, except that it has a negative effect on the teaching day. On one particular day, which coincided with a minimum day, classes were 12 minutes long, while the assembly remained its traditional three hour length.

Setting aside one day a week for all these activities would preserve the rest of the week. It would be less confusing, more consistent, and would make a statement that instructional time takes precedence Tuesday through Friday. Plus, most school holidays fall on Mondays, so students would lose only teacher-free days and not the days with their teachers during the rest of the week.

Instead of Monday being the black sheep of weekdays, students would begin looking forward to it. All school assemblies and field trips could be held on Monday with parateachers serving as chaperones. Sometimes students take so many trips that they can miss up to ten school days each year. No doubt, field trips are vitally important in that they provide new learning experiences for students; however, not all teachers feel that way. So by scheduling field trips only on Mondays, the rest of the week would remain undisturbed.

Students could spend time on Mondays studying or receiving tutoring from the parateachers. A weekly plan could be developed each Monday that allows students to reflect on how well the week went and what new goals to establish. At the high school level, registering for the following year's classes uses up instructional time. With the four-day week, students could work with counselors on Mondays.

By teaching four times a week, teachers would be able to interact with colleagues, thus expanding and enriching their pedogogical knowledge. Faculty and department meetings could be held, teachers could attend conferences and workshops—eliminating their frequent absences from the classroom, and teachers would have the time to research what they are doing, perhaps by reading professional journals. Elementary schools would retain the five-day workweek, with teachers working collaboratively in the afternoon hours.

A middle high school teacher from Ohio thinks that a four-day workweek would be "a marvelous thing just to do the paperwork alone."

The most difficult aspect to the four-day workweek would be finding space for teachers to meet because they wouldn't be able to do so in their classrooms. This should not be the reason for not implementing it, however. If need be, teachers could meet in the library or even in each other's homes.

The real concern if such a plan were to be implemented would be to ensure that the district did not control those Mondays, that if any type of formal meetings were to occur, they would happen only in the morning hours. It is crucial that teachers not be herded from one meeting to the next; rather, they should be entrusted with open-ended time to use as they wish. A ceiling of 90 minutes for structured meeting time would be sufficient.

Having monthly meetings does not produce substantive change, nor does it promote collegiality. The best and only way for this breakthrough to occur is if teacher interaction time is integrated into the work schedule. And this means teachers not teaching school five days a week.

As Linda Darling-Hammond points out, "The master schedule—the master of all possibilities in schools—must change before schools can support serious teaching and learning for both students and their teachers" (1999, p. 2).

Plan 4: The Dream Scenario—All of the Above

If all three of these proposals were implemented, teachers would have a very manageable 75-student workload. While more teachers would be needed, fewer teachers would leave because conditions would be less stressful.

No matter which plan is put into action, one thing is certain: relieving the stress level of teachers will benefit everyone. Teachers would call in sick less often. As it stands, teachers tend to take more mental health days off work than actual days for illness. More teachers would remain in the profession longer, and teaching would be attractive to more people.

Redesigning the School Year

"High-quality teaching as envisioned by standards-based school reform cannot be accomplished within a 6-hour day and a 9-month school year . . . the best teachers—those whom the system needs to retain and who could be paid more—work substantially beyond these minimums" (Odden and Kelley, p. viii).

From the first day of the school year, the clock is ticking, and secondary teachers have barely 180 hours to cover a year's worth of material. That translates to one regular work month, a month to master U.S. history, to understand the formulas of algebra, to read the master-works in English literature and analyze their rhetorical elements. Teachers find themselves out of breath by the time the 3:00 bell rings, five days a week.

Rigidity of the teacher's workday allows for little planning or collaborative work. Teachers, after being re-vitalized and feeling refreshed after a well-done work-shop or conference, return to work the next day ready to fight the good fight, but they immediately get swallowed up by the school rat race. Every teacher attending a con-ference should be given the next day off to reflect on it, or the conference should include time during the day for this purpose.

Where does one carve out time to develop, plan, and integrate new ideas? With no time budgeted for these ac-tivities, all of the wonderful ideas presented the day be-fore only gather dust in a folder in a filing cabinet.

Excellent teachers know what students need, yet they feel utterly frustrated by not having the time to develop the lessons necessary for students to optimize their learn-ing experience.

The current system all too often saps teachers' energy so even the best ones resort to not assigning enough writ-ing, not reviewing and reflecting and revising daily les-son plans, not listening to their students, not perceiving their needs based on test results.

Why should a teacher assign another essay? Why should a teacher spend hours analyzing the results of a science test to see which students need remediation? It's a blessing that there are teachers who do do this.

Much of public education is on automatic pilot. So many teachers are zombies, taking out the same list of study questions, the same chapter test year after year. Once a test is done, there is little analysis of what went wrong, what should be the next plan of action. The assem-bly line never rests, it constantly moves, and teachers push on regardless of results.

The problem isn't that teachers don't know how to best serve students, it's that they aren't given time to come up with ideas.

"A Nation at Risk" asked for "seven-hour school days, as well as a 200- to 220-day school year." The long-established, antiquated, 180-day, fall-to-spring school calendar was developed originally for farmers who needed their children's help during the summer to till the fields. This no longer applies to most people.

According to the National Center for Educational Statistics, many countries whose education systems are internationally renowned keep students in school longer:

Country	Number of School Days
Korea	220
Israel	215
Japan	195
Germany	190
U.S.	180

But when we look at the number of hours spent on core subjects, the discrepancy looms larger:

Country	Number of Hours on Core Subjects
Germany	3,700
France	3,500
Japan	3,400
U.S.	1,500

If the instructional time were organized better and used more efficiently, students wouldn't need to attend school year-round. Add up all the minimum days and testing days, and you can easily end up with over a month's worth of lost teaching time.

Standardized and other state tests like New York's Regent's all erode valuable instructional time. It's not as if for each new legislated test, more time is added to the school calendar. And some tests are administered as early as the start of the second semester, when students have only studied half of the year's curriculum. No wonder so many results are discouraging.

Days reserved for standardized tests are especially damaging during the the last weeks of a school year. Noneducators think of a teacher's year as "winding down" in May or June, whereas it is actually gathering steam, when more work needs to be evaluated and grades have to be averaged.

The school calendar should come to a close when testing begins. If the College Board (which is in charge of AP testing) schedules AP tests in May, that's when those classes should finish up. Instead, in many states, courses start in September and run through the end of June, creating problems for AP teachers who fill nearly a month's worth of instructional time for a course that students have already completed. The other problem with this type of schedule is that it takes away a month of preparing for the test by having schools begin in September instead of August to provide an additional month.

If the testing frenzy doesn't subside (see chapter 9), why not just budget time for the tests by adding a testing month as the last month of the school year. Students can begin in mid-August and end instruction by early May. Then the rest of May can be used for test taking.

Extending the school year by ten days (two weeks) to 190 would provide time needed for testing without interrupting the curriculum. It would also justify paying teachers higher salaries, because they would be on the job longer. Working an additional month would not affect secondary teachers as much as elementary ones, because many of the former already teach four to six weeks of summer school.

A national poll by Recruiting New Teachers, Inc, and Louis Harris, released in the spring of 2001 found that six out of ten Americans favor lengthening the school year by two weeks (Haselkorn and Harris). Having public schools in session from mid-August to early June would mimic the schedule of many universities. Like universities, K–12 should have a more distinctive break after each semester to give teachers time to figure out grades and students time to take a mental break. In some school districts, the spring semester begins the day immediately following the last day of the fall semester.

This 42-week school year would still leave ten weeks out of the year for vacation periods and summer school.

The School Day

The idea of moving students every 45 to 55 minutes from cubicle to cubicle treats young people as if they are widgets on an assembly line. This system, which has remained unchanged for decades, creates a layer of anxiety for students and teachers alike, putting everyone a bit on edge.

Think about this: College was the only time for many teachers to have freedom from a bell schedule. All their lives, from the time they attended school as children through their working career, they have been conditioned like Pavlov's dogs to move along without much complaint, accepting groups of students marching in and marching out, every hour on the hour, with 15-minute breaks and 30-minute lunches (imagine a lifetime of eating cafeteria food).

At the secondary level, class periods need to be longer to relieve the stress of hordes of youngsters moving in and out of classrooms after such short periods of time. However, unlike block scheduling (discussed later), where classes meet on alternate days, the entire school day should be lengthened so that students see all their teachers every day.

Fifty minutes is not enough time to cover material effectively. Many teaching strategies work best with more time. Having classes be 70 minutes long would accommodate those strategies without losing students' interest, which happens in 90- or 100-minute periods.

The reason why many schools have unusual timed periods, such as 53 minutes, stems from state laws stipulating the exact number of instructional minutes for students.

Counting every single instructional minute begs the old chicken or the egg question: which came first—union contracts stipulating that teachers are not to work one second past those minutes, or districts stipulating that teachers must be on duty during those minutes? In either case, each side feeds off the other in terms of counting minutes, putting everyone on edge when a meeting runs long or a new change in the bell schedule occurs. "Make sure we don't work one more minute than we have to" comes from union members. "Make sure they don't leave the meeting early" comes from administrators. Instead of treating each other with mutual respect, everyone plays the minute game.

Former California Governor Pete Wilson once proposed lengthening the school day in California by simply not counting the five-minute passing period between classes at the secondary level, which is considered instructional (or paying) time of the teacher.

An anonymous official commented that teachers shouldn't be paid for any noninstructional minute. During their five-minute "break," teachers answer questions from their students, erase and write on the board, prepare handouts and books, move chairs, pick up trash, and the list goes on. Such an ignorant statement as that official's shows a total lack of understanding of how teachers use this time. Maybe every second is not instructional time for the student, but the teacher is working during all of it. More important, to what other profession would such a standard of *only* paying people for productive minutes apply? Every single worker must go to the bathroom—does that add to the company's productivity? What about all the surfing and buying on the Internet some people do where they work? Do teachers have the time to do such things (assuming they even have a computer)?

The focus shouldn't be on using a time clock to measure student learning. As the old saying goes, it's not the quantity but the quality. The focus should be on how those minutes are structured.

In the last ten years, block scheduling has surfaced as a way to restructure the school day.

Block Scheduling (More B.S.?)

One of the biggest trends in changing the look of the secondary school day and week has been block scheduling. Several schools have switched from a traditional school-day divided into six hourly classes to a block schedule consisting of classes meeting on alternate days for longer periods of time ("blocks"). There are many variations of block scheduling in many schools. The most variety is to have classes meet every other day in 90- to 120-minute periods. There's also the four-by-four plan in which students take four classes of similarly blocked time every day and finish the coursework in half a semester, then repeat the process three more times during the school year.

While the idea of students staying in class longer has its merits, it also raises certain problems. For example, teaching non-native speakers the English language in a two-hour block of time is challenging even for the most gifted instructor.

Part of the problem of any block scheduling is what happens to the daily hour of prep time for the teacher. Every other day, the prep time is two hours, a plus, but on the alternate days, it disappears, a minus. Teachers need to work on their craft daily. Additionally, to teach effectively for six hours one day, then four the next, creates an inconsistent level of energy needed by the teacher to practice. It puts more pressure on teachers to plan only on alternating days.

Then what happens to a student who is ill one day? Or a teacher? That would be like missing two days of class time. Think how hard it would be on the student to have a substitute for two hours.

Frankly, the real reason for block scheduling at many secondary schools is that it decreases the number of times students are roaming the hallways, and crowd control is job number one for administrators. The bottom line is fewer kids are out and about, meaning fewer traffic cop duties for principals. And who can blame them? But shouldn't a program of this magnitude be measured by its impact on students? Thus far, studies on student learning in block scheduling formats are inconclusive.

A high school biology teacher who has tried both block scheduling and traditional scheduling offered this opinion:

> As a science teacher, during a 90-minute block of time, your first reaction is, "Wow, what am I going to do with these kids!" I have been able to have a 30-minute introduction to a lab, the lab itself, have clean-up, then review the lab, all in the same period. In reality, however, there are not enough materials to do such a lesson every day. The kids get antsy, and they are ready to go on to the next class after an hour of science.

A high school teacher from California, who works in a setting where a yearlong course takes 19 weeks, said, "It makes everything go by faster, but you have to trim out a lot from the curriculum to fit the more important things in. For many students it is too fast a year."

As a teacher, seeing your students every day is a must; it adds continuity and helps keep students focused. Classes such as sports and journalism suffer without daily exposure, especially math and foreign language courses, which are sequentially organized. Plus, doing smaller amounts of homework each night is easier than doing larger amounts every other day. Yet, having enough time to finish lessons would also be beneficial. Increasing 45-, 50-, or 55-minutes period to 65 or 70 minutes would be helpful as students go through the system from middle to high school. After all, so much class time is frittered away on taking attendance and reading bulletins that students actually receive only 45 minutes of instruction in nearly one-hour-long classes. Seventy-minute classes allow even the slowest teacher to give students a solid hour of instruction.

If teachers were given fewer classes, but more time to spend with each one, that would be the most productive. Of course, the schoolday would have to be lengthened, and the question of when to start school would need to be analyzed.

Start Times

First of all, school should not begin at 8:00 A.M. and end at 3:00 P.M. With two-working-parent families the norm these days, more parents would appreciate having their children in school longer. At elementary schools, after-school programs, where young children wait until 6:00 P.M. for their parents to pick them up, are quite popular. Many older children already spend longer days, by either enrolling in 7:00 A.M. or 3:00 P.M. classes, or joining a sport or activity that requires them to be at school until 4:30.

For secondary students, the schoolday should start no earlier than 8:30 and go until at least 4:30, due to the nature of teenagers. Adolescents' bodies are still growing, so they require more sleep. Getting up earlier in the morning interrupts their normal sleep cycles. Having school start later, and end later in the afternoon, cuts into the period when half of all juvenile crime occurs, between 2:00 P.M. and 8:00 P.M., the time when most teens are at home unsupervised. U.S. Representative Zoe Lofgren (D.-Calif.) introduced a Zs to As Act H.R. 1267 that would provide grants to schools that agree to start secondary classes after 9:00 A.M. Some schools in Minnesota and Kentucky already do that, with such positive results as increased attendance, less tardiness, and more alert students.

An example of a high school schedule with 70-minute classes might look something like this:

Sample High School Bell Schedule

Period 1	8:30–9:40
Period 2	9:45–10:55
Period 3	11:00–12:10
Lunch	12:10–12:55
Period 4	1:00–2:10
Period 5	2:15–3:25
Period 6	3:30–4:40

Eliminating nutrition or snack time means that students wouldn't scarf down chips and soda, weakening their attention span for the rest of their morning classes. It would also cut out one of the two breaks during which administrators must monitor student behavior. However, lunch would be 45 minutes long, allowing a long enough break in the middle of the day. In addition, more working parents would be able to pick up their children at 4:40 instead of 3:00. Students could still enroll in after-school programs lengthening their stay until 5:30 or 6:00, an end time much more convenient for parents coming off of work.

While there would still be several passing periods when students roam the halls, the longer class sessions would balance out the hectic nature of the current shorter period schedule.

A New York teacher with 31 years' experience would like to see the following:

> The school year needs to be longer because our
> students do not come from homes that give them much

stimulation over the summer. I'd like to see academics and enrichment summer programs required for at least four weeks during July or August. I'd like to see the day lengthened, with enrichment activities offered from 3:00–4:00. Band and music lessons, choir, extra physical activity programs such as gymnastics, or art and computer programs could be offered during this time instead of the constant pullouts during the day. Our students seem to dribble in and out of the classroom, and we are constantly trying to catch individual students and figure out what discussion, activity, or direction they might have missed.

Designing Schools

When my worksite was getting a new building, the principal asked the teachers to help design the faculty lounge. This request gave teachers a sense of importance, that their opinion really mattered. After all, it was the one room in the three-story wing exclusively for their use.

While soliciting input to design classrooms would have been ideal, asking teachers for their thoughts on anything was quite generous.

While government buildings may not win architectural awards, educational buildings look the worst: less money goes into designing and building a school than a city hall or courthouse, even a prison. Not only are these buildings the least appealing to the eye, they are also the last on the list to be renovated or replaced. It's estimated that the average age of a school is 40 years old (Zernike, 2001b). This is especially true with urban schools, all the more reason to make sure the facilities look inviting to the students.

Teachers should be involved in school design. This is not necessarily a new idea, but it is an extremely important one. To do their job effectively, teachers must have some control over their working environment. Problems such as overcrowding, inadequate storage space, inadequate room for display, and lack of planning for new technology not only can hamper the learning process, they can stop it dead. It's just common sense to allow teachers a voice in the planning process to avoid these difficulties.

Why not tap such a rich resource for ideas? Teachers tend to have creative minds. Since they spend their entire working careers in these spaces, it makes perfect sense to have them help design them. "During the programming phase, architects help teachers articulate their spatial requirements," said Laura Wernick, vice president of HMFC Architects, one of the architectural firms in the nation that has designed hundreds of schools.

This is how one Los Angeles teacher would design her workspace.

> I would have the following: more closet space, an office with a glass or window divider with a computer and Internet service, telephone, fax, maybe a copier. The classroom would be big enough to have work areas or stations for students. Stations would be: a reading center with about four comfortable chairs, an art station with a round table for four or five with all the necessities, such as a sink, paints, paper, etc. Another station would be for students to work on computers. They would have Internet access to research things for the class.

Some schools have enlisted the ideas of their teachers. In recent years there has been an effort by many school districts to involve teachers in school design. This practice needs to be implemented in every district across the country. To get an idea of how beneficial it can be, let's look at a few examples of projects that have been completed or are in the process of being built.

Kent Island High in Stevensville, Maryland, like all of the schools discussed here, was designed with the participation of teachers and administrators. School boards and architects are slowly coming to the realization that school design needs to be guided by the people who will use the site. By accepting input from these groups, the architects were able to create a plan with the potential to foster a dynamic and flexible learning environment.

An important concept that guided the planning process was the clustering of classrooms around decentralized administrative areas. In the words of the architectural firm Grimm and Parker, as published on Designshare.com's website:

> The design creates a sense of community and provides interdisciplinary cluster teaming with career focuses. This cluster concept integrates groups of students with [the] facility to create a smaller community feeling within a larger school. This grouping fosters a sense of identity and belonging. Each cluster is organized around a decentralized administration area and interdisciplinary planning area where teachers, administrators and students can work together for longer periods and get to know each other. Such an arrangement will facilitate interdisciplinary teaming opportunities between academic subjects and career focused programs. The design allows the academic, career and technology teachers to be distributed throughout each cluster which utilizes classroom space more efficiently. This makes the opportunity available to change the educational and teaching setting and program for future curriculums.

One of the most important aspects of this plan is that it allows teachers to work together. Without having to attend meetings after school or on weekends, without having to make time in their schedules for retreats and seminars, teachers have the opportunity to discuss curriculum, exchange ideas, and to get to know each other better. There won't be a need to encourage teamwork; the design of the school makes teamwork a fact of daily life. In addition to bringing teachers closer together, note that the classroom layout is also intended to build closer relationships between principals and students. Rather than having the administrators be a remote, unseen presence, hidden behind the doors of "the office," the decentralized concept makes them a part of the educational process. This gives them a clearer idea of the practical problems teachers face, and makes them more aware of the work teachers are doing to educate students. As it now stands, administrators mostly deal with teachers on issues relating to management or discipline. Bringing them into the classroom environment gives them a better sense of all aspects of a teacher's performance.

The design for Central Tree Middle School in Rutland, Massachusetts, built in 1998, dealt with some of the same issues as Kent Island High and came up with some of the same solutions. But let's look at this school from a different point of view: aesthetics. Many people say that aesthetics are not central to the educational process and, therefore, are of secondary importance, especially if building a more beautiful school results in significantly higher costs. Because most school districts have taken this view for decades, students are housed in buildings that are often bleak and depressing, encouraging the attitude that school is a prison.

To quote from HMFH Architects, who designed Central Tree Middle School:

> The physical appearance of the building was found
> to make a significant contribution to the users'
> experience of the building. Both teachers and students
> reported feeling that the colorful atmosphere affected
> their mood, made the students feel that the building
> was designed for them, and made the building seem
> "kid-friendly." Many design features were seen as
> "fun" and the building overall was seen as appearing
> "important."

What a novel idea! Creating a learning environment that raises peoples spirits rather than lowering them. A setting where education might be fun.

But let's hear more from the people responsible for the design of Central Tree:

> Upon entering the building parents are received in an open reception area. Chairs and a table provide a place to sit and feel welcome. Additionally, attractive conference rooms in which teachers, parents and students meet also make the point that parental involvement is important to the school's philosophy.

To appreciate how unique and how important this approach is, listen to the words of someone who worked in a Los Angeles–area elementary school for seven years:

> The school was always trying to put out the message that parents needed to get involved. They sent out bulletins, they scheduled special events trying to lure the parents to the school. But the day-to-day reality was that parents visiting the school were often treated like intruders. Security was a concern, which is understandable, but often parents weren't even able to enter the school after the doors were locked in the morning. If they did get in and couldn't see the principal right away, they had to sit in a tiny, cramped office which was often crowded with other people. This was especially hard on parents who brought small children with them.

It isn't enough for schools to send out bulletins encouraging parent involvement; schools must show parents that they are welcome.

In looking at a third school, Davidson Elementary School in Davidson, North Carolina, consider another aspect of school design: health. Davidson Elementary was designed to allow for natural ventilation and daylight. As we hear more and more about "sick-building syndrome," we realize that in addition to the benefits air conditioning offers, there are health concerns. Making natural ventilation a built-in aspect of the school's design may help to reduce health problems. And anyone who has worked in an office lit only by fluorescent lights will appreciate what a difference a little daylight can make.

In fact, a study by the California Board for Energy Efficiency found that "students in classrooms with the most daylight improved 20 percent faster on math tests and 26 percent faster on reading tests over one year than students in classrooms with the least" (Zernike, 2001b).

Even if it costs more money to build schools like these, isn't it worth it to have the kids feel good about their surroundings? How much is it worth when teachers feel comfortable in their classroom rather than feeling oppressed by it? Is it possible to calculate the return they will get on this investment?

But does it cost more money to build more pleasing schools? No, according to HMFH's Laura Wernick. "The cost should be the same since the primary expense is square footage per student. Architectural firms work under the same cost constraints in Massachusetts or Indiana or Vermont since the pursestrings are tightly held. Good architecture costs no more than bad architecture."

Why then don't more districts build more desirable schools? "Districts are scared of innovation. It's very easy to do what's been done before. It's more difficult to do what's creative and different. If you're trained to teach a certain way, then you'll build schools the same way you've been building them."

If aesthetics alone is not enough of a reason to build exciting school campuses, what about instilling pride in the students and the staff? "Students and teachers are more apt to take care of their environment, leading to lower upkeep expenses in covering up vandalism," said Wernick.

Charter Schools

Charter schools allow forward-thinking educators to use innovate salary structures and curriculum guides to reinvent and improve public education. Usually teachers have more of a say in how a charter school is run than a traditional one.

There are fewer than 2,000 charter schools in the United States, serving nearly 400,000 students. Charter schools receive the bulk of their money from states and local school districts with the provision that no funds go to capital costs, such as real estate, student desks, or supplies. This is where the innovation of the charter school founders is needed, getting contributions from the community and the private sector.

Despite intense interference by school boards and teachers unions, some charter schools are thriving.

- Yvonne Chan began Vaughn Next Century Learning Center in Los Angeles, which houses 1,200 lower economic minority students. The school earned the National Blue Ribbon title two years after opening. Yet, Ms. Chan still has to go begging for funding at LAUSD meetings where board members seem jealous of her success with creative and nontraditional ways of running a school. Even the union does not support her and forced teachers working at Vaughn to lose union protection.
- In Kingsburg, California, the superintendent made the entire school district a charter one.
- Edison Schools Inc. manages more than 113 schools nationwide. They hire both traditionally and alternatively certified teachers. Teachers are given scheduled time to collaborate on lessons. Molly Stevens, a recruiter from Edison said, "The salaries are usually slightly above the local public school salaries to compensate for a longer day and longer year."

It's still too early to see if charter schools will lead the way for public school reform.

One of the newfangled ways of describing the cumulative role of students is as self-directed learners and independent thinkers, who have been taught all the necessary tools to succeed no matter what endeavor they choose. How ironic that teachers who teach students these tools aren't able to exercise the same behaviors in their own profession.

Teachers are not viewed as independent thinkers. Instead, they are looked down on as people who are best dictated to, told when to show up for work, what forms to fill out, what meetings to attend, when to turn grades in, where to go at what time.

Teachers should be more like partners in a law firm rather than clerks in a department store. Sandra Feldman, American Federation of Teachers president, said in a *Newsweek* article, "schools need to become more like dot-com outfits where people sit around and brainstorm and figure out what to do next."

What would it cost to implement any of these changes? The following chapter details how such plans could be put into motion. Money is not the issue; what is at issue is handing over the steering wheel to teachers. Will politicians and school boards allow this? Do they trust teachers? And, if they don't trust teachers to be in command of their own profession, why are they allowed to be in the classroom teaching young people?

PART 3

What Stands in the Way?

If we paid teachers based on their ability to teach, made sure they are trained appropriately with more class time under their belt, offered incentives for the best teachers not to exit the profession in the first few years, and handed over the reins of public education to the teachers, teaching would become a full-fledged profession. Of course, it's not that easy.

The old reasoning why public education has weaknesses stems from insufficient financing. Fund schools properly and watch the problems go away.

Well, thanks to the unprecedented decade-long prosperity of the 1990s, public schools have received a record $350 billion each year during the last decade. No longer is it a question of how much money; rather, it is how to spend it. With so much money floating around, no wonder everyone from consultants to publishers wants a piece of the education money pie.

Unions have negotiated double-digit contracts for their members, but are teachers any better off in terms of controlling their profession? Will those with real power in education—politicians, school boards—give more control to teachers, the ones with the least power but the most impact? Paying teachers more money, in essence, is empowering them.

Remember, the idea behind paying teachers $100,000 is that not all teachers would earn that kind of money. Redistributing the money, paying better teachers more and weaker teachers less, would not increase property taxes. In addition, the money needed to improve working conditions, provide sufficient supplies and equipment, and hire secretaries and parateachers, is already there. Programs like Title I and other categorical types of funding should be closed down, and the money should be sent to schools to best figure out where the money could be used most effectively.

If the money is there, then who could say no to higher teacher salaries as long as teachers were evaluated? Who wouldn't want more rigorous training to weed out weaker candidates? Who wouldn't like to see more talented people enter the teacher workforce? Who wouldn't want America's children to have the best possible public school education? Unfortunately, the groups that wield the power are the exact ones that would oppose such reforms: politicians and teachers unions.

One can understand why politicians want to legislate what teachers do in their classrooms; that's what they're in the business of doing—telling everybody else how to do their jobs. But for teachers unions not to embrace peer review, authentic performance evaluations, and career ladders for their own constituents goes beyond credulity.

People who have written critically about teachers unions take the "throwing the baby out with the bath water" tactic: All unions do bad things; therefore, they are all bad. This is not the case. Teachers associations have had a great deal to do with why teachers are paid as much as they are today and why they have any time to prepare for their classes. But that was back in the '70s and '80s. Now they must fight the hardest battle of all: for professional control and prestige.

That control and prestige rest more with school administrators than classroom teachers. Society tends to pay more regard to high school principals than high school history teachers. And salaries bear that out. However, what are administrators but teachers who have taken a dozen more college courses? Yet to observe the dynamics of the administrator-teacher relationship, an outsider would think each of them came from vastly different backgrounds.

And teachers are partly to blame for allowing themselves to be treated with so little respect and viewed negatively by administrators. There are things that teachers need to do to clean up their act and put "pro" into the word "professional."

CHAPTER 7

Funding: Not a Problem

Is paying good teachers $100,000, providing adequate supplies and equipment, improving school facilities, and ensuring that students have textbooks going to cost money? You bet. Will it raise taxes? Not necessarily, even though some surveys show a surprisingly large number of people would be willing to pay higher taxes to improve schools. In a 2000 national poll released last year, more than eight in ten people favor paying an additional $10 a year in taxes to bring teacher salaries more in line with other professions of equal education (Haselkorn and Harris, p. 20).

During the last four decades, local funding has decreased as a percentage of public school revenues, while state and federal contributions have increased, with the federal share nearly doubling, from 4 percent in 1960 to almost 8 percent today.

Clearly, the problem hasn't been that education in the United States is inadequately funded. From 1960 to 1990, real educational expenditures per pupil increased by more than 200 percent, according to the National Center for Education Statistics. Sixty percent of every education dollar is spent on instructional services, which includes teacher pay. The statistics do not show any measurable difference in the way a large metropolitan and small rural district spends their money.

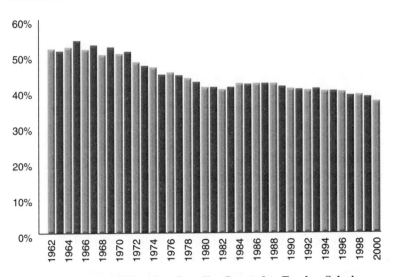

Figure 14. Percent of Education Spending Devoted to Teacher Salaries
Source: *Survey & Analysis of Teacher Salary Trends 2000*

Look at figure 14, which shows the percentage of education expenditures used for teachers. According to AFT's
Salary Trends 2000, "Teacher salaries today account for a
smaller proportion of total education spending than they
did 40 years ago." The average education expenditure devoted to teacher salaries has decreased from 51 percent in
1960–61 to 39.2 percent in 1999–2000.

Most new school revenues during the past 30 years
have been spent on teacher specialists and other services
for special-needs students—low income, disabled, English
language learners—at the expense of the primary service
providers—classroom teachers. Teacher specialists are
all former classroom teachers, who get paid more money
to perform a variety of tasks, from providing staff development to proctoring tests. From 1960 to 1984, there was a
500 percent increase in curriculum specialists and instructional supervisors. Teacher's aides have ballooned
from 700,000 in 1960 to more than 2.5 million today (Gross,
p. 31). The proportion of all professional staff represented
by teachers fell between 1950 and 1995, from 70 percent to

52 percent, according to the National Commission on Teaching and America's Future. However, "only 43 percent of education staff are classroom teachers. In other industrialized nations, about three-fourths of education resources are spent directly on instruction, and classroom teachers represent from 60 to 80 percent of all staff" (Darling-Hammond, 1997a, p. 3).

Studies have shown only modest positive results from all this extra specialist spending, not a lot of bang for the buck. So, while education funding has risen in the past decades, the regular teacher teaching the regular curriculum has received proportionally less money.

> Other countries invest more of their resources in supporting the efforts of better paid, better prepared teachers who are given them and responsibility for managing most of the work in schools. In the United States, however, schools have invested in a relatively smaller number of lower-paid, often less well-prepared teachers, directed and augmented by large numbers of administrators, supervisors, specialists, and other noninstructional staff. As a result, fewer school employees are available in the U.S. to engage in schools' primary function: teaching [Darling-Hammond, 1999, p. 3].

What follows are specific ways to fund six-figure salaries for qualified teachers. With redistribution of current funding programs and smarter management, paying the best teachers $100,000 can be done without raising taxes and with some money left over for upgrading the rest of the teachers' work environment.

Pool Categorical Money Together and Watch the Billions Pile Up

More funding for public schools today comes from state sources than from local property taxes, leading to more state-controlled than locally-controlled school districts.

Myriad strings are attached to these categorical funds, so you may have a school rich in computer hardware and adult aides, but poor in the upkeep of the school's infrastructure. Consolidating the money from state programs into one pot and distributing it to local districts with no strings attached would allow for more local control.

The last several years have seen an explosion of grants. Illinois schools received $5.6 billion in fiscal year 2000. However, an additional $1 billion was available in categorical grants. The money is there, but only if it is spent in a certain way for certain things. Rarely can grants be used for books, supplies, copiers, or secretarial help. If all this money were pooled together and distributed to the worst-performing schools, these schools could afford to attract better teachers, and students could receive a better education.

There's money for experts and consultants to train teachers on test-taking tips, but no books on the core curriculum so students can get authentic practice, not just artificial, daily, five-minute practice tests.

There's money to remodel administrators' offices, but no toilet paper for student bathrooms.

Too much money and time are spent on peripheral programs, not on the nuts and bolts of learning. That's why block grants are better than categorical programs, because the former allow schools to decide how best to spend the money.

One amendment that failed the final cut of the education packages passed by Congress in 2001 would have allowed governors to obtain waivers from the strings attached to federal funding. How many strings are there on the $57 billion? The House and Senate bills were 1,032 pages and 796 pages, respectively.

Eliminate the Title I Program

Over $185 billion has been spent on Title I, the Elementary and Secondary Education Act signed into law in

1965 providing money for poor schools, with little to show for it. Enacted during President Lyndon Johnson's War on Poverty, Title I was meant to diminish the achievement gap between economically disadvantaged children and the wealthier counterparts.

Allocated to schools with a majority of students in the free lunch program, Title I cost $8.7 billion in 2001, more than the entire budget of the nation's second-largest school district, Los Angeles Unified.

And what have been the results during the past 36 years? Half of the 90 percent of Title I money spent on instruction and support has been "wasted on unskilled though well-meaning teacher aides, who are often more baby-sitter than instructor," according to a staff editorial in the *Los Angeles Times*. Current Secretary of Education Rod Paige concurs: "After spending $125 billion of Title I money over 25 years, we have virtually nothing to show for it."

In fact, studies have shown that when poor kids attend middle-class neighborhood schools they do just fine, in some cases even better than their wealthier peers. It has finally become clear that it's not the individual students so much as the entire education experience given to these children: campuses that look like prisons with 10-foot-high steel bar fencing, metal detectors that students must walk through each day, run-down facilities with broken drinking fountains and poorly maintained restrooms, and, most important, green teachers fresh off the truck, many with no credentials, many whose very first time in front of a live audience is the student's first day with them. And where has the money gone? New computers, useless curriculum materials, and more adult instructional aides.

"Well-prepared teachers are affordable if most education funds are invested in classroom teaching rather than in a panoply of special programs and peripheral jobs that do not directly improve teaching (and are often created to offset the effects of inadequate teacher preparation)," writes Linda Darling-Hammond (1997b, p. 304).

Based on three million teachers and an average salary of $50,000, if 5 percent of the teachers qualified for the top salary of $100,000, each of those 150,000 teachers would double their pay, costing around $7.5 billion. Therefore, Title I could completely fund such salaries by itself, without even considering the savings garnered when high-priced, low-competency teachers get their pay reduced by one-third. And what happens to the teacher specialists, adult aides, and computers paid for via Title I? Some of the specialists go back to the classroom, and some of the aides remain as teachers' secretaries or are retrained as parateachers.

Smarter District Spending

Many people, especially teachers unions, feel that the district administration budget is inflated and should be cut. However, when education is compared to other industries, public school administrative expenses tend to be lower than in private industry. The issue lies in how the money is used.

1) Implement performance-pay salaries. In paying better teachers more and less-qualified teachers less using a performance-pay method instead of the single salary schedule, districts can easily afford $100,000 salaries, because money for the teachers in the higher positions would come from redistributing the money from instructors in lower positions.

   The problem is, whenever a new contract is signed, *all* teachers get a raise, causing a huge drain on district resources. If only the deserving ones received raises, districts would not have to cut money from other areas to fund salary increases. And after every newly signed teacher contract, a ripple effect occurs when all other school employees, from principals to custodians, demand the same percentage increase—a me-too raise— without putting forth the effort the teachers unions do to get it. Teachers fight for new contracts, and everybody else gets to piggyback for free without feeling the public relations heat.

2) Eliminate the wasteful spending plaguing so many school districts. Hire MBAs to manage larger districts. For example, the Los Angeles Unified School District spent $175 million on a new high school, the Belmont Learning Center, only to shut it down when it was half-way finished—with the likelihood that the school will never open because of potentially explosive gases underneath the site.

3) Contract work out to private companies. Just like the military excesses that came to light during the 1980s (remember $500 hammers and $5,000 toilets?), it costs districts ridiculous amounts of money to perform the work themselves. In one classroom, what should have been a $250 electrical job escalated into a $5,700 district expense. "If schools contracted out the work, it would be done on time, at a faster rate and correctly, not to mention more cheaply," said a Los Angeles teacher.

4) Relinquish budgets to school sites. One cannot equate high per pupil spending with high achievement. Look at the state of New York: with the highest per pupil spending of close to $10,000 (the 1999–2000 national average was $7,000), more than half of fourth graders failed an essay test in 1999.

Determining how money is to be spent is best left in the hands of the individual school. Some schools may need to hire 20 master teachers, whereas others may need only five. Some campuses would build new buildings, others might need copiers. Let those working alongside the students decide how best to spend the money on them.

Encourage More Corporate Partnerships

There's only so much property tax revenue to go around, making corporate partnerships with schools practically essential today. But these companies can do even more. They have a vested interest in ensuring that their future employee pool has been schooled properly. Many companies already benefit schools through adopt-a-school programs. Apple and IBM, for example, have donated computers and software to thousands of schools over the past decade. With nearly one-third of newly hired employees tagged as job-illiterate, corporations annually spend $50 billion to train them in basic English, math, and computer skills that should have been taught in the schools (Gross, p. 6). Clearly, the private sector can no longer take a backseat to helping fund education.

Continued private-sector participation could be a key factor in transforming public education this century. After all, Peter O'Malley could no longer do it alone as sole owner of the Los Angeles Dodgers; he needed a Rupert Murdoch conglomerate to take over. Likewise, schools can no longer be funded solely by property taxes.

In fact, businesses have sprung up that help bridge partnerships between schools and businesses. According to the *New York Times,* "Corporate contributions to non-profit organizations have more than doubled since the early 1980's" (Halpert). Schools have become dependent on these private-sector associations, with some collecting more than $100,000 each year from snack machines placed in the schools to pay for athletics and clubs. The Chula Vista School District located near San Diego cut a $4.45 million, ten-year exclusive deal with Pepsi for its soda products.

Just recently, Coca-Cola announced it would no longer seek exclusive contracts with schools for the sale of its beverages, and would use nondescript covers for its large vending machines to cut down on commercialism (an answer to consumer complaints). This brings up potential hazards to having unrestricted corporate sponsorship. If the Boston subway can auction off corporate naming rights to its stations, what's so farfetched about doing the same with public schools? That's what museums are doing: the General Motors Center for African American

Art in Detroit, the McDonald's Please Touch Museum in Philadelphia, and the Emerson Electric Children's Zoo in St. Louis. Who would want to drop off his third grader at the Doritos Elementary School (when considering children's dietary habits, however, it would be apropos)? Corporate names do not have to be that blatant. Have a logo built into student desks or on a small corner of a blackboard or whiteboard, very similar to the way portions of the TV screen are sold today. Yet the reality of today's advertising market is that corporate imprints on school grounds will not vanish.

Plain old philanthropy works well, too. The only problem is that the big spenders traditionally give their money to universities, not the K–12 system. Two notable exceptions are Walter Annenberg and Bill Gates, who have donated millions of dollars to public schools. If a difference is truly to be made, it has to begin at the K–12 level. The astronomical amounts given to colleges have a great deal to do with why U.S. postsecondary institutions are some of the best in the world.

And, Finally, Start Charging Minimally for Public Education for the Vast Majority Who Can Afford It

If students know something is free—that is, doesn't cost them anything—then the value to them of that item is zero. In my journalism classes, I used to order newspapers for them donated by subscribers. Very few students took advantage of the free papers, so I canceled them to avoid throwing away dozens of leftovers each day. Yet, when my English students purchase their own books, even used ones, they make sure they don't leave them in their lockers or lose them on their way to school, because they had to pay for them.

Why public schools don't at least demand a nominal deposit fee for all books checked out at the beginning of the school year is a mystery. Unreturned books account for the most expensive debits of any school's yearly budget. The fact that students check out $70 textbooks without as much as a token $5 book deposit generates huge debts for schools when some of those books are never returned. If parents had to pay for books, or put down a deposit, suddenly the value of losing a book is not lost on a student. Attaching a price to "free" services will help students and parents understand the value of education. If consequences are involved, rewards will increase. "Free fosters no respect for books or materials," said one New York teacher. "I make my students buy paper for one cent a sheet if they don't bring their own. I found that just handing things out meant waste."

Putting down a deposit on books shouldn't be a stretch. Parents already shell out money for their children's athletic uniforms, band instruments, and elaborate overnight school trips. Many affluent parents raise tens of thousands of dollars each year for their children's schools.

The aim here is not to spell out step-by-step exactly how higher salaries and better working conditions can be paid for, but to offer a framework for putting such plans into action. The issue isn't can it be done, but will it be done.

Education was a key issue in the 2000 election. People want change. Now we need leaders with vision, who can devise a strategy to educate our children for the century ahead. It's easy to brandish the moniker, "Education President," but it isn't so easy to show the courage to really be that person, to go to the American people and explain what needs to be done to restructure the whole public education system.

The most courageous act is to have the American people sacrifice for it. And Americans have a history of sacrificing for causes that are clearly spelled out for them and are shown to have positive results.

We wouldn't have to increase property taxes to implement the programs discussed in this book. In fact, raising taxes would be the cheap and easy way to fund these programs, instead of taking a hard look at what is currently funded in public education and dismantling the programs that haven't worked.

About eight out of every ten Americans agree strongly that a "high national priority" should be placed on recruiting and preparing teachers who can deliver a quality education—even if it means spending more money to achieve it. The same percentage of people agree strongly that "we should ensure that all children, including those who are economically disadvantaged, have teachers who are fully qualified, even if that means spending more money to achieve it" (Haselkorn and Harris, p. 12). If the people in charge are willing to set the tone, then it can be accomplished. And those people are union leaders, politicians, and school administrators.

In today's schools, there is no scarcity of funding, only scarcity of critical thinking. There are so many funded programs that do not fit together, do not complement one other, and sometimes are at odds with each other. Some schools have several specialists who are in charge of these programs, but rarely speak to one another.

The image one gets is of that old vaudevillian act that used to appear on *The Ed Sullivan Show* showing a man twirling plates precariously at the end of five-foot-high sticks. Just as one plate was slowing down and seemed to fall to the ground, the entertainer quickly moved to it and spun it again to keep it from breaking. Schools are run the same way. They are implementing many programs, with funding from a plethora of sources. No one stops to think about the possibility of giving teachers—you know, those people who are with the kids all day long, the people who are trained to educate—the power to decide what's good for the kids, what might be useful to try, or what resources might be needed to maximize kids' learning potential.

CHAPTER 8

Unions: Political or Professional?

It's perfectly understandable why teachers huddle beneath the shield of their unions: as an employee group, they have little control over their profession. This overall sense of powerlessness helps to explain the fanaticism of some teachers about their union—it's the one outlet teachers have to exercise power and be listened to by districts and state and federal education officials. This, perhaps, is the union's worthiest role: giving voice to teachers' concerns.

This is why I do not perceive unions as the "evil empire" as others do, and am not in favor of disbanding them as some critics have demanded. It's much easier to change what already exists than to create something new. Teachers unions and associations already have the ear of teachers, districts, and politicians. However, unions need to mature and move past their blue-collar perspective to that of a white-collar professional group. The dynamics of the teacher/district relationship resemble those of labor/management. In this factory model, the district is clearly in charge, and the teachers hold no authority. This has to change.

Teachers have a unique opportunity to do what doctors accomplished early in the last century—gain control of their profession. Unfortunately, unions are doing little to accomplish this. Teachers unions have created a long distance race that offers members guaranteed lifetime employment to those who reach the finish line; the only hurdles are a few inconsequential evaluations.

Protecting all teachers, regardless of their quality, needs to end now. The American people think unions serve a role, but they want bad teachers to be fired, not be given a lifetime job without the possibility of a termination.

According to RNT's 2001 report, *The Essential Profession*, "although nearly six in ten (58 percent) Americans believe teacher unions support high standards for teachers, a higher 72 percent agree that too often teacher unions stand in the way of removing incompetent ones" (Hasselkorn and Harris, p. 5).

Union culture is so pervasive at schools that teachers have been brainwashed to swallow everything their associations sell them, lock, stock, and barrel, without questioning what's best for the profession in the long run.

For a teacher to criticize teachers unions is akin to a National Rifle Association member supporting gun control: it's just not done. And if it is, it's always surreptitious. There is good reason why unions are hard to bargain with: they are powerful lobbies. The two-and-a-half-million-member National Education Association, combined with the one-million-member American Federation of Teachers (AFT), represents revenues exceeding $1 billion annually.

No doubt, when teachers first became unionized, their collective numbers helped the teachers corps of the past negotiate respectable salaries and working conditions. Teachers are no longer expected to work during their breaks; they now have "duty-free lunch." But time has passed them by. Slowly, the unions are waking up to the growing notion that not all teachers deserve higher pay, that some accountability is necessary if for no other reason than to satisfy the public's wishes, and that the tenet of job protection may have to be abandoned. Yet, defining good teaching skills is an issue unions shun.

Only recently, under much legislative pressure, have a few union heads reluctantly considered the notion of peer review, allowing colleagues to evaluate new and poor-performing teachers. Now, unions are trying to embrace the concept so they can control as much of the process as possible.

In 2000, riding the crest of a decade-long booming economy, double-digit pay raises were part of several new teacher contracts, due mainly to the greatest economic prosperity in our country's history. Union membership is sure to soar, but what percentage of union members deserve to be called professional and earn higher pay? Not 100 percent, that's for sure.

The unions' rhetorical message repeats like some annoying TV commercial: we are professionals; pay us professional wages. But to ask taxpayers to pay $60,000 to teachers who couldn't pass a high school exit exam after 15 years on the job, and every year there after, is insulting to new teachers who work three times as hard and are much more eager to improve, yet earn less than half of that teacher's salary. Unfortunately, the union is not interested in their story.

What about the bright college students who had an inspiring high school teacher whom they would love to emulate, but when they look at the rigid, nonrewarding salary schedules, they choose to opt out of teaching? Unfortunately, the union is not interested in their story.

What about the 10-year veterans who have finished receiving annual pay raises and are facing a decision about whether to continue in a profession with only three more pay raises left in their career, as more and more work is asked of them? Unfortunately, the union is not interested in their story.

From the district's point of view, throwing dollars in front of teachers keeps them quiet and placated—yet no more teacher authority is gained.

Some teachers are quick to take out their union contract and shove it in the face of their principal as a
weapon against any task that is asked of them beyond the
contractual minutes, and every time a criticism of their
work is discussed. This is the reaction of a factory worker
on the assembly line, more than that of a highly educated
pro. Instead of ensuring that teachers are compensated
for every extra minute worked, union representatives
should focus their attention on gaining more managerial
power for their members.

First, unions should earn the respect of the public by
lobbying for instructors with stronger skills to earn more
money. Unions historically have opposed any distinction
of good teachers from bad ones. They feel it would bring
out the competitive nature of teachers. Well, guess what—
teachers are already competitive—just look at how they'll
do anything to get ahead of someone else in line for the
copying machine.

Besides paying raises only to those teachers who earn
them, unions need to stop protecting incompetent instructors. In their pursuit of contracts that follow the Three
Musketeers' motto—all for one and one for all—they have
failed America's parents and children by allowing the proliferation of mediocre teachers, granting them tenure few
people in other professions enjoy.

No matter how hard principals may try to rid their
campus of terrible teachers, despite the number of student and parent complaints, once tenure is granted after
the second or third year of employment—barring convic-
tion of some heinous crime—these teachers remain in the
school district until they retire. And it is these teachers
in particular who wrap themselves up with the union
security blanket, defending themselves in principals'
offices "with union-hired lawyers contesting even well-
documented evidence of poor teacher performance and
behavior" (Bigler and Lockhard, p. 112).

By using labor unions such as the AFL-CIO as their
model, rather than such professional organizations as the

American Medical Association (AMA), teachers unions have created an antagonistic and adversarial relationship with school districts, a collective "us against them" mentality. Woe to teachers who aren't card-carrying members. On my very first workday as a teacher at Garfield High School, an unknown teacher introduced herself to me and said, with a stern face, "We all belong to the union on this floor."

In recent years, the unions have spent a great deal of their time lobbying on the issue of agency fees, which force nonunion teachers to pay union dues. This is a pot of gold for those unions that have been able to get such a requirement into contracts. Agency fees have become the law of the land for all union professions in many states, including Hawaii, Minnesota, New York, and California.

In some cases, if teachers refuse to pay an agency fee, they no longer have job protection and can be fired—that quickly and easily. It's interesting how unions would rather protect the lifetime employment of a person who wastes classroom time, reads the newspaper while students chit-chat, doesn't return student work, and doesn't follow the curriculum, *but* is a card-carrying member, than a gifted educator who desires the freedom to join or not.

Unions are more political animals than professional organizations. Many teachers oppose the political actions of the state and federal branches of their local unions; but as long as they get raises from time to time, they allow the union machine to continue at the expense of quality in the profession. It is more important that the union have real power among legislative bodies, than for the profession to be more professional.

"According to the Federal Election Commission, 98 percent of the money dispensed by the teachers unions' political action groups—NEA-PAC and AFTCOP—goes to Democrats" (Gross, p. 216). In 1998, 11 percent of the delegates to the Democratic National Convention were NEA members, the single largest group. This assumes that all teachers favor only Democratic Party candidates. However, a Carnegie Institute survey "revealed that the union's [political] endorsements may not accurately reflect the political philosophies of teachers": 42 percent classified themselves as conservative, and 29 percent moderate. Despite their members varying philosophies, unions unabashedly claim "to speak for the entire teaching profession" (Bigler and Lockard, p. 108).

Even when Republicans sign legislation favorable to unions, they can't win their support. Former California Governor Pete Wilson signed into law classroom size reduction classes in grades K–3, an action long sought by teachers and their unions. Did he get credit for it? No. He was criticized for also signing into law a teacher accountability act that his current Democratic successor Gray Davis is implementing with little condemnation.

In terms of national organizations, the NEA and AFT differ philosophically on which direction to take teaching. The NEA, founded in 1857 by school superintendents, began as an anti-union organization and continued that way for the next 100 years. The AFT, on the other hand, has worked with some Republican and conservative politicians. Founded in 1916, and an affiliate of the AFL-CIO, AFT now represents bus drivers, cafeteria workers, and nurses, in addition to teachers.

The AFT was started by the Chicago Teachers Federation and was able to get teacher associations from New York City; Gary, Indiana; Oklahoma City; Washington, D.C.; and Scranton, Pennsylvania, to form an alliance, which they called the American Federation of Teachers.

While teachers founded the AFT, superintendents started the NEA. For many decades, teachers who were encouraged to join the NEA weren't able to make much headway with their agendas because school administrators controlled all actions.

Both the NEA and AFT really didn't take off in terms of membership or clout until the 1960s, when they began using collective bargaining and acceptance of teachers' right to strike. Also, teachers could no longer belong only to their local association. Union dues had to be paid to the local, state, and national branches of the organization. Until then, the NEA was more a professional association than a industrial-style labor union whose members were predominantly nonteachers. Executive director from 1973 to 1983, Terry Herndon, was responsible for building the organization into a powerful political force, and for injecting liberal politics into the NEA. At one time during his tenure, the union encouraged students to get signatures for an antinuclear weapon petition.

Albert Shanker, AFT's president from 1974 to 1997, who is seen as a visionary or an eccentric, depending on one's point of view, started in the 1980s to move the AFT toward previously unchartered areas for teacher unions. These included:

- firing incompetent teachers;
- career ladders;
- peer review;
- a national exam for teachers so rigorous that only 20 percent of teachers would pass it because "there are teachers teaching in this country who are illiterate and who shouldn't be in the classroom"; and
- a published directory of board-certified teachers akin to the Michelin guide.

In defending his endorsement of the Toledo Federation of Teachers' peer-assistance program, Shanker said, "We don't have the right to be called professionals—and we will never convince the public that we are—unless we are prepared honestly to decide what constitutes competence in our profession and what constitutes incompetence and apply those definitions to ourselves and our colleagues" (Toch, p. 143). Unfortunately, many of his ideas never came to pass.

There has been some movement toward making teachers unions less adversarial and more professional. The

Teacher Union Reform Network (TURN), as part of its
mission statement, seeks a more "we are all in this together" philosophy "to promote reforms that ultimately
will lead to better learning and higher achievement for
America's children." Besides affiliations with the NEA
and AFT, it also counts as members more than 20 metropolitan teacher associations.

For the past five years, NEA and AFT have been
discussing a merger. The first substantive discussions
about a possible merger between the two largest national
teacher unions took place in 1996. A jurisdictional agreement was signed by both sides to explore the possibility
further. As of July 2001, the NEA's Representative Assembly and the AFT's Executive Council approved an
NEAFT Partnership Agreement.

According to a prepared statement by AFT President
Sandra Feldman, "The agreement provides a framework
for more regular and focused cooperation between the two
unions by creating a joint council composed of 15 members
of each organization. This council will decide on the partnership's activities, including holding conferences on topics of common interest and coordinating legislative and legal actions." Whether the two groups actually merge into
one unified organization remains to be seen. However, it is
likely that the more maverick views of the AFT would
have to be toned down to be more palatable to the much
larger NEA's old-time union traditionalists.

During the summer of 2001, New York City Public
Schools' teachers union, the United Federation of
Teachers, was trying to reach agreement with Mayor
Rudolph W. Giuliani. Union president Randi Weingarten
is willing to accept easier dismissal of incompetent teachers in exchange for higher rewards for the most competent. Giuliani wants teachers to work longer hours. The
union is asking for a 20 percent pay increase that would
cost the city $1 billion. More problematic, if teachers do
get most of the increase they are seeking, other city

unions, such as the police, will want identical terms. This is what makes it so difficult when a union goes after an across-the-board pay raise instead of only giving raises to those teachers who deserve them.

Kathryn S. Wylde, president of the New York City Partnership observed in a *New York Times* article, "Our competitiveness in a knowledge-based economy absolutely depend[s] on getting the public education system fixed and doing it now" (Greenhouse, 2001).

Unions are missing a golden, perhaps once-in-a-lifetime, opportunity to help overhaul the most anachronistic social structure in our society. If they do not change course very soon, they miss a true opportunity to gain real teacher reform: control of the profession.

As Shanker said in 1985 regarding unions' role, "Unless we go beyond collective bargaining to teacher professionalism, we will fail in our major objectives: to preserve public education in the United States and to improve the status of teachers economically, socially, and politically" (Toch, p. 141).

Unions have had a positive impact on teacher salaries and working conditions in the past. If it weren't for them, salaries would be lower, teachers would still do yard duty, and many would work without mandated preparation time. Now, however, their goals need to reach to a loftier level. Union leaders must come to realize that their future depends on strong teachers leading the fight toward professional pay and working conditions.

Half of those polled in 1998 (*The Essential Profession*) agreed that "teacher unions too often stand in the way of real reform" (p. 4). To accomplish real reform, unions must focus on professional working conditions and act as a professional association like the American Medical Association, instead of a trade union like the United Auto Workers, with its emphasis on salary, benefits, and work rules.

Teachers unions should focus their energy and their money on establishing their independence; as long as unions want the status quo relationship (a little salary increase here, a little less power there), they will always finish second, with the district retaining the upper hand.

CHAPTER 9

The System: Politicians, Administrators, and Teachers

The public understands who controls public education, and it's not the teachers (see figure 15).

When asked who has the power to improve public education, the top five responses are all politicians or politically charged bodies such as school boards. Teachers ranked a dismal seventh out of 12 groups.

Lack of funding can be overcome, unions can be won over, but the biggest obstacles to professionalization of the teaching profession are those who wield the real power in public education: politicians.

Politicians

These are teachers' real bosses. Politicians do not trust teachers to do their job. Otherwise, why would they pass so much legislation dictating what should go on in the classroom.

Politicians from both sides of the aisle pass reforms that in reality become more taxpayer-subsidized programs of no proven value. When debating what should be done for public education, rarely do they "ask teachers to make such determinations for their field . . . because they do not

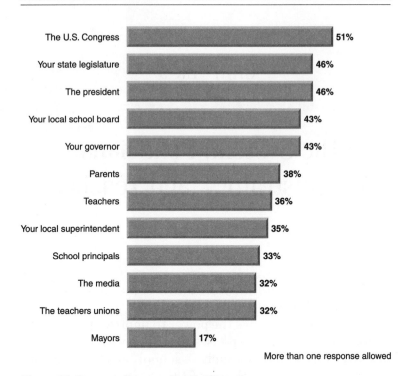

Figure 15. Power to Improve Public Education
Source: Recruiting New Teachers, Inc.

expect teachers to have the knowledge to do so" (Darling-Hammond, 1997, p. 298).

It's scary to realize how few people make policy decisions that reverberate throughout classrooms in America. And working teachers are not part of this education
elite.

What gives them a right to tell teachers how to do their
job? A question often brought up when looking at the
small but significant proportion of public school teachers
who have their children in private schools is: if public
schools are so good, why don't the teachers at public
schools send their own children there? The same test could
be applied to lawmakers. How many of their children attend public schools? Yet, all of them make policies that di-

rectly affect the education of public school children. Politicians act as silent partners in the classroom, deciding which textbooks to place in the teacher's hands, which laws to post on the teacher's bulletin board, and even which writing standards to put on the teacher's chalkboard. They need to let the teachers do the teaching.

The Standards Movement

At the behest of politicians, during the last decade, state departments of education have been required to define exactly what students should be learning and what teachers should be teaching, grade by grade, course by course. This standards movement arose because too many mediocre teachers were doing their own thing in their classroom and not following the curriculum. Course curricula have always existed, acting more as outlines of what a teacher needs to teach. The standards go one step further, spelling out exactly what skills students need to master year after year. Every state but Iowa has content standards.

For example, there are 25 standards for Algebra I in California. Standard 20.0 reads, "Students use the quadratic formula to find the roots of a second-degree polynomial and to solve quadratic equations." And California's Grade Six World History standard 6.6: Students analyze the geographic, political, economic, religious, and social structures of the early civilizations of China.

On the face of it, standards appear to be beneficial, fleshing out for instructors what needs to be done and eliminating nagging questions about specific learning objectives. It has taken a long time for educational administrators to define clearly what the best teachers have been doing already.

Defining standards for courses strengthen the argument that teaching in and of itself is a subject worthy of study, further justifying it as a true, quantifiable profession. Having standards adds legitimacy to the profession.

The teachers who benefit the most from following standards are new instructors and struggling ones who need direction.

Just having standards published in a book and given to every teacher does not ensure that everyone understands them, let alone is able to synthesize them and develop effective lesson plans around them. Many schools pass out reams of materials on standards and how to develop standards-based lesson planning. It takes time to go through all such material and even more to prove that good lessons apply to the standards.

One disturbing outgrowth of standards has been the proliferation of standardized tests that seek to determine whether students are being taught these skills. While mainly focusing on student acquisition of skills, they're also a way of checking up on teachers. The bottom line is that if there were enough competent teachers following the curriculum in the first place, there wouldn't have been a demand for the standards.

Standardized Testing

State testing is the biggest public education scam. Many people, especially politicians, like standardized tests because they are a simple way to track student progress from year to year and, in some cases, state to state. Why do politicians love testing so much? Because the tests are multiple choice, with answer keys that can be read by high-speed machines, they provide quick results for a large body of students. If given in May, all results can be posted on the Internet as early as the next month. Also, testing makes politicians look good. It gives the impression that they are doing their job of ensuring parents that the teaching of the standards is occurring. Poor test results make the teachers look bad, not the politicians, even though the teachers didn't devise the tests.

The intense pressure placed on teachers affects students as well, putting them under so much stress that performing at their best is difficult. Imagine if you were given only one way to reveal to a stranger how much you knew about a subject. This runs counter to one of the current hot trends in education—differentiating instruction. What this means is that effective teachers don't use just one way to teach something. They differentiate their lessons in ways that maximize the learning potential of all their students, each of whom has a unique way of traveling down a path to get to the destination—the lesson's objective. Yet, by offering a multiple-choice test as the sole barometer of what students have learned, an assessment tool unanimously frowned on in education research literature, students who have different ways of expressing their knowledge are denied success. That's why essay-type questions are preferable; they allow students to reveal exactly what they know.

Some schools make sure that all disciplines share in administering standardized tests, while other schools lean on the English and math teachers to conduct all the testing. Having the testing occur in these core classes means that English and math teachers lose those hours of instruction because they have to proctor the test. How ironic that the classes considered to be the most important end up with instructional time eliminated to give the test. Meanwhile, health and guidance and ceramics classes end up with more class time. One year the English department where I work lost nine instructional days, nearly two weeks' worth, to standardized testing, class registration, and photo ID day.

At the same time that teachers are pulled toward higher standards and more rigorous curricula, standardized tests require time to administer (days that are not added to the already overcrowded testing calendar of APs, SATs, Stanford-9s, regents, and exit exams) as well as time to prepare the students. Not all these tests are even aligned with those new standards; but teachers are pulled out of classrooms to learn strategies on how to implement state standards for test taking, and they end up with less and less time to accomplish the core of their job—teach.

Isn't it crazy that, at a time when schools are under intense pressure to show results, teachers are spending less time in the classroom and students less time on the curriculum?

California created the High School Exit Exam (CAHSEE) partly to address this issue of testing the standards in math and English. The first time this test was administered on a pilot basis, the results were so dismal that the length of the test was cut nearly in half. In the spring of 2001, the test was given again, and the results still weren't impressive: less than 45 percent of ninth graders and less than 25 percent of Latinos and African-Americans passed.

According to Larry Cuban, professor of education at Stanford, after a while, states will be forced to create easier tests and lower passing scores, as Massachusetts, Virginia, and Arizona have already done.

The cornerstone of President George W. Bush's education plan is a nationwide standardized test. If put into law, children in grades three through eight would take part in national testing. States would have three years to implement the testing, portrayed euphemistically by politicians as, not a national test, but 50 state tests monitored by the federal government. This is the wrong path to take.

Politicians are quick to pass bills demanding that districts test students, without thinking about the money and time needed to administer such tests. As in other public education "reforms," someone from on high comes up with a new idea, legislates it into law, and expects results in a short time. Never mind how intrusive the whole process may be to those who have to do the work.

There is such a demand for more and more tests, a "tests race" if you will, that publishers of the tests are hard-pressed to meet the demand without incurring major scoring glitches.

A May 2001 *New York Times* multipart series on testing by Diana B. Henriques and Jacques Steinberg, entitled "None of the Above," explored what happens to an industry that is suddenly asked to produce 50 percent more testing than ever before. "An examination of recent mistakes and interviews with more than 120 people involved in the testing process suggest that the industry cannot guarantee the kind of error-free, high-speed testing that parents, educators and politicians seem to take for granted." Politicians frequently have unrealistic timetables for developing new tests, so that many companies opt out on even bidding for the jobs. A case in point was when Gov. Gray Davis signed a bill in 1999 to create the California High School Exit Exam that gave companies the grand total of ten days to submit proposals. No one did until more time was allotted.

The higher the stakes states place on standardized test results, the more chance that a minor scoring error may negatively affect a student's chance of graduating from high school. In the last three years, the country's largest testing company, NCS Pearson, whose revenues exceeded $620 million in 1999, "produced a flawed answer key that incorrectly lowered multiple-choice scores for 12,000 Arizona studies, erred in adding up scores of essay tests for students in Michigan, and was forced with another company to rescore 204,000 essay tests in Washington because the state found the scores too generous" (Henrique and Steinberg). Of course, it's important to remember that NCS's Measurement Services unit scored almost 300 million answer sheets in 2000 with hardly a mishap. But would you want one of the few mishaps to be your child's test?

Part of the problem lies in getting enough competent people to score the tests. A temporary job at $9 an hour may not attract the brightest individuals, something not foreign to teachers who have their own low-paying temporary employee group called substitute teachers. One such scorer admitted to the *New York Times* that "lots of people don't even read the whole test—the time pressure and scoring pressure are just too great" (Ibid.).

The problem is never funding the test, but, as mentioned earlier, finding the time. Teachers are not given the time to familiarize themselves with the new idea. So, when the results are not there, the teachers, are blamed. You can't alter their work without providing them time to assimilate the changes.

Do politicians understand what they are asking of teachers? To take away precious days from the cramped 180-day school calendar not only to administer the tests, but prep the students on them, and then to pull the teachers from their classrooms to instruct them on the new tests and strategies, leaves students with less time to learn the curriculum and less time with their teachers.

Preparing for statewide standardized tests requires an immense amount of time, as does the physical management of teachers picking up testing materials, distributing them to students, then collecting everything every single testing day. Sixty-six percent of teachers surveyed by *Education Week* said that they were concentrating on the tests "to the detriment of important areas of learning" (Steinberg). Currently, about half of all states have mandated these tests, which affect students' promotion or graduation. In 2001, New York required all its high school graduates to pass the English and math Regent's tests, not just those bound for college.

Some schools prohibit teachers from assigning homework or giving other tests during the state testing days. As a consequence, teachers lose classroom time in administering the test, falling behind in the curriculum while the education process remains in "pause" mode.

Many experts in the testing field have spoken out against having students take one exam to represent their breadth of knowledge. Standardized tests are based on the assumption that a new immigrant student in San Antonio and a native English-speaking student in South Bend, Indiana, would have a similar likelihood of success taking the same test based on the same core of knowledge, despite studies that prove an inherent bias in all standardized tests. How can the immigrant student, in this country for one year, possibly know what "prairie" means?

If students can't read English, they *will* do poorly on the test. If students come from a home where education holds little value, they *will* do poorly. If students work on creative projects that expand their minds and stimulate high levels of thinking beyond rote recall, and they have this knowledge assessed in essay tests instead of true-false ones, they *may* do poorly.

Some states, like Texas, offer financial rewards to schools and teachers who meet a certain threshold of student achievement. The higher the stakes placed on standardized tests, the more pressure is on principals and teachers to show results or else. A few teachers and principals have resorted to outright cheating to gain a state's financial rewards.

In this era of accountability, the one person who is supposed to benefit from this testing, the student, is least accountable. In fact, teachers have been told to lie to students—"Colleges will know how you do on these tests!"—to convince them to take the tests seriously. California has gone one step further by providing money to students who score well on their standardized tests. Teachers (of course!) are the ones who are really being tested—on how well they have taught the standards. It's like putting a gun to the head of teachers to get them to push students to do well on the test, not because it benefits the students (it doesn't), but because it benefits teachers (financially, that is) and principals (their job). And this is how accountability is enacted in public education.

Teachers are trained in credential programs to assess their students by asking questions and devising assignments that probe the higher-level thinking skills of evaluation and synthesis and avoid the "when" something happened or "who" was involved rote type of learning. Then why should so much time be expended in force-feeding students tests that only measure those lower-level thinking skills?

Learning is a task that takes time to foster, shape, mold. Having students take practice tests wrongly focuses their energy. How tremendous the results would be if this same amount of energy went into having the best teachers at a school mentor the weaker ones. And how tremendous the results would be if this same amount of money was offered as a carrot for teachers to better their in-class work and to those bright college graduates who view teaching as only a back-up plan.

It's perfectly understandable that parents and politicians want to see results (current code name: *accountability*) from public education. Giving one test to all children seems a simple and easy way to measure yearly progress. But if the public wants to see progress, parents should examine their children's report cards. They are the best barometer to how they are performing. Though report cards may be subjective, if teachers are held to a higher standard of competence, the public will have confidence in the teacher's professional assessment of each child's achievement level.

Concerned that preparation for standardized test consumes too much classroom time, teachers, parents, and others have begun efforts to thwart such exams. Most notably, two-thirds of the eighth-grade class at Scarsdale Middle School in New York boycotted standardized testing in the spring of 2001. The affluent area traditionally boasts some of the nation's highest test scores. According to the *New York Times* (Zernike), parents there say such testing has bred "a test prep culture and . . . lock-step instruction," stifling creativity and forcing teachers "to abandon the very programs that have made the schools excel." School board members and the PTSA, and even the superintendent, agree with the parents about the negative impacts of standardized testing as "unnecessary and intrusive," creating undue stress among students. As Scarsdale superintendent Michael V. McGill said, "They've diverted attention from important local goals, highlighted simplistic and sometimes inappropriate tests, needlessly promoted similarity in curriculum and teaching . . . [and] . . . they've undermined excellence."

In states such as Illinois, Maryland, Massachusetts, and Virginia, students have started their own form of protest either by refusing to take the tests or purposely bubbling in wrong answers. In Colton, California, a group of teachers who earned bonuses for their school's increased test results are hiring an antitesting consultant to speak to parents.

There's even the National Center for Fair and Open Testing (Fair Test) that advocates an end to "the abuses, misuses, and flaws of standardized testing and to make certain that evaluation of students and workers is fair, open, accurate, accountable, and educationally sound," according to its mission statement.

In his book *Standardized Minds: The High Price of America's Testing Culture and What We Can Do to Change It,* Peter Sacks describes the key problems with standardized testing:

- Standardized tests generally have questionable ability to predict one's academic success.
- Standardized test scores tend to be highly correlated with socioeconomic class.
- Standardized tests reward passive, superficial learning, drive instruction in undesirable directions, and thwart meaningful educational reform.

These tests hurt students most by requiring too much time. To ask teachers to use precious instructional minutes on prepackaged test preparation kits is more than foolhardy—it's antilearning. Besides, the students who need the most attention, lower-economic minority children, are hurt the most by these tests.

When all mandatory tests, including AP exams, are taken into account, to paraphrase the old saying, a test day here and a test day there, and soon you're talking real instructional time lost to testing. Teaching at schools grinds to an abrupt halt during parts of April and May, the home stretch of the school year when a teacher is bringing everything together from the entire year; the momentum breaks, the rhythm is lost.

"Our schools are morphing into test-taking factories," said former U.S. Secretary of Labor Robert B. Reich in his *Education Week* article from June 20, 2001, "Standards for What?" "Politicians like tests because they don't cost much money and they reassure the public that children are at least learning something."

As Reich points out, "It's far more important to learn how to identify and solve new problems, think critically, and challenge assumptions" than "regurgitate facts.

"Our new obsession with standardized tests runs exactly counter to the new demands of the modern economy. It is training a generation of young people to become exquisitely competent at taking standardized tests, and a generation of teachers to become exceedingly good at teaching how to take them. Neither of these competencies has much to do with preparing young people for what they will encounter when they leave our schools."

What a shame that at such an opportune time, when the nation's economy had been growing at unprecedented rates for nearly a decade, and education has been the number one concern of the public, statewide and now nationwide testing is perceived as the best "solution" for public school improvement. The money is there, the focus is there, but the solution isn't.

The only meaningful results are those that use multiple measures of assessment. Knowledgeable teachers must develop well-thought-out lessons that allow students to think beyond the best of four choices, and create assignments that give them opportunities to work in heterogeneous groups. This is a more effective display that students are learning than a one-size-fits-all test. There isn't a simple buzzword or acronym for traditional learning methods, such as students using their listening, speaking, reading, and writing skills; otherwise, an awful lot of publishing houses and consulting groups would make even more money than they do already on the big business of standardized testing.

So what we have in public education is the following: a teaching talent pool that is stretched precariously thin due to class size reductions of the past few years in elementary and secondary schools; and greater numbers of inexperienced teachers in the classrooms who are increasingly teaching non-native-English-speaking students how to improve their performance on a test that bears little resemblance to what goes on during the rest of the school year.

Yes, the taxpaying public deserves to see results from schools, but not at the expense of real content-embedded lesson plans. Smart teachers are better off paying lip service to mandated testing, and doing what the best teachers have always done about each new fad that's supposed to cure education that comes crashing down on them: close their doors, roll up their sleeves, and get on with the gritty business of true teaching.

Implementation of content standards and follow-up testing is nothing short of enforcing teachers to teach to a regimental schedule. It's complete control over the educator's planning book because the system does not trust its teachers to do their job. Testing is not the answer; teaching is. In the 2000 RNT poll, 60 percent of people stated that teacher quality has the greatest influence on learning, more so than academic standards (28 percent) and standardized tests (11 percent).

At a time when politicians are demanding accountability, and state education departments want new standards, teachers can't get supplies, phones, books, or clean rooms. If legislative bodies spent their time working on these issues, then teachers could concentrate on teaching to their students. Politicians needs to leave the teaching to the teachers.

Voucher Programs

The idea behind vouchers—giving parents money to take
their children to whatever school they wish—is that
public schools are not doing the job. The inherent message is that private schools are superior. Of course, private schools have little in common with public ones. It's
not a simple matter of comparing apples to oranges;
rather, it's more like comparing a low-cost housing com-
plex to a gated community. Private schools are not gov-
erned by states, do not have to follow any policies such as
the standards or testing, and do not have to accept all
children. In fact, private schools can expel troubled and
special education students. One is not going to find a
4,000-student private high school academy with 40 students in a class. One also is likely to come across teachers
who lack credentials.

Only 15,000 of the country's 53 million schoolchildren
use vouchers, particularly in Cleveland, Milwaukee (the
oldest and largest program, where only low-income families can participate), and Pensacola, Florida. Some studies do show higher achievement at private schools. But
one must remember that having to pay money for school
creates a vested interest in what the school is doing. Parent involvement in these schools is higher than in the
public sector, which has a great deal to do with higher
student achievement.

It's perfectly understandable for taxpaying parents
fed-up with their children's public schools to punish the
big bad system by taking money away and putting it into
private schooling.

Unions and educators fear that if enough parents
choose private schools, public education would lose large
sums of money since the voucher (in most cases $4,000) is
paid out of public education funding. Such a fear is un-
founded when one looks at public opinion polls and ballot
measures that show people enthusiastically support their
local schools.

When asked which is the better way to improve schools, 84 percent of people surveyed chose the selection, "doing what it takes to put fully qualified teachers in every public school classroom in America" over "allowing parents to use public education money to send their children to a private or parochial school" (Haselkorn and Harris, p. 24). When given a choice between qualified teachers and charter schools, the percentage was even higher, 90 percent versus 7 percent.

And dozens of states have defeated voucher initiatives or delayed enabling legislation. During the last presidential election, California and Michigan voted down voucher initiatives by nearly 70 percent. Such lopsided losses cannot be accounted for simply by union money.

No study in the limited use of voucher systems has shown that Johnny, who can't read, can do any better outside a public school. There is enough good teaching and learning being conducted in public schools to nullify such disruptive campaigns. Since its inception in 1982, the National Academic Decathlon competition has never been won by a private school.

True choice is to enroll your child where the best teachers are. Of course, if many of the proposals in this book are implemented, no wise parents would want to remove their child from the public school system.

Administrators

In surveys, teachers say time and again that what hinders their work most are incompetent and uncooperative administrators, a heavy workload, and a lack of materials and resources. The materials shortage can be fixed with better money management, and the workload can be negotiated, but the administrative hurdle is harder to solve.

Let's face the hard-to-swallow truth: There are simply not enough smart people in the field of education, and the smartest people are not necessarily in charge. Remember, if a majority of teachers have average SAT scores, so do the administrators running the schools.

Criticism from highly respected and truly qualified superiors would be constructive and taken to heart. But when you have people who were average instructors or former coaches who know very little about core academic classes making the decisions that affect teachers' daily instruction, then you've got a problem. When a mediocre teacher becomes a mediocre administrator, who then hires new mediocre teachers, a cyclical effect occurs where mediocrity reigns supreme.

Administrators, for the most part, are decent, hardworking people. Yet something twists their view of teachers once they walk into an office instead of a classroom. A layer of distrust and disrespect of teachers permeates the administrative fold in schools so deeply that few administrators can detect it. All one needs to do is to attend a meeting to be faced with a chilly antiteacher air.

The administrator-teacher relationship has soured in recent years with the increasing pressure they have to bear. "Administrators are no longer faculty-friendly because they are in a perpetual CYA [cover your ass] mode," said one Georgia educator.

Administrators spend so much time determining whether teachers attend meetings or leave work early that one wonders where they find the time in their hectic schedules to do it. "It's demeaning to sign in for every meeting every time," said a teacher working in her fourth decade of education. It's hard to imagine a conference of physicians where the speaker berates the doctors for not signing in. It's more than unprofessional—it's demoralizing.

Perhaps the priorities are wrong. Is the meeting more important than practicing with the youth orchestra or prepping students for an AP test? And, more important, why should teachers have to explain their absences as if they were students?

It's another way of treating teachers like children, just as they have to have their work checked with their principals, from daily lesson plans to masters they want to photocopy. This type of treatment maddens teachers and breaks their spirit. It's simply a power play, one that administrators will never relinquish until teachers take command of their profession.

To Protect and to Serve?

A major reason for weak administrative talent is what the job of principal has become over recent years: more of a security guard than a curriculum expert. The job is no longer attracting people with true leadership skills, with a vision on how a school should be run.

Walk on any school campus these days and administrators are easy to spot: look for the Secret Service type. The modern administrator's accessories include pager, cell phone, and walkie-talkie. Such a "uniform" clearly draws the line between administrators and teachers, creating an unsettling atmosphere, as if one is working at a prison. Teachers are not privileged enough to be given equipment or inside information on what's being discussed. This form of communication reaches its most ridiculous level when overhearing conversations such as "I'm in the room next to you; I'll be there in ten paces."

No matter one's benevolent intentions, as soon as a person enters administrator-land, the job molds one's outlook on things. Not a day goes by when administrators don't yell at kids or have to talk to parents. Their blood pressure always rises as the day wears on, since their paramount concern is making sure students aren't roaming hallways, cutting class, or starting fights. No wonder they overwhelmingly favor block scheduling, which cuts in half the amount of time students are out of class. The students who are sent to principals' offices generally are the troublemakers.

So much of these negative activities eat up administrators' days that they have little time to focus on the programs at the school, what science projects students are working on, the work kids are doing in art class, the music children are practicing, the singing in the choir room. Rarely do they get an opportunity to enjoy students from the learning perspective, as teachers. It is vitally important if not healthy for them to visit classrooms regularly, not just to evaluate teachers, but to observe the children. The farther administrators stray away from the classroom, the more disconnected they become from their teachers. What soon develops is an "us vs. them" mentality, because neither side understands what the other is all about.

Perhaps an even deeper reason for the division between administrators and teachers is that each doubts the other has the ability to carry out his or her job effectively. What is surprising is how quickly everyone forgets that teachers and administrators came from the same place.

As teachers serve students, so should administrators serve teachers, doing all they can to make overworked teachers' workplace as hospitable and stressfree as possible. Sometimes this support isn't available. A high school English teacher from Florida said:

> One day a group of football players were pounding on my door as I was teaching a class. They demanded their test results. So I called and asked for help from the office to have them removed. No response. I called again and said, "Look I'm upset, will you please help me?" I went outside and there around the corner was an assistant principal standing with his walkie-talkie as if he were hiding. I asked him why he didn't come to my room. He said, "Someone else was going to come." Well, I started to cry I was so distraught. I told him, "What is wrong with you?" He's in the system for 30 years. He should be able to handle a class.

Part of the problem with people in education is that most teachers and administrators never worked in the private sector. All they know is school and the two roles in a school: student and teacher, which later become teacher and administrator. Just as many teachers do not realize how unprofessionally they are treated, neither do administrators realize how unprofessionally they treat teachers.

When informed of the added time commitment a controversial new student evaluation process would require from teachers, the principal at one school responded, "Teachers are given a full day to do grades, and the parking lot is empty after the morning." Translation: Those lazy teachers are getting time off so why not give them something else to do? Did it occur to this principal that teachers may have used that day as an incentive to work harder in the evening to get a breather before the start of the next semester?

A first-year English teacher was given a note from her principal after he visited her class. She was showing a filmed version of *Of Mice and Men* to her students after they had studied the John Steinbeck novel. This is a common closure activity to enhance students' understanding of the book. Also, it provides an excellent writing opportunity for teachers to have their students practice comparison/contrast between the original and the filmed adaptation. The note read that it was "an inappropriate use of class time" and that he "never wanted to see that again."

Besides the fact that he was wrong about the validity of such a lesson (commonly taught to new English teachers in methods classes), what was more alarming was his tone, especially in his closing remark. Remember, this was a new teacher who needed nurturing not lecturing.

Good teachers must fight constantly against this hostility, which is even more painful than outsiders' criticisms of the profession, since all administrators were former teachers.

Sometimes teachers are put in uncomfortable positions by their superiors, such as being asked to change grades. From a California educator:

When I first started at my school we had an assistant principal who wanted me to change the grades of two seniors because they were going to have trouble getting into some Ivy League schools. The reasoning was that they had taken a higher-level language class after mine and gotten As. I was disgusted with her and the students. I would not change the grades. I had the girls take the same final they had taken two years earlier in my class in which one had received a D and the other an F. They took the test over and got the exact same grades and this after taking upper-level classes and passing with an A. Incredible! After this the assistant principal never questioned my grades.

A teacher from Georgia says, "I was told on three separate occasions that I would have to give the son of a major business partner of the school makeup work. [As] if that weren't bad enough, I got this message from the assistant principal, not the principal."

Other times teachers are asked to disregard certain policies. A middle school teacher from the South was told to ignore the ban on social promotion, where students automatically move from one grade up to the next. "Even though the state and the governor have said no social promotion, my principal told me, 'We will not have middle-school students driving to school.' A major criterion whether to retain a student is how large he is. If the student is physically small, there is more of a likelihood he will be retained."

Most disturbing is when a form of sexual harassment occurs. A female Spanish teacher relates her troubles with some male administrators. "I've had some [administrators] say things to me in a suggestive way or just look at me with a dirty sexual look that is disgusting. I don't dress in a sexy way or seductive way to work [n]or have I ever even done or said anything that would call for that kind of behavior. I'd say that would be disrespectful."

"What We Have Here Is a Failure to Communicate"

The worst quality of administrators is when they don't keep the teaching staff informed. This shows a complete lack of respect and trust. For example, teachers and students commonly receive important information late with little prior warning. By receiving insufficient advance notice of what is happening at their worksite, teachers quickly end up shuffling around their lesson plans. It is unprofessional simply not to warn teachers days, if not weeks, ahead of time of what is happening where they work. It's not uncommon for teachers to receive a memo in their boxes informing them that an assembly is occuring that same day. How can teachers do their job properly when they are kept in the dark?

Such poor communication causes severe anxiety for teachers when they only find out at the last minute what classes they will teach. In what other field do professionals know at the last minute what work they are going to perform? While student numbers can fluctuate over the course of the summer and into September, not telling teachers what they are going to teach until the last minute creates unnecessary anxiety. If teachers want to prepare lessons and units for the entire year on their own time during the summer, they may find out later that all that work was for naught, when they discover they are no longer teaching those grades or classes. Now those teachers are totally unprepared for their students and must work extremely hard to stay a couple of days ahead of them. And who suffers more than the teacher? The students. Is that any way to ensure good teaching? It's simply treating teachers in the most highly unprofessional way, with a total disregard for what they need to do to be effective instructors.

One time I wasn't informed about a change in my teaching schedule until the printouts of the new student rosters were made available at 3:30 P.M. the Friday before school was to begin. And I was head of the department. In fact, as department chair, I am usually the last to find out information. Many times a teacher will come to me regarding a mid-year class change. I'm standing there with egg on my face because, as department chair, at the very least I should know about these things, and be in on the decisions. Whether purposeful or unintentional, such lack of communication undermines the authority of the department chair. Just when one feels a sense of pride about being in charge of something, *boom,* you're right back to that old "you're just a teacher" saw.

Equally frustrating is how infrequently administrators respond to notes, e-mails, or voicemail messages. Here's one example from a high school English instructor from Florida: "I e-mailed the administrator about a student of mine who had been a no-show for a few days. Two months later, school had ended and I still hadn't received a response."

The problem with some administrators is not that they don't communicate, but that they don't know how to do it *effectively.* Administrators are afraid of approaching teachers. Many times they ask teachers to do their work for them, and they search for ways to avoid confronting teachers who are not doing their jobs.

A veteran elementary teacher with 28 years' experience views administrators as more a "structural problem than an individual problem," while a middle school teacher believes that "administrative talent has definitely gone down in recent years. They no longer talk to individual teachers about issues, so whatever thing is bothering them gets said to the entire faculty at staff meetings. It's because they are afraid of the unions."

If a particular teacher doesn't leave lesson plans, then the administrator should talk to that teacher, not the department chair. Why should a big stink be made at a department meeting when only one out of 20 teachers is involved? Such broad admonishment only serves to discourage hard-working teachers who are blamed for others' shortcomings. Incompetent teachers are the ones who make the job harder for the good ones. It's the old "one student did something wrong so all must be punished" syndrome. If a few teachers don't follow the rules or aren't doing what they are told, everybody else gets painted with the same brush.

Several times teacher input is requested but not acted on, making teachers feel their voices don't count. Even when administrators mean well, their plates are so full that all they can do in response to a problem is create yet another committee. Administrators form committees as frequently as traffic cops hand out tickets—there must be a quota. Forming a committee gives the appearance that a problem is being addressed. If you're really lucky, a committee will beget a task force, and a task force will beget a plan, and the plan either is never realized or the top brass's original idea is implemented (surprise!).

One of the more bizarre meetings I've ever attended involved which supplies should be ordered for teachers. A supply committee was formed to determine which supplies to purchase. What followed was a five-minute heated discussion over what color the pens should be since there wasn't enough money to buy a variety of colors.

A Los Angeles high school teacher said, "Some administrators are very supportive, especially those who have not forgotten what it is like to be a teacher. Others leave something to be desired. Some principals prefer to side with parents rather than with teachers, thinking this will resolve the issue and keep them in good standing with the parents."

Many veteran teachers agree that the main quality separating past principals from current ones is the inability to make a decision. What this means is that more and more schools are actually run from the district office. As the accountability of standardized tests ratchets up, more district administrators tighten the screws on their principals who, in turn, do likewise on their teachers, adding yet another layer of stress to everybody's already maxed out anxiety levels.

Administrators should work alongside teachers, be the lead teachers on a campus, observe teachers frequently, even teach some classes so that classroom teachers learn from their teaching skills.

Districts don't have aggressive administrator recruitment programs, even though the current shortage of good teachers has led to a shortage of good administrators. Model administrative degrees on the best of MBA programs at Harvard Business School or Northwestern University. Put teachers who wish to be administrators through them. Actually try to make the job attractive through both salary incentives and better working conditions and the ability to make site-based decisions without district interference. Better-trained principals will relieve the traditionally strained relationships that now exist.

And, finally, give principals control over their own schools. How can they be effective when it has been estimated that they make only 25 percent of all decisions affecting a school.

Unless the administrative ranks are filled with highly knowledgeable people, former exemplary teachers themselves who can manage effectively, schools are doomed to house ineffective bosses.

Just as an exceptional teacher can lead students beyond learning horizons never reached before, so can exceptional administrators lead a faculty to heights of excellence never attained before. The best quality in administrators, as with all superlative leaders, is vision, a vision of what the school can become. Once everyone buys into that vision, any hard medicine to remedy the school's problems can go down much more easily (like a "spoonful of sugar").

Teachers

Teachers are often their own worst enemy. Here are some characteristics of teachers who make the whole profession look bad.

• *Not Responding to Messages*

The lack of response from teachers to memos and e-mails is astronomical. I wonder if a memo were sent out stating that, by simply checking off a box a teacher would receive $1,000, there would be more than a few takers. Of course, teachers are inundated with mail, and, yes, there is an excessive number of memos and junk mail envelopes filling their cubbyholes daily. The demands on teachers' time are daunting. Imagine you've just arrived at work and five people immediately pounce on you asking for input. That's how it feels when memo after memo after memo is stuffed into teachers' mailboxes.

Still, no matter what business you are in, it is a lack of respect not to respond to someone. It is a definite sign that teachers tune out and no longer pay attention to things they have deemed to be unimportant or trivial. Yet, only by tuning in will teachers be able to capture control of their own field.

• *Not Attending Meetings*

As mentioned earlier, just because people show up on time for a meeting doesn't mean they are good teachers; it just means they are punctual. And certainly the point was made earlier about how unproductive meetings can be. But not to attend any of them? It behooves teachers to act professionally by attending meetings as often as they can, especially if their principals want them to be there.

Administrators very quickly generalize about teachers based on how teachers treat rudimentary things such as signing in or appearing at meetings. While neither one is a valid test of teachers' ability, why *not* reply to a message or attend a meeting? It serves to maintain a level of professionalism.

• *Having a Bad Attitude*

Often, teachers have good reason to feel wary of a new program—they were never involved at the ground level and are simply being asked to vote yes or no on something someone higher up developed. This does not mean teachers should be rude or act childishly. A faculty meeting shouldn't turn into an episode of the *Jerry Springer Show*.

A common theme heard from veteran teachers is how students aren't as (fill in the blank: smart, nice, well-behaved, etc.) as they used to be. Instead of focusing on what they can change, these instructors prefer a daily "bitch" session and usually hang around with others to commiserate with.

A veteran California teacher said, "Some teachers feel that they always need to get their way because they have the most seniority, and [they] even go as far as to threaten or present a lawsuit. This is just plain lunacy and childish. How are people supposed to respect some-one like this?"

- *Dressing Down*

Teachers enjoy brandishing the term, "professional," as if uttering the word alone garners respect. Well, teach-ers need to dress professionally if they want students and other adults to look up to them.

Many teachers dress for work as they would for the beach. Do these people look in the mirror before leaving their house in the morning and actually say to themselves, "I'm ready for work!"? While a recent trend in the busi-ness world is casual Fridays, for many teachers every day is casual day. Male teachers tend to dress worse than fe-males, probably because it's harder for a woman to dress down than a man. Unkempt hair, unshaven faces, tattered T-shirts, dirty shorts, white socks, and tennis shoes is how some male teachers come to work.

A high school teacher from California said, "Some teachers do help to bring down respect for the profession. For example, the way some teachers dress. There are male teachers whom I have worked with who wear sweats to school all the time and they are not coaches. Some female teachers dress like they're going to a bar rather than [to] work."

While no connection exists between how one dresses and how one teaches, teachers should take their status as role models seriously. Several times I have been asked by students and even teachers why I dress in a tie and sport jacket. I tell them, "I'm at work." I've lost track of how often one of my colleagues comments to me, "Why are you so dressed up?" or "You look nice. What's the occasion?" How does one answer these questions? I'm not suggesting that teachers dress formally, as if they were attending a wedding, only that they dress differently from their clientele. Some teachers dress as if they are still in school themselves, and what this does is erode respect for the teacher, reinforcing the perception of teacher as glorified tutor, not as professional educator.

Instead of showing apathy in manner and dress, teachers should jump in when asked by a principal to join a committee or to attend a conference to improve the whole school. When teachers do get more involved, at least they have a sense that they are having an impact and some semblance of control. It's the professional thing to do.

Believe it or not, some teachers like things exactly as they are. The old Psychology 101 maxim that you can't get respect unless you respect yourself is not embraced by enough teachers. Educators are often passive by nature and do not want to rock the administrative boat or the union juggernaut. They wish to help children learn and find it uncomfortable to speak out against insensitive policies and insulting attitudes. They choose to close their classroom doors. People who are treated as inferiors soon grow into their subordinate role, and this is exactly what has happened with teachers.

Shaking the status quo loose from its foundation to enable true public school reform is possible but may not be probable. The only sure bet is that everyone in public education must admit how important and powerful an impact classroom teachers have on student learning. If all parties recognized this fact, then the door to true change would begin to let some light through.

This is not about making teachers rich or having them become all-powerful. It's about what everyone always likes to say it is about: the kids. It's too easy and cheap to keep bringing up schoolchildren when postulating on how to fix public education. But good teachers truly enjoy working with young people. They want the very best for them. They want the very best for themselves. And they want to do the job they know they could do if they were given the chance to do it.

Whenever one hears about teachers who show their students R-rated films, teachers who show the same film-strip three days in a row, or teachers who read from a textbook in a monotone voice without looking up from their desks to see a poker game going on in the back of the room, good instructors cringe because it is these bad ones who contribute to the negative stereotype of the teaching profession. It can't just be nonchalantly disregarded as "all professions have a few rotten eggs," because, with teaching, children's education is at stake. "A few rotten eggs" is not acceptable.

"Respect is not shown," according to Berliner and Biddle, "when top-down forms of innovation are imposed on teachers by school boards, superintendents, state departments of education, or federal mandates" (p. 337).

The system must respect its teachers before society can. It must release its stranglehold on teachers in the classroom and give them their freedom. Emancipate them.

CLASS DISMISSED

Is Teaching Worth It?

I have already put much time into attending orientation meetings, getting my fingerprints and TB tests taken, filling out several forms, taking the verbal and essay tests, getting four recommendations and paying out money. But I don't see the point of throwing out good money after bad. And so I have come to the realization and conclusion that it isn't worth becoming a high school teacher. In a way, I should thank the credential office, for they gave me a good lesson in futility, bureaucracy and utter frustration. If this is any indication of what being in public education is going to be, then I don't want any part of it. It has left a bitter taste in my mouth, and I'm going to wash it out now before it starts decaying the rest of me.—Brian Crosby, 1982

That was part of an opinion piece I wrote for my college newspaper as a graduating senior right before I was to start my student teaching, the bread and butter of any training program. It was then when I decided not to finish my credential work after becoming utterly frustrated at how the program was structured to accommodate only students who did not have to work.

One class met on Thursdays at 8:30 A.M., while my English methods class (the most relevant of all credential coursework focusing on lessons for a teacher's specific subject area) met on the same day at 7:00 P.M. And these were the only sections of each course the university offered. This meant that I would have had to have been on campus from 8:30 A.M. until 10:00 P.M. Even if a person didn't have to work, it was a tremendously long time to be on campus, or to be available for class.

Twenty years ago there was a demand for English, math, and science teachers just as there is today, so one would think the credential office would have bent over backward to accommodate qualified candidates. Keep in mind that I could have gotten an immediate job through LAUSD on an emergency credential without having to go through this hassle. But the college credential office warned severely against jumping ship, that a candidate with a license was more likely to get a better position.

As I mentioned earlier, the starting pay was $13,000 in Los Angeles, and I was earning $18,000 as a part-time word processor. I figured it out on paper, and no way could have I paid for a $500 a month apartment along with the rest of my bills on a teacher's salary.

When I pleaded my case to one of the credential program administrators, suggesting that I take one of the classes next semester or do an independent study, she suggested that I find a job from midnight until 7:00 A.M.

Curiously, several of the educators in the credential program asked how much money I earned in my job as a word processor. That should have been my first indicator of "the writing on the wall."

I decided to remain a word processor until teachers' salaries improved enough that I could live off my paycheck. Seven years later, starting salaries had increased significantly, so that I could pay my bills despite taking a small pay cut—and that's when I went into teaching.

A student asked me one time as I pushed a cart of English anthologies up a ramp in my sportcoat and tie, drenched in perspiration, "Mr. Crosby, why do you do that?" And why would he want to do it as well?

Much of this book paints a dreary picture of what it's like being a teacher today. While many of my points may come across as overly critical, I deeply care about public education in this country. It's too easy to throw darts at it.

With such a negative portrait, why would anyone, especially extremely intelligent people, voluntarily put themselves in this situation, devote their professional lives to an institution still stuck in an early twentieth-century factory model, one rife with obstacles, offering few financial rewards? Because teaching can be exhilarating. Nothing else in the job market quite matches the high points in a teaching career:

- When a student finally understands how to compose a thesis statement, or begins to connect the science lesson to an everyday occurrence in the kitchen.
- A card in your cubbyhole on the last day of school from a student who says, "My memories of your class will stay with me forever."
- The thank-you letter during the summer from a former student who got into college with the help of your recommendation.
- The guest speaker whom you invited to your class and came year after year, lighting the flame of learning.
- The parent who on Back-to-School night tells you that her daughter in college sends a "hello" and a "thank you" for giving her skills that have helped her do well.
- The student who gets very excited to see you in a situation outside the classroom, such as at a movie or a sporting event, and introduces you to his friends and family as some sort of celebrity.
- The superintendent who sends a note of thanks to a teacher who was highlighted in the newspaper. "It showed me that the superintendent knew I existed," said the teacher, still proud of the mailing years later.

- The time a colleague tells you that your name was used by a student in a paper entitled, "My Favorite Teacher."
- When a sales clerk in a department store, upon inquiring what you do for a living, reacts with a "God bless you" and "we need more people like you."
- The strangely mature adult walking into your room whose name fails you, but whose face brings back a wonderful memory of that precocious young boy many years ago.
- The brand-new student who on the very first day blurts out as attendance is taken, "I've heard you're hard but good," and you use all of your might to avoid breaking into a huge smile.

Here is a real-life reward story from a high school biology teacher in Pennsylvania:

I had a young lady in my academic biology (college prep) class this past school year. She is a student who excels in school, works hard, and is always prepared. She is used to getting all A's. However, my class was one that she found to be difficult and challenging. She said she has never had to work this hard, and she did not want to get a B. At one point she even asked me to approve her dropping the class to take the lower-level general biology class. I asked her if she wanted to go to college. She responded by saying yes. So I explained to her that this course was going to prepare her for freshman college-level bio. I had to encourage her to stay with some extra tutoring and many "pats on the back." She EARNED all B's, but I told her the letter grade did not matter. It was the information and useful, meaningful knowledge that she could apply to her life in and out of school that was important.

At the end of the year, she asked me if she could sign my yearbook. In my yearbook, she thanked me for supporting her. She thanked me for encouraging her to stay in academic biology. She thanked me for taking time to tutor her and reinforce ideas and concepts. She told me that those B's in biology were the "proudest" B's she had ever earned. She felt like she really learned something this year in science. And that made all the difference!

When I think about this particular student, it makes me feel good. It makes me smile. It gives me that feeling of accomplishment. It is not often that we know who we were able to reach, but this young lady let me know that I was appreciated as her biology teacher!

The renewal process in education is unlike any other job. Every year there is a beginning and an end to the work you do from September to June, giving educators a more profound sense of the passage of time than other professionals. A teacher can see the physical and emotional development of a high school freshman who is transformed into a young adult. A few weeks off before the start of school can also allow a hard-working instructor to refuel before the new school year begins.

Those teachers who have students for longer than a year feel like foster parents given the guardianship of caring educationally for young people. There is a sense of emptiness and melancholy at the end of the school year when the students leave the room, leaving the teacher behind.

What motivates teachers to open up their wallets for every school fund-raising event?

What motivates teachers to tutor in the early morning or late afternoon hours?

What motivates 400 teachers to give up a Saturday morning to attend a workshop so they have time later to take their students to the symphony?

What motivates an entire school's faculty to donate money to a student's needy family?

The students.

Ultimately, it is not the money or the status or the working conditions. When it comes down to it, teaching is the greatest giving profession there is. And, unfortunately, it is that giving nature that has placed teachers in weak standing among the professions.

A teacher is teaching the future. When I look out at my students, I see the people who will be fixing my car, becoming my doctor, helping me in a department store, etc.

In a time of tragedy, society turns to those professions—firefighters, police officers, school teachers—for help and leadership. The loss of emergency service personnel on September 11, 2001, reminded everyone the important job those people do. In a less dramatic way, teachers comforted children in schools and day-care centers that day, especially those near the areas of devastation. It was reassuring for the nation to know that its children were safe at school with their teachers. Public education takes care of the country's young people.

In teaching, clichés are no longer clichés. The future of America does indeed depend on how it educates its youth. Teachers hold the key to the American dream, but they are given nightmarish conditions under which to perform the act. But as rewarding as teaching can be on an emotional level, it is not for everyone nor should it be. Just as many of us would not take a surgical tool to another person's body, many aren't able to perform in front of young people and unlock their minds to get them to understand and be excited about knowledge.

What will today's teachers do tomorrow? Will they unite? Will they abandon their roles as public servants and form private professional groups, say, an American Educational Association, outside the auspices of the unions if their current associations don't take the initiative first? Will national board-certified teachers take charge? Will teachers walk out for issues other than money? Will politicians back away and allow people much more knowledgeable about education than they are to run the show? Will superintendents support teachers and ensure that support through site administrators? Will more parents and students respect teachers? Will teachers respect themselves?

And who will fill those two million teaching positions in the next ten years? Where will those people come from? What will their academic background be? Will they be honors students, or students who barely passed? Will teaching be something they've wanted to do since childhood, or will it be a third or fourth choice after other aspirations have fallen through? Will they feel confident the first day they stand in front of students in a classroom, or will they feel inadequate, underprepared, lost? Once they have a couple of years of teaching under their belt, will they gain confidence, begin to have a sense of how important their job is, feel appreciated that they are doing an important job, be motivated to push themselves harder than ever before because they know that such work will be rewarded in ways beyond a simple "thank you"? Will they teach year after year because other challenging opportunities are there for them? Or will they get another job, any job, as fast as they can, feeling unworthy, not receiving help when they need it most, feeling overworked and underappreciated, feeling depressed by their surroundings, with a sense that there is no place for them to go beyond their current classroom job?

States and districts around the country, like South Carolina's Teacher Cadet program for high school honors students, are trying to come up with ways to make teaching look attractive. What will really get students interested, however, is by a) having dynamic teachers who demonstrate through their teaching their excitement about what they do, and b) being surrounded by a pleasant school environment, a place they, too, enjoy coming to. That is what will bring students to teaching, not just after-school clubs or one-day job shadowing programs.

The first time I experienced what it was like being a teacher was back in the third grade when my teacher, Mrs. Hockings, asked me to tutor a new student from Mexico named Emilio. For one hour a day, Emilio and I would sit in the back of the room; I would read to him and have him read to me. No epiphany hit me then; I just remember the good feeling that came from helping someone else.

As I progressed through school, whenever I had a teacher I admired, it made me admire teachers and what they did. Two teachers in particular were my secret mentors: my ninth-grade geometry teacher, Sidney Kolpas, and my tenth-grade English teacher, John Sage.

Being a shy boy, I would enjoy staying in Mr. Kolpas's classroom during lunch, helping him pass out papers for his next class or just talking to him about life. It was a difficult time for me because my father was dying of lung cancer and school provided me a refuge from dealing with that harsh reality.

During my first year in high school I was in Mr. Sage's English X class (X was the euphemism for honors, Y for average, and Z . . . well, you know). He was older than Mr. Kolpas but more proper, almost British. I was having another bad year personally and had to be hospitalized for a month. Mr. Sage visited me twice during my stay, giving me presents of fine literature to read while I was there.

While I didn't analyze it back then, I can see similarities between the two men now. They both dressed professionally, always in tie and sport jacket. They had a seriousness about them that told the class, "This is important what I am talking about," that made you pay attention and learn. They both had a sense of humor, the younger man hipper, the older man more subtle. And most important of all, they believed that the knowledge they had to impart was meaningful to you and to them. They deeply cared about their subject and it showed. I wanted to be like them.

Everyone has a teacher who has left a mark, an imprint for life, a teacher one can get choked up over, always remembering his name and even his way of speaking and of dress. Considering the impact that teachers have on people, it's shameful the profession isn't turning away future candidates instead of accepting anyone with a pulse.

Recruiting New Teachers' 2001 report, *The Essential Profession: American Education at the Crossroads,* concluded, "Americans are saying fix teaching first. Raise standards in the profession. Pay teachers more. Hold teachers accountable and remove those who fail to make the grade. Treat teaching as the honored and respected profession it must become if the promise of public education is to be achieved. And most of all ensure that all children, particularly low-income and minority school children, are taught by fully qualified teachers in every subject and every classroom every year" (p. 5).

Students are the ultimate beneficiaries of the professionalization of teaching. More government programs, more staff development, more grants, more school choice, and more standardized testing combined cannot equal the power of solid teaching.

Pay is going to have to be increased, career ladders need to be established, means of evaluating teachers to hold them accountable need to be in place, teacher training needs to be retooled, and power needs to be handed over to those who do the work of educating—the teacher.

> "The prestige and the income of the teaching profession must reflect the high importance of education in the modern society. Education must both attract and celebrate the best."
>
> —John Kenneth Galbraith
> *The Good Society: The Humane Agenda*

If a teacher revolution does not occur soon, its lack could well reverberate during the next several decades.

In the blink of an eye, 2102 will arrive, and there will still be public education in America. Most Americans will still send their children to them. More books will be written about teaching and the public schools. Will there be a tome looking back at the twenty-first century and wondering why more effort wasn't made to elevate teaching at such an opportune time, lamenting why so many people still leave the profession, why so many students score poorly on standardized tests, and why so few people enter teaching? Or will the book look back at the twentieth century in amazement at what teaching used to be like, how far it has come during the last 100 years, and how much students learn?

REFERENCES

Archer, Jeff. "Competition is Fierce for Minority Teachers." *Quality Counts 2000: Who Should Teach? Education Week,* 17 July 2001a. www.edweek.org

Archer, Jeff. "Earning Their Stripes." *Quality Counts 2000: Who Should Teach? Education Week,* 18 July 2001b. www.edweek.org

Atkinson, Richard C., and Charles B. Reed. "Higher Education Helps Drive the Economy." *Los Angeles Times,* 1 October 2000.

Baron, Christine. "Novice, Veteran Teachers Share Job Frustration." *Los Angeles Times,* 12 May 1999.

Berliner, David C., and Bruce J. Biddle. *The Manufactured Crisis: Myths, Fraud, and the Attack on America's Public Schools.* Reading, Mass.: Addison-Wesley, 1995.

Bigler, Philip, and Karen Lockard. *Failing Grades: A Teacher's Report Card on Education in America.* Arlington, Va.: Vandamere Press, 1992.

Blair, Julie. "Cincinnati Board Approves Pay-for-Performance Initiative." *Education Week,* 24 May 2000.

Blair, Julie. "Lawmakers Plunge into Teacher Pay." *Education Week,* 21 February 2001.

Bradley, Ann. "The Gatekeeping Challenge." *Quality Counts 2000: Who Should Teach?, Education Week,* 17 July 2001. www.edweek.org

Bronner, Ethan. "Long a Leader, U.S. Now Lags in High School Graduate Rate." *New York Times,* 24 November 1998.

Cetron, Marvin, and Margaret Gayle. *Educational Renaissance: Our Schools at the Turn of the Century.* New York: St. Martin's Press, 1991.

Coeyman, Marjorie. "America's Widening Teacher Gap." *Christian Science Monitor,* 18 July 2001.

Colvin, Richard Lee. "States Not Raising Teacher Standards, Study Finds." *Los Angeles Times,* 26 May 1999a.

Colvin, Richard Lee. "U.S. Could Take Lessons From Asian Teachers." *Los Angeles Times,* 11 August 1999b.

Colvin, Richard Lee. "Opposing Forces Tug on Teachers." *Los Angeles Times,* 8 December 1999c.

Cooper, Kenneth J. "20% of Teachers Quit Profession within 3 Years, Study Shows." *Los Angeles Times,* 9 February 2000.

Danielson, Charlotte. *Enhancing Professional Practice: A Framework for Teaching.* Alexandria, Va.: Association for Supervision and Curriculum Development, 1996.

Darling-Hammond, Linda. *Doing What Matters Most: Investing in Quality Teaching.* New York: The National Commission on Teaching and America's Future, November 1997a.

Darling-Hammond, Linda. *The Right to Learn: A Blueprint for Creating Schools that Work.* San Francisco: Jossey-Bass, 1997.

Darling-Hammond, Linda. "Target Time Towards Teachers." *Journal of Staff Development,* 20, No. 2 (Spring 1999). www.nsdc.org

The Essential Profession: A Survey of Public Attitudes in California toward Teaching, Educational Opportunity and School Reform. 14 October 1998. www.cftl.org/essentialprofession.html

Ferguson, Ronald. "Paying for Public Education: New Evidence on How and Why Money Matters." *Harvard Journal of Legislation 28* (Summer 1991).

Finn Jr., Chester E. *We Must Take Charge: Our Schools and Our Future.* New York: Free Press, 1991.

Galbraith, John Kenneth. *The Good Society: The Humane Agenda.* Wilmington, Mass.: Houghton Mifflin, 1996.

Giordano, Joseph. "LAUSD Recruiting Gets Boost." *Los Angeles Daily News,* 23 July 2001.

Goodnough, Abby. "Teaching by the Book, No Asides Allowed." *New York Times,* 23 May 2001.

Grant, Gerald, and Christine E. Murray. *Teaching in America: The Slow Revolution.* Cambridge: Harvard University Press, 1999.

Greenhouse, Steven. "New York City and Teachers Far Apart on Money Issues and Tenure in Contract." *New York Times,* 13 November 2000.

Greenhouse, Steven. "Chance for Change, if City and Teachers Agree." *New York Times,* 5 June 2001.

Gross, Martin L. *Conspiracy of Ignorance: The Failure of American Public Schools.* New York: Harper-Collins, 1999.

Groves, Martha, and Jessica Garrison. "State's Standardized Test Spurs Scattered Backlash." *Los Angeles Times* 24 May 2001.

Halpert, Julie Edelson. "Dr. Pepper Hospital? Perhaps, for a Price." *New York Times,* 18 February 2001.

Hanushek, Eric A. "The Trade-Off between Child Quantity and Quality." *Journal of Political Economy,* 1992.

Hart, Peter D., and Robert M. Teeter. *A Measured Response: Americans Speak on Education Reform.* Educational Testing Service, 2001.

Haselkorn, David, and Louis Harris. *The Essential Profession: American Education at the Crossroads.* Belmont, Mass.: Recruiting New Teachers, Inc., 2001.

Haycock, Kati. "Good Teaching Matters . . . A Lot." *Thinking K–16* 3, No. 2 (Summer 1998).

Henriques, Diana B., and Jacques Steinberg. "None of the Above." *New York Times,* 20 May 2001.

Hirsch, Jr., E.D. *The Schools We Need and Why We Don't Have Them.* New York: Doubleday, 1996.

Holloway, Lynette. "Temporary Housing Sought to Help Recruit Teachers." *New York Times,* 8 March 2001.

Honan, William H. "Nearly Fifth of Teachers Say They Feel Unqualified." *New York Times,* 29 January 1999.

Japanese Education Today. 30 May 2001. www.carson. enc.org

Johnson, Susan Moore. *Teachers at Work: Achieving Success in Our Schools.* New York: Basic Books, 1991.

Kantrowitz, Barbara, and Pat Wingert. "Teachers Wanted." *Newsweek,* 2 October 2000.

Kelley, Carolyn. *Douglas County Colorado Performance Pay Plan.* Madison, Wisc.: Consortium for Policy Research in Education, May 2000. www/wcer.wisc. edu/cpre

Kerr, Jennifer. "Downside to New Class Size." *Los Angeles Daily News,* 23 June 1999.

Kohn, Alfie. *The Schools Our Children Deserve: Moving beyond Traditional Classrooms and "Tougher Standards."* Boston: Houghton Mifflin, 1999.

Kramer, Rita. *Ed School Follies: The Miseducation of America's Teachers.* New York: Free Press, 1991.

Labaree, David F. *How to Succeed in School without Really Learning: The Credentials Race in American Education.* New Haven: Yale University Press, 1997.

"Let's Grade School Aid." *Los Angeles Times.* 12 March 2000.

Levine, Arthur E. "For Lasting School Reform, First Look to the Teachers." *Los Angeles Times,* 3 January 2000.

Lieberman, Myron. *Public Education: An Autopsy.* Cambridge: Harvard University Press, 1993.

Lieberman, Myron. *The Teacher Unions: How the NEA and AFT Sabotage Reform and Hold Students, Parents, Teachers, and Taxpayers Hostage to Bureaucracy.* New York: Free Press, 1997.

Mitchell, Ruth, and Patte Barth. "How Teacher Licensing Tests Fall Short." *Thinking K–16* 3, No. 1 (Spring 1999).

Morse, Jodie. "Do Charter Schools Pass the Test?" *Time,* 4 June 2001.

Murnane, Richard J., Judith D. Singer, John B. Willett, James J. Kemple, and Randall J. Olsen. *Who Will Teach? Policies That Matter.* Cambridge: University Press, 1991.

Nelson, F. Howard. *International Comparison of Teacher Salaries and Conditions of Employment,* December 1994. www.aft.org/research/reports/internl.htm

Odden, Allan. *Cincinnati's Teacher Evaluation and Compensation System.* University of Wisconsin–Madison: The Consortium for Policy Research in Education, 15 November 2000a. www/wcer/wisc.edu/cpre

Odden, Allan. *Vaughn Learning Center's Pay Performance Plan.* University of Wisconsin–Madison: The Consortium for Policy Research in Education, 15 November 2000b. www/wcer.wisc.edu/cpre

Odden, Allan, and Carolyn Kelley. *Paying Teachers for What They Know and Do: New and Smarter Compensation Strategies to Improve Schools.* Thousand Oaks, Calif.: Corwin Press, 1997.

Olson, Lynn. "Finding and Keeping Competent Teachers." *Quality Counts 2000: Who Should Teach? Education Week,* 17 July 2001a. www.edweek.org

Olson, Lynn. "Sweetening the Pot." *Quality Counts 2000: Who Should Teach? Education Week,* 17 July 2001b. www.edweek.org

Olson, Lynn. "Taking a Different Road to Teaching." *Quality Counts 2000: Who Should Teach? Education Week,* 17 July 2001c. www.edweek.org

Philadelphia, Desa. "Rookie Teacher, Age 50." *Time,* 9 April 2001.

Posnick-Goodwin, Sherry. "Emergency Permit Teachers." *California Educator* 5, No. 9 (June 2001).

Reich, Robert B. "Standards for What?" *Education Week.* 20 June 2001.

Robbinsdale Area Schools Skill Based Salary Schedule. University of Wisconsin–Madison: The Consortium for Policy Research in Education, 24 June 2001. www.wcer. wisc.edu/cpre/tcomp/state/mn/robbinsdale.asp

Roza, Marguerite. "It's the Teachers, Stupid." *The Christian Science Monitor,* 19 April 2001.

Steinberg, Jacques. "Survey Finds Teacher Support for Standards but Skepticism on Tests." *New York Times,* 11 January 2001.

Stigler, James W., and Harold W. Stevenson. "How Asian Teachers Polish Each Lesson to Perfection." *American Educator,* Spring 1991.

Survey & Analysis of Teacher Salary Trends 1999. Research and Information Services, American Federation of Teachers, AFL-CIO, 15 Nov. 2000. www.aft.org/research/ survey9/index.html

Survey & Analysis of Teacher Salary Trends 2000. Research and Information Services, American Federation of Teachers, AFL-CIO, 10 July 2001. www.aft.org/research

"Teachers with National Board Certification Outperform Others in 11 of 13 Areas, Significantly Enhance Student Achievement, Study Finds." *The Professional Standard* (Fall 2000).

Teaching and California's Future: The Status of the Teaching Profession. Summary Report. Santa Cruz, Calif.: Center for the Future of Teaching and Learning, 1998.

Toch, Thomas. *In the Name of Excellence: The Struggle to Reform the Nation's Schools, Why It's Failing, and What Should Be Done.* New York: Oxford University Press, 1991.

Uses of the Educational Dollar: Expenditure Patterns. 15 November 2000. www.wcer.wisc.edu/cpre/finance.htm

Weiss, Kenneth R. "College Leaders Urged to Improve Teacher Training." *Los Angeles Times,* 25 October 1999.

What Matters Most: Teaching for America's Future. National Commission on Teaching & America's Future. Columbia University, New York. 28 June 2001. www.nctaf.org

Zernike, Kate. "Suburban Mothers Succeed in Their Boycott of an 8th Grade Test." *New York Times,* 4 May 2001a.

Zernike, Kate. "The Feng Shui of Schools." *New York Times,* 5 August 2001b.

INDEX